Gerald Suster was born in London in 1951. He attended
Highgate School, later taking an MA in Philosophy and
Law at Cambridge University. After Cambridge, he
worked as an advertising executive and history teacher
before taking up writing full time. In addition to history
and the occult, his interests include the arts, politics,
psychology, conversation, boxing and his wife, with
whom he lives in London.

Also by Gerald Suster in Sphere Books.

THE DEVIL'S MAZE
THE ELECT

Hitler and the Age of Horus

GERALD SUSTER

SPHERE BOOKS LIMITED
30-32 Gray's Inn Road, London WC1X 8JL

First published in Great Britain by
Sphere Books Ltd 1981
Copyright © 1980 by Gerald Suster
Published by arrangement with the author and his agents

TO MY PARENTS
and in memory of D. C.

TRADE
MARK

Set in Lasercomp Times

Printed and bound in Great Britain by
©ollins, Glasgow

CONTENTS

LIST OF ILLUSTRATIONS

ACKNOWLEDGEMENTS

To the Hamlyn Group Ltd for permission to reproduce material from *Hitler: A Study in Tyranny* by Alan Bullock; to Macmillan, London and Basingstoke for permission to reproduce material from *The Last Days of Hitler* by Hugh Trevor-Roper; to Michael Yeats and the Macmillan Company for permission to quote from *The Second Coming* by William Butler Yeats; to Granada Publishing Ltd for permission to quote from *Satan and Swastika* by Francis King; to A. D. Peters & Co. Ltd for permission to quote from *The Decisive Battles of the Western World* by J. F. C. Fuller; to W. H. Allen & Co. Ltd for permission to quote from *Ladies and Gentlemen: Lenny Bruce* by Albert Goldman; to Martin Secker and Warburg Ltd for permission to quote from *The Rise and Fall of the Third Reich* by William Shirer; to Weidenfeld (Publishers) Ltd for permission to quote from *Rasputin* by Colin Wilson and *The Face of the Third Reich* by Joachim C. Fest; to the Hutchinson Publishing Group Ltd for permission to quote from *Witchcraft Today* by Gerald Gardner and Hitler's *Mein Kampf,* translated by Ralph Manheim; to Futura Publications Ltd for permission to quote from *Occult Reich* by J. H. Brennan; to the Radio Times Hulton Picture Library for the photograph of Aleister Crowley; to the Imperial War Museum for two photographs and one reproduction of a painting of Adolf Hitler and photographs of Himmler, Goering and a Nuremberg Rally. While publisher and author have made every effort to clear permissions, in some cases this has not been possible, and the publisher would be happy to hear from those, where difficulty has been experienced in tracing the ownership of rights.

PREFACE

Hitler: Orthodox Version

Few men have been the subject of such excellent historical writing as Adolf Hitler. Four books in particular stand out as masterpieces: Alan Bullock's *Hitler: A Study in Tyranny*, surely the classic biography of Hitler; William Shirer's *The Rise and Fall of the the Third Reich*, the standard history of Nazism; Hugh Trevor-Roper's *The Last Days of Hitler*, an unsurpassed study of the twilight of the Third Reich; and Joachim C. Fest's admirable analysis of the men and mood responsible for National Socialism, *The Face of the Third Reich*. There are numerous other books on the subject, none of which attain the exalted heights of these, but most of which are of an unusually high standard. It can be argued that the work of recognised orthodox historians has rendered any subsequent efforts completely redundant.

How Do They Do It?

The authors cited above have achieved deserved renown for their work. They have been fortunate, perhaps, in the intrinsic fascination of their subject-matter, but then so has everyone who has attempted the task of comprehending the Hitler phenomenon. What distinguishes Bullock, Shirer, Trevor-Roper and Fest is firstly, their enviable prose styles, and secondly, their acute powers of analysis.

There is a third similarity: their historical method. It is above all a method based upon rationality. Let us leave aside, laudable though it is, their talent for original research and the integrity which moves them to check the accuracy of every source. I am referring more to the very nature of their approach, which consists of endeavouring to tackle their subject without conscious preconceptions.

It used to be fashionable to invoke some ethereal 'spirit of history'. Even today, there is a school of historians that invokes an equally ethereal 'spirit of economic forces'. The men we are discussing will have none of this, and resolutely shun the temptation to impose upon their work an all-embracing theory of history. Instead they present us with the facts, and from these facts they draw logical deductions. No one could in consequence criticise their writings for being 'unscientific' – except possibly a determined propagandist. Nor is there present in their books any element that a rational mind would automatically question and reject.

Yet, as E. H. Carr has shown in his excellent *What Is History?*, the art of the historian does not consist of relating the facts, since everything that has ever happened is a fact, but in *selecting* the facts which, consciously or unconsciously, he thinks are significant. To some, therefore, the fact that at least on one occasion, Hitler consulted an astrological horoscope may be extremely important: to others it is too trivial to be worth mention, save possibly in a footnote.

The historian, in other words, emphasises the facts which he feels are important, and neglects the others. This emphasis may be consciously exerted, as in the case of Marxist historians, who are determined to fit history into a preconceived pattern: or it may be unconscious, and determined by the conviction that history is a rational process. Irrationalities and oddities will therefore be played down or forgotten. Thus, there is no such thing as *objective* history, any more than there is *objective* journalism. Everything depends on the facts which the historian selects from the infinite number available to him, and on the emphasis he gives those facts, and the result is the pattern which the historian has seen, which may be explicit or implicit in his narrative.

Do We Now Understand Adolf Hitler?

The pattern which emerges from the works I have cited is a rational pattern. That is to say that everything is explained in terms which a rational-humanist mind can grasp. The question is whether at the end of these and similar works, we understand the phenomenon of Adolf Hitler.

Despite the brilliance of the studies I have cited, it is my conviction that these works alone do not ultimately enable us to understand either Hitler himself or the Third Reich. After studying the mechanism by which Hitler attained power, the uses to which he put his power, his writings, his speeches and his actions, I hold that one is still baffled by a flood of unanswered questions.

Why did a civilised nation of the twentieth century abruptly revert to barbarism? How could a shabby ex-dropout, so manifestly third-rate in all matters of the intellect, have achieved such unparalleled power? Why did the Germans come to venerate Hitler as a god? Why do he and his associates, Himmler, Goering, and Goebbels, still exert a mystique that is so conspicuously absent when we study Mussolini, Ciano and Starace, or Stalin, Molotov and Beria? Why does one feel that the Third Reich stood for a radically different kind of civilisation? Most fascinating of all, what drove Adolf Hitler, what motivated him, what went on in his mind that resulted in consequences of such magnitude?

Hitler, Unorthodox Version: or, Now At Last The Truth Can Be Told!

These, and so many similar questions, have resulted in a spate of books which furnish a bizarre contrast to the works I have mentioned. The first of these is that extraordinary work, *The Dawn of Magic* by Louis Pauwels and Jacques Bergier, which has exercised a profound effect upon what is loosely termed the alternative culture. Part Two of the book, 'A Few Years In The Absolute Elsewhere', brings to light a vast number of facts, rumours, coincidences and hypotheses, all of which point to an involvement of Hitler and his associates with the occult. The authors speak of an eruption of the irrational with Hitler as its mediumistic prophet, of influential societies dedicated to the pursuit of magic, and of bizarre beliefs from the darkest hinterlands of the occult which obsessed the minds of Germany's leaders.

This thesis is not entirely original. Many years before, during the Second World War, Lewis Spence had published *The Occult Causes of the Present War*, which portrayed the Nazis as black magicians in the purest Satanic tradition. But whereas Spence had based his not very convincing arguments upon pre-twentieth century occult groups, the utterances of Alfred Rosenberg, anti-German prejudice and pro-Christian propaganda, Pauwels and Bergier cited a disturbing number of illustrations from the period 1919–45 which really did make one pause to consider whether they had stumbled upon the extra-ordinary truth.

The Dawn of Magic prepared the way for other books of a similar nature. J. H. Brennan's *Occult Reich*, brought to our attention a large number of facts ignored by ortho-dox historians, which again pointed convincingly to a strong connection between the Nazis and the world of magic.

In *Satan and Swastika*, Francis King attempted a rational and dispassionate analysis of the connection between Nazism and the Occult, and made clear that there was, beyond all doubt, such a connection. Mr King, a good and reputable historian, did not hesitate to lean towards the side of caution whenever there was the possibility of a rational explanation, with the result that his more extraordinary assertions are always fully substantiated.

Finally, there are the works of Hermann Rauschning, the former Nazi Gauleiter of Danzig to whom Hitler revealed some of his most secret beliefs and desires, and who in consequence fled to Britain. No one, to my knowledge, has impugned the authenticity of Rauschning's books, which make plain the magical world-view of Hitler: instead, the books have been for the most part studiously ignored. It is no use opposing to Rauschning's testimony a rag-bag of supposedly anti occult public statements by Hitler: of course Hitler did not parade his magical obsessions before an uncomprehending crowd. As Rauschning tells us, Hitler spoke frankly only to those select intimates whom he felt might understand him.

Now, the books I have just mentioned are not, as works

of history, in the same class as those of the best recognised historians. Nevertheless, they do contain much information which the latter have neglected or dismissed. They do make comprehensible certain things about Hitler which had hitherto made no sense at all. They do answer many of the questions which were left us by orthodox historians. They do emphasise those very facts which seem closest to the baffling National Socialist mystique, and so bring us closer to a total understanding of Nazism and of Hitler. Therefore we cannot afford to neglect them.

What Are We To Conclude?

Why have such superb historians as those whom we have praised implicitly denied the existence of the close relationship between the Nazis and the occult? It is because their outlook is a rationalist's outlook, which can make no sense whatever of what strikes them as being a collection of bizarre lunacies. One almost feels in the background the existence of a mad syllogism: occultists never enjoy historical significance; Hitler enjoyed historical significance; therefore, Hitler was not an occultist. Others may argue that there is precious little evidence to demonstrate Hitler's passion for the esoteric: but the evidence is very plainly there, as I shall show, and this argues the existence of a certain wilful blindness.

In short, the orthodox historian is determined to demonstrate that however strange the Hitler era might at times have been, ultimately all the events conformed to a rational pattern. The heretical historian denies this, and emphasises facts which upset this pattern. Some have gone further and imposed their own pattern, which, to the orthodox historian, is completely 'irrational'.

One of the prime motives behind this book has been to use the available facts so that the nature of Hitler and of Nazism can be fully comprehended. Many of these facts have been shunned by orthodox historians, but it is my conviction that this attitude has been mistaken, though to their writings I owe an enormous debt. I am greatly indebted too, and I have acknowledged this where appropriate, to the historial heretics. I have concentrated on the darker and lesser known side of Hitlerism, and I venture the suggestion that the resulting work supplies a truer insight into the subject than has hitherto been available.

Shall We Take A Theory For Our Guide?

Inevitably one does, even if it is only a subconscious faith that history is entirely explicable in terms of the concepts of the majority of people living in the post-1945 world, which faith, I confess, I look upon as a curious superstition. Just because we choose to be rationalists is no reason why others should automatically be so, or why Life itself should be rational. I have contemplated the facts before me, and I have sought for a theory which would satisfactorily explain them. I believe that I have found it.

How Was It Arrived At?

Given what has been said, it is tempting to speak of intuition: where, after all, do original ideas come from? But such has not really been the case. To my mind, intuition is wholly untrustworthy unless it has a firm basis in reality. My methods have therefore consisted of logical deduction from the facts I considered significant, and of induction. To explain this last term: if we wake up one morning and see a grey sky and a wet street, we are justified in arguing that it has been raining, even though we have not seen it actually doing so; we have learned what the signs of rain are. Similarly, if I see Hitler saying and doing all the things which occultists say and do, then I am justified in arguing that he was an occultist, even though in some cases this is not immediately apparent; I have learned what the signs of occultism are.

Is This 'Occult History'?

No, if by 'occult history' is meant an ill-written jumble of odd facts, scraps of fiction, irrational prejudices, secret and mystical information sources, and a pretence at complete omniscience. Nor would I care to be labelled as an occultist, a term which most occultists have brought into a richly deserved contempt. Like all orthodox historians, I have done my utmost to understand my subject and to present what I believe to be the truth about it. Occultism forms a significant part of this narrative because it is there.

Hitler and the Age of Horus

In the course of endeavouring to comprehend the nature of Hitlerism, one inevitably contemplates the entire tale of the decline and fall of Europe and the values it represented. One confronts the question of Hitler's role in Europe's collapse. One perceives the values which accompanied the collapse and notes their relation to Hitler. For my part, I saw the two themes as being intertwined.

What Is the Age of Horus?

The further I pursued this theme, the stronger became the belief that the twentieth century is that of the greatest crisis in human affairs for very many centuries. This is hardly a novel announcement: it has been said so often that it is virtually a platitude. My belief differs from the common-place only in my comprehension of the nature of this crisis which, I will argue, has been both a crisis of the breakdown of a civilisation and a spiritual crisis of the most profound significance. For reasons subsequently explained, I have poetically termed this crisis the onset of the Age of Horus. I have also implicitly asserted that we shall find a real insight into this phenomenon in the work of artists, poets, writers and all who are concerned with the world of the unconscious.

What This Book Is About

It is about Hitler, it is about the Age of Horus, and it is about the relationship between Hitler and the Age of Horus.

Is There a Spirit of World Historic Destiny?

Like most twentieth-century historians, I dislike grandiose terms such as the above, but the issue must be faced and dealt with. Either events conform to some kind of order outside the historian's mind, or they do not. If they do not, everything that happens, happens purely by chance, there can consequently be no such thing as science, and the historian's job becomes one of making sense out of random chaos, a job no different from writing fiction. If, on the other hand, there are laws of history, or there is some order in accordance with which events occur, there is no excuse for not trying to discover what it is. Christians may see in history the workings of God, of Christ, of the Devil: Marxists may discern the immutable workings of economic forces, of the class struggle, of the machinations of capitalism; and so on. I too have discerned a form of order. In common with other historians, I believe that the evidence points to the pattern I have discerned, and not to any other.

'Why Did He Write It?'

Because 'those who do not learn from history are condemned to repeat it'.

PART ONE

The Rise
of Horus

CHAPTER ONE

1889

'These are fools that men adore; both their
gods and their men are fools.'
The Book Of The Law I 11

'Coming events cast their shadow before.'
Goethe

Adolf Hitler was born in Braunau-am-Inn in the Empire of
Austria-Hungary at 6.30 pm on 20 April 1889. The world
into which he was born differs so hugely from our own, that
were there a meeting between a representative figure from
each, they would accuse one another of ignorance,
savagery and barbarism. It was a world which Hitler later
vowed he would destroy; it was a world which he was to
play a leading part in destroying and the last of which died
with him; yet it was a world which had absolutely no
intention of being destroyed, and which regarded so im-
probable an occurrence as a subject for jest and contempt.

In 1889, it was possible to do without aeroplanes,
motorcars, television, radio, mass journalism, free and
compulsory education, prefabricated concrete, frozen and
tinned foodstuffs, and telephones: everybody did. But the
men and women of this age did not merely do things
differently, they also thought about things differently. In
1889, the average Englishman, for example, believed firmly
in God, Christianity, Empire, Free Trade, Capitalism,
Civilisation, Conscience, Liberty, Justice, Reason, Explanation, Peace and Progress, as moral absolutes.
Western men and women of 1889 thought their age to be
superior to any that had gone before, and believed in all
seriousness that things could only get better.

There was every rational ground for this optimism.

3

Western civilisation had made extraordinary industrial progress, before which the rest of the world could only bow in humble recognition of its obvious superiority; and since the young United States of America was only beginning to consolidate its power, Western civilisation meant Europe, the Europe that had struggled to birth from the ruins of the Roman Empire. Confident in their supremacy, and impelled by economic necessity, the great powers of Europe had extended their influence to include much of Asia and the Middle East, and most of Africa.

Of all the great powers, the most self-confident was Great Britain, ruler of a mighty commercial empire that would by 1900 cover one fifth of the entire world's land surface. By virtue of its invincible Navy, which had ruled the waves since the battle of Trafalgar, Great Britain was able to maintain a Pax Britannica equal in effectiveness to the fabled Pax Romana. Trade was good for England, peace was good for trade, therefore there would be peace throughout the world. Though Great Britain's Army was negligibly small, peace was maintained throughout her domains by the simple expedient of efficient government, which enabled her to exploit both the natural resources and the labour forces of her colonies without provoking rebellion. No great power dared offend the imperial majesty of the nation which had broken Napoleon: all suspected that to change radically the direction of Western civilisation required the destruction of the British Empire: and all knew such an eventuality to be impossible.

To be British was to be best in 1889. It was to be a citizen of the most civilised nation on God's earth, the longevity of whose institutions of government put all other nations to shame. Queen Victoria presided over a government led by Lord Salisbury and opposed by William Ewart Gladstone. Both men, in their separate ways, believed that Christian civilisation and Christian values always would endure.

On the Continent, there was an impressive stability. The French Third Republic had survived and would survive all manner of crises, partly because there was no credible alternative, and partly because the majority of its citizens could subscribe to the values it upheld. The ageing Empire

4

of Austria-Hungary looked as though it would outlive the nationalism of the minorities it governed. The recently unified Italy was eager to enter the exclusive club of great powers. The Turkish Empire was weak and crumbling, but Great Britain was propping it up. Russia had recently colonised Northern Asia, and though there were revolutionaries, these despaired at the difficulty of radicalising the apathetic peasants, and were hunted down by an efficient secret police.

Finally there was the German Empire, which Otto von Bismarck had created and united. It was the greatest military power in Europe, and was soon to challenge Great Britain for industrial and commercial supremacy. Bismarck, its brilliant and audacious Chancellor, was a conservative who desired permanent European peace and who strove ardently towards its continuance through a series of wily diplomatic alliances and secret treaties. Like the other leaders of Europe, of whom he was the most intelligent, he desired a stable and ordered world with stable and ordered values.

The healthy political and economic future of Europe seemed to have been secured. Asia, South America, and Africa had no means by which they could challenge it, and the United States remained aloof, except in the Far East. Certainly there were occasional crises; equally certainly, these were resolved by civilised diplomacy. Certainly, in some countries, government was cruel, unrepresentative and unjust; equally certainly, matters would in time improve. Certainly there were still questions; equally certainly, there would soon be satisfactory answers.

In the world of art, the public applauded faithful depictions of persons and objects, poems which exalted the platitudinous, music which induced sleep rather than awareness, novels which described things just as people believed them to be, and plays which were dialogues of inconsequential trivia. Culture was geared to the needs of the dominant class of stockbrokers, bankers and industrialists. And if imagination could be denied in the world of art, it is easy to understand how this could occur in that of science. It was held that there was no longer any mystery

5

about the universe, and that everything worth knowing was already known. Matter was conceived of as being something solid, permanent, and dead. Inventors who produced designs for aeroplanes, bombs or radio transmitters were hounded to untimely graves and dismissed as insane cranks. The universe had been understood, and could be explained. If there were one or two gaps in this explanation, these would no doubt be filled unspectacularly by the end of the century.

The world of 1889 was in consequence a complacent world, possessed by an abhorrence of change. Its values were those of a lax Christianity; its methods were those of a rational mind blinkered to all except rational things. Reason crowned the mind and Jesus Christ the soul. Of course, practice was as inferior to theory as it always is in human affairs, but certainly, if the man of 1889 violated the social consensus, he was always very much aware of what it was that he was violating.

Self-appointed seers looked ahead and saw progress, a world which would evolve gradually towards perfection, a world in which all difficulties would be reasonably resolved, a world which would come ever closer to the practice of the values to which it paid continuous lip-service. The great powers held the keys to the planet's continued stability, their scientists held the keys to a universe that was no longer a mystery, and their values were the keys to Western superiority as was proved beyond all doubt by the West's domination of the world.

Such was the world into which Adolf Hitler was born and which he did so much to change. Had someone uttered a prophecy of his future in 1889, then the lunatic asylum would have claimed another victim. Had someone written a work of science-fiction which described the career of someone like Hitler, he would have been ostracised by publishers as a hopeless fool. With our hindsight, we can censure the world of 1889, confident in our knowledge that the impossible can happen, and that the impossible does happen. With an arrogance born of an acquaintance with history, we can even point out the signs that the people of 1889 should have noticed and did not: we can then proceed to ignore the signs of our own age's latent changes, and congratulate ourselves on our superiority to previous eras, for that is only what those of 1889 did.

The signs to which we refer were the seeds of the nineteenth century's destruction. Three men of Jewish race are often cited as the destroyers of this world: Einstein, who with his Theory of Relativity removed from physics and astronomy all possibility of static matter and absolute truth; Marx, who assaulted the great god capitalism, with logic rather than emotion, and who gave to the hungry a vision with which to combat the overfed; and Freud, who demonstrated that reason is but a justification of an unconscious mind concerning which we know virtually nothing. To this we must add the effects of the discoveries of Max Planck, set forth in his Quantum Theory, and those of Herz in physics and Haeckel in biology.

Historians have usually shown their awareness of these things, but one wonders whether they were the most important things. Is technology our only index of change? Or are the things that men believe of themselves and of the world and of the best ways of thinking and acting in the world, of greater fundamental importance? The three individuals whom we shall consider were not men of science, but it is arguable that what they wrote had a greater effect upon mankind. Also, and this is not unimportant, they were all three German.

The German Empire known as the Second Reich had been created recently, after the Franco-Prussian War of 1870–1. As British propagandists later alleged, Germany was the least Christian state in Western Europe. It had never been conquered by Ancient Rome, it had resisted or bullied the Popes, it had been the first battleground of Martin Luther's Reformation, and it had been the cemetery of the Thirty Years War. The many states that had existed prior to Bismarck's unification had harboured all manner of strange ideologies: it was the Western European nation closest to the borders of irrationality; perhaps this is why its university professors clung with such dogmatic desperation to logic and the rule of reason despite the work of Kant, Fichte and Hegel. Nevertheless, three prophets blew three trumpets in a country which esteemed the Herr Doktor.

The first of these was Schopenauer, one of the few who had studied the religious writings of the East with the respect that they merited. A pessimist, an atheist, a Buddhist, Schopenauer taught that existence was a wheel of suffering, and agreed with Gautama Buddha that the only cure was cessation of existence, or Nirvana. For this philosopher, the meaning of life could be reduced to 'a blind striving of the will', and the only experience open to human beings that is not futile is simply the actual, physical experience of will power. The terms *good* and *evil* therefore possess no meaning whatever.

Friedrich Nietzsche, the second prophet, was initially impressed and inspired by Schopenauer, but soon ventured beyond him, guided by a formidable talent for destructive reasoning, a capacity for mystical experiences, and a genius for inspired writing. Nietzsche allowed that the existence of most was so pitiful an affair that it was true to a certain extent that existence is suffering: yet he affirmed that for those with eyes to see, existence was joy. He maintained that one could enjoy the actual physical experience of will power, and one who did so permanently would be the next stage in mankind's evolution, the Superman.

He concentrated his attack upon the values which his world held to be absolute. With Schopenauer, he declared that there was no such thing as good or evil: all values are relative to the point of view of the individual who holds them. Beyond limitations like good and evil is the will: man must overcome himself, his values, his limitations, and identify with the will. Then he will achieve the goal of the evolution of his species, which is to be the Superman.

In *Thus Spake Zarathustra, Beyond Good and Evil, Twilight of the Idols, The Will to Power* and other works of genius, Nietzsche reduced the edifices of previous philosophers to rubble. Especially, he savaged Christianity, 'the one great curse, the one enormous and innermost perversion', which he called 'the one immortal blemish on mankind'. He despised mediocrity, equality, democracy and pacifism. He exalted ecstasy, elites, Supermen and struggle. He prophesied the advent of the Superman and of a master race of Supermen, but, contrary to popular opinion, he despised Germans as conforming maniacs and despaired of their evolutionary possibilities.

It was left to the third prophet, Richard Wagner, to declare that the coming master race was that of the Germans. Originally, Nietzsche had delighted in Wagner's music, but the latter's obsessive anti-semitism and conversion to an Aryanised Christianity caused him to denounce the composer with every twist of biting irony at his command. The great mass of people, however, were to respond more to Wagner's music than to Nietzsche's difficult writings, partly because it was great and inspired music and partly because its maker had resurrected the mythology of the German race.

It is said that myths are the truest expression of a race's spirit and culture, and in *The Ring* of Wagner, Teutonic Supermen bestrode a stage wherein was war, treachery, courage, blood and fire, climaxed by a stupendous *Goettedämmerung*: the world of Wotan and Thor, heroes and giants, great deeds, great victories, and great destruction had never been expressed with such power.

The beauty of Wagner's music moved men to such an extent that Hitler would declare that to understand National Socialist Germany one must first know Wagner. For Wagner believed that the virtues of the Teuton tribes had atrophied with the coming of industrial civilisation; that courage and will had been poisoned or emasculated by capitalism and race pollution; that the Jews were responsible for the ennervation and enslavement of the German spirit; and that a new Siegfried must arise to lead the Germans to an awareness of their greatness and their glory.

Schopenauer destroyed the meaning of values, Nietzsche proclaimed the need for passing beyond them, and Wagner supplied a new set to replace the old. These three men, renowned more posthumously than in their own lifetimes, challenged the world of 1889 and became in time the favourites of Adolf Hitler. From them he derived what fundamental values he possessed.

It is impossible to tell whether these men expressed what they felt around them, or what they sensed would be the future; or whether they were determined to stamp their wills upon the world. Were they prophets? Or were they magicians? We know that Nietzsche derived much of his inspiration from mystical trances which possessed him without warning, and that his greatest work, *Thus Spake Zarathustra*, was inspired by one such experience in the winter of 1882–3. We know also that Wagner claimed that the sources of his inspiration flowed from similar suprarational experiences, and the effect of this can be seen in that extraordinary mystical opera, *Parsival*. Whatever the truth, it is at least certain that much of what they foretold, later came to pass.

Yet the world of 1889 ignored these insignificant portents of change. People continued to live as though nothing important had happened or would happen, and no one so much as deigned to notice the birth of Adolf Hitler. Treaties and contracts were made and broken; money was won and lost; children were educated as though all was absolutely certain. Books were written and read which taught Christian, bourgeois, industrial capitalist, materialist, humanist European values as if no other could ever be of the slightest relevance.

And yet it was these books which lacked all relevance; Nietzsche, who knew the true spirit of his age and of the age to come, wrote:

'And what doeth the saint in the forest?' asked Zarathustra.

The saint answered: 'I make hymns and sing them; and in making hymns I laugh and weep and mumble: thus do I praise God.

'With singing, weeping, laughing, and mumbling do I praise the God who is my God. But what dost thou bring us as a gift?'

When Zarathustra had heard these words, he bowed to the saint and said: 'What should I have to give thee! Let me

10

rather hurry hence lest I take aught away from thee!' And thus they parted from one another, the old man and Zarathustra, laughing like schoolboys.

When Zarathustra was alone, however, he said to his heart: 'Could it be possible! This old saint in the forest hath not yet heard of it, that *God is dead*!'[1]

CHAPTER TWO

The Assault Upon the Idols

'Abrogate are all rituals, all ordeals, all words
and signs. Ra-Hoor-Khuit hath taken his seat
in the East at the Equinox of the Gods;'
The Book of the Law I 49

'To arms, citizens! Reason is dead.'
Jules Laforgue

Adolf Hitler's birthplace, Braunau-am-Inn, on the border
of the German and Austro-Hungarian Empires, had the
reputation of producing mediums. The nurse who suckled
that remarkable medium, Willy Schneider, also suckled
Hitler, a fact which, according to some, endowed the baby
with psychic powers. Whatever the truth of this assertion,
the baby would express the unconscious desires of millions.

By definition, the unconscious is that which is normally
suppressed. European rationalism had produced a suppression greater than any which the human species had
previously experienced. Only the conscious mind could
boast of its freedom, and Freud was about to demonstrate
that that is barely one tenth of what it is that makes one
human. The unconscious feelings that surrounded the child
Adolf Hitler would later be expressed by him, since their
manifestation was all around him.

Firstly, there was the scientific assault upon the world of
1889, which made of science something opposed to
common sense, and which has been superbly expressed by
Louis Pauwels and Jacques Bergier in *The Dawn of Magic*:

'The principle of the conservation of energy was
established as a certainty, solid as a rock. And yet here was
radium, producing energy without acquiring it from any

source. No one doubted that light and electricity were identical: they could only proceed in a straight line and were incapable of traversing any obstacle. And yet here were X-rays which could go through solid objects. In the discharge tubes matter seemed to disappear or be transformed into particles of energy. The transmutation of the elements was taking place in nature: radium turns into helium or lead. And so the Temple of Consecrated Beliefs is ready to collapse; Reason no longer reigns supreme! It seemed that anything was possible. The scientists who were supposed to have the monopoly of knowledge suddenly ceased to make a distinction between physics and metaphysics – between fact and fantasy. The pillars of the Temple dissolve into clouds, and the High Priests of Descartes are dumbfounded. If the theory of conservation of energy is false, what is there to prevent a medium from manufacturing an ectoplasm out of nothing? If magnetic waves can traverse the earth, why should thought-transmission not be possible? If all known bodies emit invisible forces, why should there not be astral bodies? If there is a fourth dimension, could this be the spirits' world?"[1]

Secondly, there was the artistic assault. The artist had no place in the world of 1889 that was compatible with his traditional role, for the world of 1889 was concerned not with what was true or beautiful, but with what was useful. The Church and the aristocracy no longer possessed the security which had enabled them to patronise artists opposed to their predominance, and the new plutocracy had no interest in useless visions, demanding instead to be amused and flattered, or earnestly instructed in values with which they already agreed. Those without a private income were forced to rely upon pleasing an anonymous public, which, in the words of G. M. Trevelyan, had been taught how to read, but was unable to distinguish what was worth reading. The optimism of the early Romantics had been shattered by the failure of the liberal revolutions of 1848: their vision of a better world had faded before the reality of a world that was remarkable only for its homage to

13

ugliness: the aggression of the Marquis de Sade had become the wistfulness of Leopold von Sacher-Masoch.

When we do remember the 1890s, we remember them for their decadence, even though the vast majority of people at the time thought this a temporary, negligible, and deeply regrettable aberration. Although few were involved in this artistic movement, it characterised an epoch, and took strongest hold in the most powerful, most industrialised, and most civilised countries, France, Great Britain, and Germany. Its most important aspects were its hostility to prevailing values, its worship of art for its own sake, its exaltation of style, its attraction to the evil and exotic, and its belief that the 1890s, far from being the springboard of progress, represented the twilight of empires such as had been seen when the power of Ancient Rome and of Byzantium had begun to wane.

In France, Baudelaire had already proclaimed the ecstasy of evil, and the necessity for exoticism. Artists had already cut themselves adrift from society. Now an entire group of artists were determined to express themselves, and nothing but themselves. J-K Huysmans wrote the bible of the decadence, *Against Nature*, in which a decadent aristocrat lives only for the beautiful, the useless, the artificial, the perverse; and *Down There*, in which he plunged into Satanism. He was followed by Verlaine, Rimbaud, Barbey d'Aurevilly, Mirbeau, Sar Peladan, Moreau, Redon, and others. Poets exalted the corrupted; painters sought strange and unfamiliar means of representing reality; and the world of art prepared to go mad.

The movement spread to Great Britain, where Whistler had proclaimed 'art for art's sake', Pater that 'all arts aspire to the condition of music', and Swinburne that Christianity had denied life. 1886 had seen the publication of a work loathed by all decent-minded Englishmen, especially if they had not read it, George Moore's *Confessions of a Young Man*, in which the author had declared sentiments which were in time to be put into practice:

'Art is the direct antithesis to democracy . . . Pity, that most vile of all vile virtues, has never been known to me.

14

The great pagan world I love knew it not. Now the world proposes to interrupt the terrible austere laws of nature which ordain that the weak shall be trampled upon, shall be ground into death and dust, that the strong shall be really strong – that the strong shall be glorious, sublime . . . Hither the world has been drifting since the coming of the pale socialist of Galilee; and this is why I hate Him and deny His divinity . . . Man would not be man but for injustice. Hail, therefore, to the thrice glorious virtue, injustice. What care I that some millions of wretched Israelites died under Pharaoh's lash or Egypt's sun? It was well that they died that I might have the pyramids to look upon . . . Oh for excess, for crime . . . we are weary of pity, we are weary of being good; we are weary of tears and effusion . . .'[2]

There followed the works of Dowson, Le Gallienne, Crackanthorpe and Davidson, the sparkling irreverence of Oscar Wilde, the bizarre drawings of Aubrey Beardsley, and though Wilde was sacrificed upon the altar of prurient propriety, and sentenced to penal servitude for homosexuality in 1895, that which the decadents expressed, continued.

Nor was the young nation of Italy left unaffected. Its foremost creative writer, Gabriele d'Annunzio, openly worshipped the world of the senses, bloodshed, barbarism, corruption, and inequality:

'Do you wish to fight? To kill?
To see streams of blood?
Great heaps of gold?
Herds of captive women?
Slaves?'

Later, his work would inspire Mussolini to essay the implementation of his thought. Indeed, it was as though virtually all serious artists believed that the world they knew was coming to an end, and regarded this as being a cause, not for sorrow, but for celebration. In a curiously prophetic work of 1896, the English author, M. P. Shiel, wrote a tale about a group of Supermen who roamed through Europe, murdering those whose flaws impeded the evolution of humanity: the story was entitled *The S.S.*

Beyond the arts and the sciences, however, there was a third assault, the assault of magic. The world of magic was most aggressively denied, therefore the world of magic, one of the most primitive and fundamental in the human psyche, would sooner or later exact a terrible revenge. The Church had persecuted magic, scientists now refused to admit its possibility, and men in the street laughed at it: even so, magic was afoot.

Just as the West was colonising the East, the East quietly proceeded to invade the West, and the superior communications of the West enabled a speedy transmission of ideas. Schopenauer had been the East's first messenger, but its most active propagandist was that most extraordinary personage, Madame Blavatsky.

Helena Petrovna Blavatsky was born in the Ukraine in 1831, and after various wanderings and adventures, including marriage, landed in New York in 1873, proclaiming an interest in, and knowledge of, Eastern esoteric doctrines. There she met Colonel Olcott, and with his assistance founded the Theosophical Society two years later. Its avowed aim was the study of Hidden Wisdom, and unfashionable though this pursuit then was, it still survives today. In 1878, Madame Blavatsky and Colonel Olcott sailed to India, where the Theosophical Society met with unexpected success. After some years of acclaim, and then a series of scandals involving allegations that Blavatsky's boasted mediumistic powers were fraudulent, she returned to Europe, where she died in 1891.

After her death, the Theosophical Society fell into the hands of Anna Kingsford and Edward Maitland, but continued to flourish until Annie Besant and C. W. Leadbeater produced a bogus World Messiah, Krishnamurti, who was eventually moved to repudiate publicly the role thrust upon him. This brought Theosophy into a richly deserved ridicule from which it never fully recovered, though even today it has a considerable following.

The Theosophical Society was, and is, of little consequence in itself, and is significant only insofar as it transmitted on a very large scale the doctrines contained in Madame Blavatsky's astonishing books, *Isis Unveiled* (1877) and *The Secret Doctrine* (1888). Madame Blavatsky went so far as to claim that the composition of her books was assisted by clairvoyance, and that obscure works and quotations had suddenly appeared in obedience to her needs and desires; that she was familiar with 'the oldest book in the world', the incalculably ancient *Stanzas of Dzyan*; and that Hidden Masters were in regular communication with her person. Needless to say, these claims have been disputed, but whatever the sources of Blavatsky's inspiration, and whatever else she may have been, the woman was not a mere charlatan, for no charlatan could possibly have written her exquisite mystical masterpiece, *The Voice of The Silence*.

The fact remains that Madame Blavatsky's writings had influence far beyond that which is usually assigned to them. They challenged Christianity, which Blavatsky loathed, and proclaimed in its stead a Westernised Hinduism, with its attractive doctrines of reincarnation and karma. They led people to seek alternatives to the Christian religion, and to suspect the existence of non-material occult forces, as mysterious and intangible as electricity, thus preparing the way in the popular mind for future scientific investigation.

However, three assertions in particular demand our attention. Whereas Nietzsche taught that the Superman is the imminent next stage in human evolution, Blavatsky announced that Supermen already existed, that they were the Hidden Masters who inhabited Central Asia, and that they could be contacted telepathically by those who had been initiated into their mysteries. Whereas the chemists and physicists taught that there was little more to learn about a universe of matter, Blavatsky insisted that there was much more to learn about a universe of spirit, which could act upon the former. And whereas biologists taught that man evolved from the apes, Blavatsky proclaimed that there have been four root races prior to our own, which included the ancient civilisations of lost Lemuria and Atlantis, that evolution has been assisted by divine kings

17

from the stars, that the Aryans are the purest of the fifth root race, and, more sinisterly, that the Jews are a degenerate link between the fourth and fifth root races, and hence are sub-human, a proposition with which Adolf Hitler concurred.

Although Theosophy taught that the use of ceremonial magic to aid evolution was dangerous and to be eschewed, this also was to have a renaissance, aided partly by an increasing acceptance of theosophical doctrines. The Eastern esoteric tradition began to pervade the West at roughly the same time that the West's own slumbering esoteric tradition began to awaken. This tradition was an amalgam of lore drawn from the Magic of Egypt and Chaldea, the Hebrew Qabalah, the Tarot, the works of medieval magicians, wizards and alchemists, Rosicrucianism, and Freemasonry. This tradition was kept alive in the middle of the nineteenth century by Alphonse Louis Constant, better known as Eliphas Levi, in France, by Lord Edward Bulwer-Lytton in England, and by various obscure groups in Germany.

Eliphas Levi was the author of three important books: *The Ritual and Doctrine of High Magic*, *The Key of the Mysteries*, and *The History of Magic*, important because they were read by many of the French decadents, some of whom interpreted magic as being satanic and opposed utterly to the Catholic Church, and who then embraced it more sweetly. J-K Huysmans joined a magical order for a brief while and dabbled in Satanism, the effect being to intoxicate his disciples with diablerie; Sar Peladan became a Rosicrucian, hailed Wagner as 'a natural magician', and influenced Symboliste painting; and Stanislas de Guiata and Dr Gerard Encausse, which latter wrote an influential book on the Tarot under the name of Papus, revived French interest in magic. This interest, which lent to the decadence its aura of the forbidden, still survives.

Nor was the revival of the tradition any less significant in England. Although Bulwer-Lytton achieved renown as a politician, esteem as a friend of Dickens and Disraeli, and fame as the author of *The Last Days of Pompeii*, his true interest was magic, and he proceeded to express both his fascination and his understanding in two novels, *Zanoni* and *A Strange Story*, and in a magnificent and unusual ghost-story, *The Haunted and the Haunters: Or, the House and the Brain*. Those who read them, and there were many, including a most enthusiastic Richard Wagner, learned that materialism was utterly false; that magic was a path to becoming the Superman; that Supermen lived in the world as semi-immortal initiates who even now took pupils; and that the instrument whereby we can evolve is that thing of vast and unknown potential, the human brain.

These tales changed the lives of many in the 1890s, and it is not surprising to learn that Lytton knew, and was respected by, Eliphas Levi. Yet the work of his which had most influence enjoyed it neither in France nor in Great Britain, but in Germany. It was entitled *The Coming Race*. In this story, a man discovers that beneath the caverns of the earth exists a vast civilisation, far superior to our own in every respect, which has developed a superhuman psychic power known as *vril*, and which can, as a result, easily perform what we would call 'miracles'. One day this race of Supermen will emerge from the earth and rule us or destroy us. It is not known whether Lytton believed his own tale, but certainly many Nazis subsequently did.

Although there are some similarities between the ideas of Lytton and those of Madame Blavatsky, Lytton would have repudiated much of Theosophy. He advocated a scientific approach to ceremonial magic, in which every statement could be tested by experiment and experience, and would have found nothing to commend in Blavatsky's dubious strictures concerning the Jews. At the time, though, Lytton was but one of a handful of men, like Fred Hockley, Kenneth MacKenzie and Robert Wentworth Little, who kept alive an interest in Masonry, Rosicrucianism, occultism and the unknown. It was, however, from this nucleus, that the most influential occult organisation of the twentieth century would evolve, the Hermetic Order Of The Golden Dawn.

The origins of this order are still a matter for dispute. Somehow or other, some coded manuscripts fell into the hands of two gentlemen interested in the occult, Dr

Woodford and Dr Wynn Westcott. When deciphered, these manuscripts turned out to consist of some skeletonic rituals, and the address of a certain adept, one Anna Sprengel, who lived in Nuremberg. Dr Westcott asked an occult scholar, S. L. Mathers, to assist him; Mathers agreed to write a series of suitable rituals based upon the skeletons; and Westcott wrote to Anna Sprengel, and received a charter to found an Order, and much occult teaching. Now, it has been alleged that Anna Sprengel never existed, and that the Golden Dawn was the creation of Westcott and Mathers, but this does not really matter: the Golden Dawn is important for what it was and not for who founded it. We can at least state that it was founded in 1888.

In 1891, it was claimed that Anna Sprengel had died, that her successors in Nuremberg had broken off all correspondence, and that they had urged the English magicians to formulate their own links with *the Secret Chiefs*. Who or what were these mysterious beings? It seems that they were the same as the Hidden Masters of Blavatsky or Unknown Supermen of Lytton. In 1892, S. L. Mathers claimed to have formulated a link with them, and his description is of interest:

'Concerning the Secret Chiefs of the Order, to whom I make reference . . . I can tell you *nothing*. I know not even their earthly names. I know them only by certain secret mottoes, I have but very rarely seen them in the physical body; and on such rare occasions *the rendezvous was made astrally by them*. They met me in the flesh at the time and place appointed beforehand. For my part I believe them to be human and living on this earth; but possessing terrible superhuman powers.

When such rendezvous has been in a much frequented place there has been nothing in their personal appearance or dress to make them out as differing in any way from ordinary people except the appearance and sensation of transcendant health and vigour . . . which was their invariable accompaniment; in other words, the physical appearance which the possession of the Elixir of Life had traditionally been supposed to confer.

On the other hand when the rendezvous has been in a place free from any access by the Outer World they have usually been in symbolic robes and insignia.

But my physical intercourse with them on these rare occasions has shown me how difficult it is for a Mortal, even though advanced in Occultism, to support the presence of an Adept in the physical body . . . the sensation was that of being in contact with so terrible a force that I can only compare it to the continued effect of that usually experienced momentarily by any person close to whom a flash of lightning passes during a violent storm; coupled with a difficulty in respiration similar to the half strangling effect produced by ether; and if such was the result produced on one as tested as I have been in Occult work, I cannot conceive a much less advanced Initiate being able to support such a strain, even for five minutes without death ensuing.'[3]

Mathers emerged as the Order's undisputed master, and though Westcott, who resigned in 1897, later claimed that a Belgian occultist rather than Unknown Supermen dictated occult knowledge to Mathers, the latter definitely believed that he was in contact with the Secret Chiefs from that moment onward. Indeed, he was a remarkable man, who devoted his life entirely to magic. He was the translator and editor of such arcane medieval classics as *The Greater Key of Solomon* and *The Sacred Magic of Abra-Melin the Mage*; of *The Qabalah Unveiled*; and of a short book on the Tarot from which most subsequent authors have borrowed without acknowledgement. Yet nowhere in these books does he display the synthetic genius which enabled him to create the system of magic practised by the Golden Dawn. He weaved together rituals, methods and knowledge from innumerable sources into something that was beautiful, harmonious, logical, and, for those who worked with it, efficaceous. The aim of Golden Dawn magic is nothing less than to become the Superman: the method is the use of light, colour, sound, scent, words and ceremonial, and of meditation, to train the human brain and focus the human will so that a transformation of the magician's life can take place, enabling him to know and use his full potential.

A strong supporter both of the hereditary principle and of authoritarian government, Mathers believed that man could become the Superman here and now, but that this course was only for the few. In 1894, he moved to Paris with his wife and founded another Order temple; meanwhile, the membership of the Golden Dawn grew to three figures, without publicity, and temples operated in London, Edinburgh, Bradford and Weston-super-Mare. English men and women, from all walks of life, studied and practised means of tapping Lytton's *vril* force, developing the unconscious, and coming into contact with the supersensible beings of another world. It is a very odd fact that when they attained to the Grade of Zelator, which was connected with the energies of the element of Earth, members learned to give a certain sign, which may or may not have been learned from Anna Sprengel and her Order in Nuremberg: this sign, which invoked the power of the soil, would become notorious as that of *Heil Hitler*!

But Mathers, remarkable as he was, and believing as he correctly did, against all odds, in the imminence of a world war, was by no means the only extraordinary figure connected with the Goldem Dawn. The man who emerged as master of the London temple was the poet and future Nobel Prize winner, William Butler Yeats.

Like Mathers, Yeats had known Madame Blavatsky; like Mathers, Yeats considered himself 'a voice of . . . a greater renaissance – the revolt of the soul against the intellect'. He insisted that 'the mystical life is the centre of all that I do and all that I think and all that I write'. He believed that by magic one could become a Superman. Rather less attractively, he gave expression to his Utopia, one which the Nazis would have adored:

'. . . an aristocratic civilisation in its most completed form, every detail of life hierarchical, every great man's door crowded at dawn by petitioners, great wealth everywhere in few men's hands, all dependent upon a few, up to the Emperor himself, who is a God dependent upon a greater God, and everywhere, in Court, in the family, an inequality made law.'⁴

Yeats endeavoured to interest Aubrey Beardsley in magic, and though Beardsley did not join the Golden Dawn, he expressed the effect a knowledge of magic had had upon him in his unique drawing, *Of a Neophyte, and of How the Black Art was Revealed Unto Him*.

Other members were hardly the mediocrities a rationalist might expect to find in a mysterious Order. They included Aleister Crowley, who would take the Golden Dawn system to pastures then unsuspected; Crowley's teachers, George Cecil Jones and Allan Bennett, which latter brought Hinayana Buddhism to Great Britain. They included men who achieved some eminence in their own time, such as Peck, Astronomer Royal of Scotland, and Gerald Kelly, subsequently knighted and made President of the Royal Academy. They included women such as Moina Bergson, wife of Mathers and daughter of the philosopher Henri Bergson, painter and clairvoyant; Florence Farr, friend of Bernard Shaw; Maud Gonne, who inspired Yeats; and Annie Horniman who did English Drama a service by founding the Gaiety Theatre. They included writers like Bram Stoker, author of *Dracula*; Sax Rohmer, author of the Fu Manchu tales and of *Brood of the Witch Queen*; Brodie Innes, author of *The Devil's Mistress*; and Algernon Blackwood, one of the greatest masters of the tale of terror. These writers broadened the awareness of all who read them, and probably the most important of this group was Arthur Machen.

A frontispiece designed by Aubrey Beardsley adorned the first edition of Machen's first tale of horror, *The Great God Pan*. The tale announced that the god Pan is not dead, and can be found even in English meadows and in English cities, for there still exist sacraments for good and for evil that are far older than Christianity. In a subsequent book, *The Three Impostors*, Machen dwelt upon the idea that these sacraments are all around us, did we but know it, and that the world is a place of magic and of mystery. His superbly written and powerful tales, suggesting as no other

23

writer has done the existence of forces far beyond our comprehension and of which the pagans knew, resulted in Dr Westcott inviting him to join the Order of the Golden Dawn, and writing a letter to him which declared:

'This book amply proves that by thought and meditation rather than through reading, you have attained a certain degree of initiation independently of orders or organisation.'[5]

If prophecy is proof of initiation, then Machen was an initiate, for the pagan frenzy of which he wrote came to pass in his own lifetime. Indeed, it is curious that other things of which he dreamed also manifested themselves.

Machen, who was initiated into the Golden Dawn in 1899, had written *The Three Impostors* in 1895. The plot had told of a pale, nervous young man with spectacles, who was pursued by three impostors who were members of an Order which practised black magic: a smooth, smiling, clean-shaven gentleman; a young lady who told bizarre and outlandish tales; and a thug. Once in the Golden Dawn, Machen encountered the pale, nervous, young man with spectacles, William Butler Yeats, and learned that he lived in fear of assault, physical or magical, by a smooth, smiling, clean-shaven gentleman, Aleister Crowley, who was alleged to practise black magic; and by a young lady who told bizarre and outlandish tales, Elaine Simpson, Crowley's mistress; and by a thug whom Crowley had hired.

Machen had come unwittingly upon the quarrel between W. B. Yeats and S. L. Mathers and his ally, Crowley, a quarrel which soon split the Golden Dawn into a group of warring sects, and which, taken with an unimportant scandal, had the effect of inducing Machen and others to leave the Order. He gave up writing, took up acting, and then journalism, and became a Christian. We will briefly return to him later, in 1914, when his power to 'dream true' asserted itself for the last time with the fantastic episode of the Angels of Mons.

Golden Dawn groups have lingered on to this day, but the Order's significant work was done by 1900. A few inhabitants of the most industrialised and rational empire in the world had acquainted themselves with the ancient and neglected arts of magic. Nor had the people of Great Britain's leading competitor for world supremacy, the German Empire, been left untouched by this sudden occult fever. Various groups, quite ferociously nationalistic, had kept going throughout the nineteenth century. In 1895, Karl Kellner, a wealthy iron-master, who had been taught by one Arab and two Hindu masters, proclaimed the establishment of the quasi-Masonic Order of the Oriental Templars, or OTO. By 1904, this Order was producing a periodical, *The Oriflamme,* and teaching a system of sexual magic based upon control of the *vril.* Though this Order became the second greatest influence upon twentieth-century esoteric thought, it was not at the time of its foundation as important as two German magicians independent of it, Guido von List and Lanz von Liebenfels.

In 1875, Guido von List, a white-bearded magus in flowing robes, celebrated the Summer Solstice by burying a number of empty wine bottles on the summit of a hill overlooking Vienna: these wine bottles were placed in the form of a sign which had not been seen in the land before; it was used as a Badge of Power in the Golden Dawn, where it was known as The Hermetic Cross; it was known also as the Hammer of Thor; it was an exclusively Aryan symbol; it was the Swastika.

In 1907, Adolf Lanz, who called himself Lanz von Liebenfels, ran up a flag from his magical temple which overlooked the Danube; it was the Swastika. The sign stood for all that List and Liebenfels believed in: an abandonment of Christianity, an embracing of neo-paganism, a desire to become or create the Superman, and an affirmation of Aryan racial superiority. We will be returning to these two strange men, who had much effect upon the views of Hitler.

Such were the ideas which were born or resurrected at around the same time as Hitler's birth. Such were the ideas which he would greedily imbibe in Vienna. Such were the ideas which began to infect a world which believed it could not be infected. Such were the ideas which played their part in making the twentieth century what it is.

One could be pardoned for observing that the values and gods of the world were entering upon their dotage, and that the gods of a new, strange, and terrible age were stirring in their sleep and about to awaken. Was there a meaning behind this assortment of signs, portents, prophecies, beliefs, omens, coincidences and lunacies? *The Second Coming* was written in or around 1921 by William Butler Yeats, but it applies more surely to the strange broth we have examined:

'Surely some revelation is at hand;
Surely the Second Coming is at hand.
The Second Coming! Hardly are those words out
When a vast image out of *Spiritus Mundi*
Troubles my sight: somewhere in sands of the desert
A shape with lion body and the head of a man
A gaze blank and pitiless as the sun
Is moving its slow thighs, while all about it
Reel shadows of the indignant desert birds.
The darkness drops again; but now I know
That twenty centuries of stony sleep
Were vexed to nightmare by a rocking cradle,
And what rough beast, its hour come round at last,
Slouches towards Bethlehem to be born?'[6]

CHAPTER THREE

The Equinox of the Gods

'Now let there be a veiling of this shrine; now let the light devour men and eat them up with blindness!'

The Book of The Law II 14

'We are at the outset of a tremendous revolution in moral ideas and man's spiritual orientation. A new age of the magic interpretation of the world is coming, an interpretation in terms of will and not the intelligence.'

Adolf Hitler

The irrationalism that we have so far examined cannot be dismissed if we wish to understand a man as irrational as Hitler, or that still more irrational thing, the breakdown of nineteenth-century Western civilisation and its imposing heritage. We therefore make no apology for continuing in our bizarre quest for clues which will enable us to understand these matters, even if it initially appears that our subject-matter is only of marginal relevance, and best left to cranks. The word 'initially' must be stressed, for subsequent events will reveal the importance of our peculiar clues; furthermore, it is an essential part of our historical method to neglect nothing, no matter how outlandish, that may better inform our comprehension.

Our first guide will be Aleister Crowley, who, though he now possesses many more disciples than ever in his own lifetime, is still dismissed by most of those who have heard of him as a charlatan, a madman, or a debauchee. Despite these dispiriting labels, he is of interest to us, for he became one of the very few men who understood the time in which he lived, a statement which requires some form of explanation.

27

Crowley was born in Warwickshire in 1875, the year of the foundation of the Theosophical Society. He survived a strict Plymouth Brethren upbringing, rebelled against it, and, after coming down from Cambridge University, was initiated into the Order of the Golden Dawn in 1898. He became involved in the 1900 quarrel between Mathers and Yeats, took the side of Mathers, fought a magical duel with Yeats, and then departed for Mexico, where he set world mountain-climbing records, wrote poetry, and tirelessly practised the magic arts, having sworn to renounce all that he possessed for the sake of illumination.

From Mexico he went to India and Ceylon, where he worked at yoga with Allan Bennett, attained to the trance known as Dhyana, and embraced the philosophy of Buddhism. After an abortive but record-setting attempt to climb the world's second highest mountain, K2, he returned to Europe, and married a woman of society, Rose Edith Kelly. The couple set out on another world tour; by this time Crowley had abandoned ceremonial magic in favour of his Buddhism.

In April 1904, Crowley and his wife were in Cairo, and she asked him to perform a magical ritual purely out of curiosity, having little interest in the subject. Soon afterwards, she became 'inspired', and declared to Crowley that 'they are waiting for you', eventually informing him that 'they' meant in particular the god Horus. A sceptical Crowley carried out a series of tests based on the traditional magical associations which this god possesses, and though Rose had no knowledge at all of occultism, she guessed correctly every time against total odds of 21,168,000 to 1. The upshot of all this was that Crowley performed an Invocation to the god Horus, the hawk-headed Egyptian god of war, and obeyed his wife's instructions to sit at a desk in his hotel room on the 8, 9 and 10 April between 12 noon and 1 o'clock. A being which announced himself as Aiwass appeared behind him on each occasion, and dictated to him the three chapters of a book called *Liber Al vel Legis* or *The Book of The Law*.

Judged on one level, *The Book of the Law* is an extraordinarily beautiful prose-poem, but it declares itself

28

to be much, much more. It proclaimed nothing less than that one age had come to an end, and another had replaced it. The old age was that of Osiris, the god who died and rose again, known also as Adonis, Attis, Dionysus, and Jesus Christ: the new age was that of Horus, the Crowned and Conquering Child. Hence *The Book of the Law* announced a new ethic for mankind.

The first and foremost command was *Do What Thou Wilt Shall Be the Whole of the Law*, which means that man must know and understand the essence of his self, his true will, and do it – and nothing else. The second, *Love is the Law, Love Under Will*, proclaimed that the nature of things is love, or the urge for union. The third, *Every man and every woman is a star*, declared that each human being is unique insofar as his or her true will is concerned, and to this was added, *The word of Sin is Restriction*, which meant that all restraints upon the true will are evil and must be destroyed.

Much of the document, however, was not as attractive as the above. In no uncertain terms it asserted that before the religion of the new age could take effect, the old aeon must be swept away as ruthlessly as was the pagan world of the Roman Empire, and that the planet would therefore be bathed in blood. Barbarism, lust and cruelty were prophesied, and the destruction of all Christian sentiments. *The Book of the Law* therefore challenged the cultural tradition of two thousand years.

It asserted the reality of magic, of mysterious and irrational forces, of Unknown Supermen, one of whom was its author. It exulted in inequality between the masters, who know and do their will, and slaves, who do not. It demanded courage, blood, fire, irresponsibility, excess and ecstasy: it denounced all old religions, democracy, mediocrity, pacifism, logic, humanitarianism and stability. It is uncomfortable reading.

Aleister Crowley was the first to find it so. As a Buddhist, he could not accept that 'Existence is pure joy'; as a Shelleyan humanist, he could not accept its exaltation of destruction; as a philosophical sceptic, he was embarrassed by its hailing of him as The Beast 666, come to destroy

29

Christianity, even though that was what his own mother had called him. He did not want to be a prophet, and deliberately lost the manuscript, though it obstinately refused to disappear permanently, and thrust itself upon his attention again in 1909, when he was finally moved to take it seriously.

But how seriously should we take *The Book of the Law*? It was certainly not the conscious composition of Aleister Crowley; some have argued that it was an automatic writing produced by his unconscious. Whatever it was, it is of unusual interest, for, as we shall see, certain of its precepts took effect in a most alarming way, and hardly in the manner that Aleister Crowley initially anticipated. Let us content ourselves with the statement that the destruction of the old world was announced in 1904, when it was also announced that world war was imminent, and that entirely new values would replace old and outmoded ones.

Of course, the people of 1904 had no idea that the Age of Horus was upon them, being only marginally less smug than in 1889. Artists, poets, musicians, novelists, magicians, mystics and madmen may have believed that a catastrophe was in the offing, but most found the very idea to be completely absurd. The great powers were now stronger rather than weaker; the artistic decadence of the 1890s was already receding in popular memory; there had been no European war since 1870–1; the colonies still disgorged their wealth; thinkers and rationalists loudly proclaimed the doctrine of progress; and it was automatically assumed that Christian civilisation would resist all changes and all onslaughts.

It is of interest that some orthodox historians, who have not read *The Book of the Law*, and who, one suspects, would rather die than read *The Book of the Law*, nevertheless regard 1904 as the year in which the death knell of European hegemony was first sounded. Their reasoning is based on the consequences of the Russo-Japanese War which broke out in that year, and which was won by Japan.

'It disrupted Russia by stimulating the virus of revolution which for long had eaten into her bowels. By liberating Germany from fear of war on her eastern flank, it freed her to concentrate on her western border, and thereby upset the balance of power in Europe. This caused Great Britain to abandon her policy of isolation, which had been the backbone of the Pax Britannica, and, in order to re-establish the balance, it drew her away from Germany towards France. Further, by challenging the supremacy of the white man over the coloured, it awakened Asia and Africa and dealt a deadly moral blow to every colonial empire . . .'[1]

'It gave the impulse in Turkey to the revolutionary activities which led to the fall of Abdul Hamid. It made an overwhelming impression in Persia, which was the first Asiatic nation to start a simultaneous struggle against its own despots and against the rapacity of European governments. The same is true of China.'[2]

'In Africa the influence was equally profound . . . it is impossible to exaggerate the effects of the Japanese victory upon the Indian mind . . . The fall of Port Arthur in 1905, like the fall of Constantinople in 1453, rightly may be numbered among the few really great events in history.'[3]

The significance of the Russo-Japanese War can only be seen in retrospect; no one was so historically acute at the time, and no one was converted by this event to a belief in the West's coming doom. In fact we find in Germany a growing belief in Teutonic racial superiority and in a predestined greatness, that seemed oblivious to the awakening of Asia. It is rewarding, however, to take a closer look at three proponents of this Pan-German nationalism, for we will find that though they did not believe that the age of European supremacy had passed, they did think that the Christian character of Europe was being eroded, should be eroded, and should be replaced by a new ethic. Their names were Houston Stewart Chamberlain, Guido von List and Lanz von Liebenfels. They were cranks, but they were also prophets.

Houston Stewart Chamberlain was an Englishman, born in 1855, who went to live in Germany in 1882, obsessed by its history, its language, its mythology, its culture, and its future. In 1905, he divorced his Prussian wife and three years later he married Richard Wagner's daughter, Eva, moving to Wagner's adopted town of Bayreuth, where he died in 1927. His most influential work, *Foundations of the Nineteenth Century*, was published in 1899. A volume of twelve hundred pages, it would sell over a quarter of a million copies.

Chamberlain's methods of composition would not elicit the approval of academics. According to William Shirer:

'Hypersensitive and neurotic and subject to frequent nervous breakdowns, Chamberlain was given to seeing demons who, by his own account, drove him on relentlessly to seek new fields of study and get on with his prodigious writings. One vision after another forced him to change from biology to botany, to the fine arts, to music, to philosophy, to biography, to history. Once, in 1896, when he was returning from Italy, the presence of a demon became so forceful that he got off the train at Gardone, shut himself up in a hotel room for eight days and . . . wrote feverishly on a biological thesis until he had the germ of the theme that would dominate all of his later works: race and history.

'There was . . . a profound unity of inspiration in all his published works and they had a remarkable coherence. Since he felt himself goaded on by demons, his books (on Wagner, Goethe, Kant, Christianity and race) were written in the grip of a terrible fever, a veritable trance, a state of self-induced intoxication, so that, as he says in his autobiography, *Lebenswege*, he was often unable to recognise them as his own work, because they surpassed his expectations.'[4]

It was Chamberlain who synthesised the views of Nietzsche and Wagner; who declared that the key to history is race; who believed that all civilisation flows from the white race and that the Teutonic peoples are its purest representatives; who taught that the Jews were the sworn enemies of the Aryans, bent on polluting their blood with inter-breeding so as to induce a degeneracy which would allow the Jews to rule; who insisted that Jesus Christ was not a Jew but an Aryan; and who advocated a new religion to replace even Aryanised Christianity, one that would fit the needs of a German master race.

Chamberlain argued that 'God builds today upon the Germans alone'. He recognised that new values were needed to assist the Germans in their triumphant evolution, but though he saw in mysticism the supreme expression of the Aryan spirit, he doubted whether this was suitable for the mass of German people. A new religion and a new god were therefore urgently required since 'the German stands apart and waits for a god to descend from Heaven'.

Foundations of the Nineteenth Century made Chamberlain famous and respected throughout Germany. Both Kaiser Wilhelm II and Adolf Hitler were to hail the author as a prophet and a sage. The Englishman's influence grew until he became the most renowned philosopher of the Second Reich, and mentor to the Kaiser himself.

We will be returning to H. S. Chamberlain. For our present purposes, however, it is necessary to pass on to two of his admirers, those devotees of the Swastika whom we have met before, List and Liebenfels. Guido von List, who was born in 1848, and who, fourteen years later, renounced his Catholic faith and vowed to build a temple to Wotan, had by 1908 acquired a following large enough to ensure the establishment of a flourishing Guido von List Society. Within this society there existed an Inner Order of 'Armanen Initiates'. For List's ideas of history and biology were similar to those of Madame Blavatsky, and like the theosophist, he claimed to be clairvoyantly inspired: he had had visions of an ancient race of German Supermen called the Armanen, the last surviving member of whom was apparently List himself.

This group of self-proclaimed initiates was ferociously nationalistic and anti-semitic. It attached great importance to the study of runes, a pastime which would also fascinate Himmler's SS, and to the sagas of the Teutonic tribes.

List's writings enjoyed widespread popularity, especially his major work, *Rita der Ario-Germanen* (Laws of the Aryan Germans), which was published in 1908, the year Hitler began his residence in Vienna. Nor was his dubious influence confined to the written word: some of his disciples would found the German Order, which insisted on measuring the skulls of prospective candidates to ensure they were of Aryan origin, and from which the Thule Group, later joined by Hitler, would derive; and List must be regarded as the true founder of *volkisch* occultism, the study of German nationalist, racist and occult folklore, to which a surprisingly large number of people were attracted.

List's ideas were to find practical expression in the Third Reich. He believed that if Germans were to be saved from their enemy, 'the hydra-headed international Jewish conspiracy', a racial state had to be constructed, in which inferior peoples would be the slaves of the Aryans. This new Reich would be divided into units called *Gaue*, each with its *Gauleiter*. Its leader would be 'a self-chosen Führer to whom (the German) willingly submits', bound to his followers by a sacred oath almost identical to those taken later by Hitler. There would be special racial laws exalting the Aryans and degrading inferiors, including stringent marriage laws to prevent 'mongrelisation'. The symbols of the new Reich would be the swastika and the double 'sig' rune, the latter being a symbol of racial purity which would in time be adopted by the SS.

The Reich would then be ready to annihilate the enemy. 'All military preparations must be made in the most complete detail,' List wrote, 'in order to fight this inevitable war which will come because it must come.' List died in the wake of Germany's defeat, on 17 May 1919, but not before penning a letter which contained a remarkable prophecy: in 1932 there would be established a racially pure community that would destroy both democracy and Jewry. The letter was signed '*mit Armanengruss und Heil*'.

Hitler came to power in 1933, whereupon Germans took to saluting each other with the *deutsche Gruss* and *Heil Hitler!* And the influence of List upon Hitler is confirmed by the dedication on the flyleaf of a book, dated 1921, in

Hitler's private library: 'To Adolf Hitler, my dear brother in Armanen'. The Armanen, we recall, constituted the Inner Order of List's Society.

List was also greatly respected by Lanz von Liebenfels, who was born plain Adolf Lanz in 1874, and who subsequently entered a monastery from which he was expelled in 1899 for harbouring 'carnal and worldly desires'. He then founded his own magical order, the Order of New Templars, which acquired a temple overlooking the Danube in 1907. One of the order's more illustrious members was the dramatist, August Strindberg. Another was Guido von List himself, whose own society Liebenfels joined in turn.

Liebenfels did not look like a magician, and descriptions of his appearance remind one of Heinrich Himmler: the two men also thought in a similar way. The ideas of Liebenfels were publicised in the magazine *Ostara*, the cover of which usually displayed a 'noble Nordic' combating a seedy 'racial degenerate'. Here one could learn of the racial superiority of the Aryans in general and the Germans in particular, and of the necessity for racial purity. Liebenfels advocated forced labour and a starvation diet for those who indulged in inter-racial sexual relationships. He also maintained that citizenship should be denied to non-Aryans; that the Aryans were responsible for all creativity in history; that they were opposed in all they did by 'Dark Forces' – Jews, Slavs and Negroes; and that the best remedy against race pollution was the castration of offenders. Many of the ideas in *Ostara* were enthusiastically adopted by Streicher's *Die Sturmer* in the 1920s, and even more enthusiastically put into practice by Himmler's SS in the 1930s and 1940s.

Why this obsessive need for racial purity? It was because Liebenfels believed that the Superman could be *bred*, and bred only from thoroughbred Aryan stock; hence he proposed the establishment of special breeding colonies. If this idea was lunacy, young Hitler did not think so. He became an avid reader of *Ostara*, which brought about a meeting with Liebenfels in 1909. He also became the owner of a curious work by Liebenfels, *The Book of German*

Psalms: The Prayerbook of Arios-Racial Mystics and Anti-Semites.

There can be no doubt that something novel and strange, irrational and repellent, was brewing in the world, and especially in the German-speaking world, in the early years of the twentieth century, something which few could have foreseen in 1889. What was happening lay far beyond the comprehension of most minds, including then that of Aleister Crowley, who would have been appalled by Chamberlain, List and Liebenfels had he known of them. He would soon come to realise that the old world would be destroyed by any means whatever that were appropriate, and that the mother of the new world would first bring forth her mangled abortions.

If there was some power, or current of energy or thought that had come into existence, then it could be tapped by individuals for their own ends, providing those ends were consistent with the idea of destruction. We must focus now on one who did precisely that, one who is about to make his entrance, one who will dominate the stage of world history, the one of whom Lanz von Liebenfels wrote to a fellow magician in 1932:

'Hitler is one of our pupils . . . You will one day experience that he, and through him we, will one day be victorious, and develop a movement that will make the world tremble . . .'[5]

CHAPTER FOUR

The Education of Adolf Hitler

'There is great danger in me; for who doth not understand these runes shall make a great miss. He shall fall down into the pit called Because, and there he shall perish with the dogs of Reason.

Now a curse upon Because and his kin!

May Because be accursed for ever!

If Will stops and cries Why, invoking Because, then Will stops & does nought.

If Power asks why, then is Power weakness.

Also reason is a lie; for there is a factor infinite & unknown; & all their words are skew-wise.

Enough of Because! Be he damned for a dog!'

The Book of the Law II 27–33

'It is impossible to understand Hitler's political plans unless one is familiar with his basic beliefs and his conviction that there is a magic relationship between Man and the Universe.'

Hermann Rauschning

'The aim of human evolution is to attain a mystic vision of the Universe.'

Adolf Hitler

I

Much of the writing about Adolf Hitler gives us no understanding whatever of the man. Some explain that he was a madman, without explaining how a madman, by definition one not responsible for his actions, could rise from the Vienna gutter to the lordship of the mighty empire he created, and be worshipped as a god. Some dismiss him as a monster, which automatically dismisses the possibility of comprehension of him as a man. Some admit that he was a genius, which apparently lets them out of examining the sources of, and reasons for his genius. Hitler is surrounded by a mystical fog. Therefore, if we wish to understand him, let us try to approach him without prejudice, at least for the time being.

He was the son of Alois Hitler, a minor Austrian customs official, born illegitimately under the name of Schiklgruber which he subsequently changed, and Klara Poelzl, who came from a family of small peasant proprietors. He was not proud of this petty-bourgeois background and in later life he refused to discuss it. He also possessed the typical petty-bourgeois fear of slipping back into the working-classes.

Alois Hitler fully intended that his son would follow him as a civil servant, but the son, though barely eleven, resolved to resist the prospect of this worthy but uninspiring career. Despite the fact that the father was authoritarian and domineering, the boy fought bitterly against his wish, and, comforted by his day-dreams, shocked his earnest parent by announcing that it was his intention to become an artist. The battle of wills continued until the father's death in 1903, when Adolf was thirteen.

Possibly as a result of this conflict, Hitler was an unimpressive pupil at the high school in Linz; at least that was his excuse. Furthermore, he detested his teachers:

'Our teachers were absolute tyrants. They had no sympathy with youth; their one object was to stuff our brains and turn us into erudite apes like themselves. If any pupil showed the slightest trace of originality, they persecuted him relentlessly . . .'[1]

There was only one exception to this sweeping condemnation (which many of us have echoed) and this was the history teacher, a fanatical German nationalist named Dr Leopold Poetsch.

38

Dr Poetsch was responsible for arousing in Hitler an impassioned German nationalism and a life-long love of history, though his school performance was only fair. So much in debt to this teacher did Hitler feel, that he visited him in 1938, just after Austria had been annexed by Germany, and remarked to his intimates, 'You cannot imagine how much I owe to that old man.'

When Hitler was sixteen, a lung ailment forced him to drop out of school without graduating. He did not return, nor did he ever forget his poor performance, and would in later life rail against the academic world and angrily justify his own failure. The impression he had made upon the school may be judged by the evidence of the science teacher, Professor Gissinger, and the French teacher, Professor Huemar. According to the former:

'As far as I was concerned Hitler left neither a favourable nor unfavourable impression in Linz . . . He was slender and erect, his face pallid and very thin, almost like that of a consumptive, his gaze unusually open, his eyes brilliant.'[2]

According to the latter:

'Hitler was certainly gifted, although only for particular subjects, but he lacked self-control and, to say the least, he was considered argumentative, autocratic, self-opinionated and bad-tempered, and unable to submit to school discipline.'[3]

From this we can build up an impression of Hitler as an awkward adolescent, probably spoiled by his mother; a wilful, obstinate introvert, unwilling to work at anything which did not interest him; an individualist remote from his school-fellows; the same can be said for the adolescence of many budding artists. This impression is supported by a boyhood friend, who recalled him as a pale, sickly youth, shy and withdrawn, who used to explode unpredictably against those who disagreed with him in a fit of temper so violent it bordered on the hysterical.

The years from 1905-8 Hitler was to describe as 'the happiest days of my life'. He was free of the school which he loathed and of the father whom he had defied, and though his mother nagged at him to obtain a job, she had lost the control over her son which would have enabled her desires to prevail. Hitler was free to follow the pursuits he loved, to visit the opera and listen to the music of his idol, Richard Wagner, to read works of history and mythology, to wander through country lanes and city streets, to dream, and to declaim the contents of his dreams to his only friend, August Kubizek. He had much in common with imaginative adolescents of all times and all places, including the incapacity to translate his fantasies into reality. He fell in love with a blonde girl called Stefanie, but for four years merely gazed at her from afar: this could have been prompted by shyness, or by the emergence of the masochistic desires he would later reveal. He buried himself in a self-created world of imagination, his dreams coloured by the facts that he was both an impassioned nationalist and an ardent Wagnerian.

Hitler persisted in his belief that he would become an artist, but in 1907 failed the entrance examination to the Vienna Academy of Fine Art. He was advised, after he had failed again the following year, to give up painting and take up architecture, but unless he could demonstrate special talent, he was barred from the Vienna School of Architecture on account of his failure to graduate from high school.

Young Hitler's world now began to fall apart. Evidently the world did not share his high opinion of his own talents. Moreover, his mother died in December 1908, and he seems to have had a genuine love for her. Despite this sudden shattering of both his dreams and his reality, Hitler vowed to leave Linz and fulfil his potential in the capital city of Austria-Hungary.

'With a suitcase of clothes and underwear in my hand, and an indomintable will in my heart, I set out for Vienna. I too hoped to wrest from fate what my father had accomplished fifty years before; I too hoped to become "something" – but in no case a civil servant.'⁴

He lacked qualifications, funds, connections, and useful talents. His sole assets were a State orphan's pension, a knowledge of history, a love of Wagner, an interest in Pan-German politics, an unwillingness to do any uninteresting work, a sense of personal destiny, and the 'indomitable will' which he spoke of.

II

For a youth of such high hopes and grandiose dreams, the experience of reality in Vienna must have been a most terrible disillusionment. From 1909–13 he lived in the civilised and cosmopolitan city without making the smallest impression upon the vast majority of its citizens:

'To me Vienna, the city which to so many is the epitome of innocent pleasure, a festive playground for merrymakers, represents, I am sorry to say, merely the living memory of the saddest period of my life.'[5]

Though he continued to design imposing buildings, Hitler made no effort to gain admittance to the School of Architecture, as if he suspected and feared another rejection. In November 1909, poverty forced him to abandon a furnished room and to break with his friend August Kubizek: the latter was achieving remarkable success at Vienna's Music Conservatoire, and Hitler's pride could not allow his former disciple to witness his failure and humiliation. He disappeared into the world of flophouses, charity soup kitchens and mens' hostels, mingling with the scum and dregs of the city. 'Hunger was then my faithful bodyguard; he never left me for a moment and partook of all I had . . .'[6]

Hunger, penury and obscurity were the lot of this young man who, like all spoilt children, had been so convinced that life would be what he desired it to be. Yet he was not prepared to find a steady job which would at least fill both his belly and his purse: it was as though he feared that this security might tempt him into mediocrity. Instead, he eked out a miserable existence as a freelance painter of scenes of Vienna, which he sold to petty traders and tourists, and of advertising posters. Though he would always consider himself an artist, his work was barely competent, uniting a mediocre technical talent with a striking lack of visual power. Meanwhile, his former neat appearance degenerated:

'Bohemian he certainly looked in those vagabond years in Vienna. Those who knew him remembered later his long black shabby overcoat which hung down to his ankles . . . They remembered his greasy black derby which he wore the year round: his matted hair brushed down over his forehead as in later years and, in the back, hanging dishevelled over his soiled collar, for he rarely appeared to have had a haircut or a shave and the sides of his face and chin were usually covered with the black stubble of an incipient beard. If one can believe Hanisch . . . "Hitler resembled an apparition such as rarely occurs among Christians."'[7]

Nowadays one can meet many young men of this appearance in any major city, and they follow similar pursuits: they used to be called 'hippies'.

Hitler had come to Vienna expecting triumph and acclaim, and instead had found contempt and abuse – when he was not merely ignored. The young man destined for great things was forced to struggle for his very existence among tramps, alcoholics, played-out pimps and petty criminals, morons, madmen and fellow-failures. His experiences fed his growing egomania and fanned his bitterness and hatred against those whom he fancied had rejected him. He became convinced that life was a struggle in which only the fittest survived; he became schooled in every trick of cunning and deceit and knowledge of human weakness which enabled him to survive; what little compassion he had was blunted; and he was confirmed in the belief that the mass of human beings was greedy, grasping and stupid, shorn of all purpose, will and individual identity. Any possibility of a relationship with another human being, especially a woman, which might have softened his acrimony, was denied him by his poverty, his appearance, his sexual unattractiveness, and his pride. He may have visited prostitutes: some hold that he caught

42

syphilis from a Jewish whore; others that he paid for his masochistic fantasies to be fulfilled; unquestionably he did not enjoy the sex-life proper to a young man, and hence his sexual energy became twisted into something monstrous.

Compelled by poverty to abstain from smoking and drinking, Hitler nevertheless spent much time in cafes: it may be true that there he supplemented his income by begging. For hours he would brood silently upon the injustice of a world which would not recognise his genius, then a chance remark by another customer would provoke an outburst of rage. Hitler would round on the unfortunate and unsuspecting man and scream and spit a tirade of argument and abuse that would leave his victim shocked, shattered and shaken by the frustration and venom released. Back at the hostel, such outbursts would provoke only derision, and Hitler had to content himself with silently spinning his own web of perverse and hateful fantasies. Whatever appealing qualities the child may have possessed were now lost forever. The struggle to survive had produced a thoroughly unpleasant young man, with illusions of grandeur nourished by an ambition that grew in inverse proportion to his failure; and fed by the warped creations of a frustrated and increasingly diseased imagination that craved for revenge upon the world which ignored it.

There have been and are many young men of identical temperaments in identical situations in European and American cities. Sometimes they die or commit suicide; if they survive, it is to continue in their aimless path and achieve nothing. Usually this is because they do no more than what we have so far seen of Adolf Hitler, and was this all that we could say of him, doubtless he would never have been heard of. But, pressed on by an ill-defined faith in some glorious destiny, despite all evidence to the contrary, Hitler was endeavouring to acquire the education which would one day enable him to fulfil every violent and obscene fantasy which his mind had ever entertained.

It was in Vienna that Hitler formulated the fundamentals of his political vision, learning from the failures and successes of the city's three major political parties, the Pan-German Nationalists, the Social Democrats and the Christian Social Party. The Pan-German Nationalists had aims with which Hitler was in full agreement: they thought that the Austro-Hungarian Empire was declining due to the growing power of the various non-German races within its borders, believed that Austro-German political supremacy would save the situation, and hoped for union with Germany. Even so, Hitler perceived that their methods were at fault and could not lead to success: they failed to win over both the masses and the powerful, established institutions.

The Social Democrats he loathed from the very beginning. He abhorred the socialist creed of equality, was bored by its economic basis, and despised the social democratic hostility to German nationalism. Nevertheless, he overcame his repulsion sufficiently to learn from them three invaluable political lessons: they knew how to create a mass movement, were masters of the art of propaganda, and realised the value of what Hitler called 'spiritual terror'.

Although Hitler could not bring himself to agree with all the policies of Vienna's Mayor, Dr Karl Lueger of the Christian Social Party, he had to admire a man who had learned these lessons, and who had added to this, formidable talents as an orator. Hitler concluded:

'The power which has always started the greatest religious and political avalanches in history rolling has from time immemorial been the magic power of the spoken word, and that alone.'[8]

All these lessons Hitler later made the most of, and he claimed too that it was during this period that he became an anti-semite. August Kubizek, on the other hand, maintained that Hitler had hated the Jews since his early teens. It is probable that Hitler had always shared the anti-semitic attitudes which were considered good form among the Austro-German bourgeoisie, but in Vienna, this prejudice became an all-devouring obsession.

Hitler's anti-semitism became such a fundamental part of his character and of his creed, that historians have felt compelled to account for it, which they have done in a variety of ways. Explanations include: perception of the Jews as the incarnation of the cultured Viennese liberalism he detested because he could not enjoy its benefits; tortured sexual envy of the Jews; or a desperate need for a scapegoat on to which he could unleash the torrent of his pent-up hatred and frustration; put together, these do much to explain the diseased sexual ravings in *Mein Kampf*, in the pages of which Hitler pictures bow-legged Jewish youths lying in wait to seduce pure German maidens. Joachim C. Fest has gone so far as to assert that Hitler projected on to the Jews all his own most despicable traits, and this does something to explain the ferocity of Hitler's feelings. He came to believe in all sincerity that the Jews were determined to destroy the German race, and that behind every manifestation of crime or of evil there lurked a profiteering Jew. This obsession was fed by the writings of the cranks and magicians whom we have met, most notably Lanz von Liebenfels, who were not only to exacerbate this insane delusion, but to give Hitler the means by which he would one day be in a position to order the Final Solution.

IV

National Socialism was never just a political movement: it was also a religion, a religion founded on ideas acquired in the years 1909–13, when its founder read ceaselessly and omnivorously. As Alan Bullock has pointed out:

'He spent much time in public libraries, but his reading was indiscriminate and unsystematic – Ancient Rome, the Eastern Religions, Yoga, Occultism, Hypnotism, Astrology . . .'[9]

Indiscriminate and unsystematic it may well initially have been, but the effects of this reading would be to give

Adolf Hitler the materials by which he could found both a new religion and a legend of infamy without parallel.

Hitler had begun as a devout Roman Catholic. Though in his teens he abandoned the Christian faith, he never lost the Catholic's love of ritual, of priesthood, and of an all-embracing ideology. Schopenauer had spurred on his rejection of Christianity, and had then proceeded to awaken his interest in the religions of the East, whilst alluringly denying the distinction between good and evil.

Now Hitler embarked upon a furious course of reading. He assured his readers in *Mein Kampf* that it was his habit to turn to books if he wished to resolve any question. He insisted that his method of reading, superior to any other, was 'to remember the essential and to forget utterly the inessential'. In theory, this method is highly efficaceous; in practice it involves defining what is essential, which in Hitler's case meant not logical analysis, but an intuitive and emotional apprehension combined with what appealed to his own prejudices.

He took from Schopenauer the fatalism and the idea of Will, but forgot the Buddhism and the pessimism. He took from Nietzsche concepts of evolution, the Will to Power, and the Superman, but forgot Nietzsche's insistence that the Superman overcomes not others, but himself. He took from Wagner the racism, the heroism and the paganism, but forgot the Aryanised Christianity. From Madame Blavatsky, H. S. Chamberlain, List and Liebenfels, he took whatever he wanted, and forgot whatever did not harmonise with his own world-view.

He studied Eastern religions, and though he could not agree that existence is a wheel of suffering, since he saw it as a struggle which the fittest survived to their joy, he perceived the same attractive thing about them that has prompted their appeal in the West in our own day, that thing with which Christianity has lost touch: they offer methods of attaining transcendant consciousness, an ecstasy beyond rational thought in which an understanding of life and of one's own place in it is experienced.

It was not long before Hitler discovered that the West also possessed an esoteric tradition, which contains methods and concepts more suited to Western minds, and which is often symbolised as the Quest for the Holy Grail. In *Hitler's Table-Talk*, a volume of almost interminable monologues of the 1940s, he displays a thorough knowledge of both Eastern and Western occultism. This knowledge was prompted too by the meeting with Lanz von Liebenfels in 1909, when Hitler went to the offices of *Ostara* to purchase some back numbers.

We know that Hitler adopted as his own many of Liebenfels's ideas, but we do not know whether Liebenfels was for a time his teacher in these matters. However, there is no doubt that Hitler came to despise secret societies and magical orders which displayed esoteric knowledge without possessing esoteric power:

'I . . . warn again and again those wandering *volkisch* scholars whose positive achievement is always nothing, but whose conceit cannot be matched . . . The characteristic of most of these natures is that they abound in *old* German heroism, that they revel in the dim past, stone axes, spear and shields, but that in their own essence they are the greatest imaginable cowards . . . I got to know these people too well not to feel disgust at this miserable comedy . Despite all proofs of their total inability these people pretend to understand everything better than anybody else . . . I have the feeling that they are sent by dark forces who do not desire the rebirth of our people.'[10]

Nevertheless, Hitler pursued his bizarre interests. Let us therefore gather together everything we know about him so far, and about the peculiar time in which he lived and learned: let us bear in mind too that this insignificant little tramp, whose mind was a morass of half-digested prejudices, will make the world tremble: given all this, and an ensuing digression on the nature of magic, let us endeavour to enter the world of Adolf Hitler.

V

It is best to begin with an act of imagination. We shall picture Hitler as a solitary, hungry and frustrated young man, with unnaturally bright eyes that stare feverishly from a pinched and pallid face. He is disgusted by the reality he sees around him, and determined to make his mark upon the world by any means whatsoever. He pores over books, frowning in manic concentration, searching for the keys that will bring him fulfilment and the power to make of his dreams a reality. He is racked by anguish, by an abhorrence for the bourgeois life, by an hostility to intellect, by desperation as he seeks for something that might perchance release his genius.

We know to our cost that Hitler's genius was released, but few have explained how. Indeed, few are able to define either genius or the factors which produce it. All agree, however, that genius is associated with extraordinary gifts and achievements which can go hand in hand with neuroses and appalling personal characteristics.

Aleister Crowley investigated the question of religious genius in his *Book Four* (1913). He pointed out that what Lao Tzu, Buddha, Christ, St Paul, Mohammed, and all other founders of the world's religions had in common was some form of ecstatic experience; that this experience transformed both the lives of these men and the societies around them; that these men were previously nobodies and had become somebodies; that other than this experience, they had no assets whatever to assist them in changing the world; and that the methods used by these men and their disciples to attain this superconsciousness bore a startling essential identity. The methods consisted of 'virtue', solitude, absence of excitement, moderation in diet, and a one-pointed concentration of the will. Crowley then described the technique of yoga, and recommended complementing this method with the practice of magic.

We have already seen how groups like the Golden Dawn revived the systematic practice of the magic arts, and it should not surprise us that Hitler was also part of this occult renaissance. For his reading told him that by a one-

48

pointed concentration of the will, whether by turning inward (yoga) or outward (magic), he could attain a mystic vision of the universe, become the Superman and fulfil his every desire. He could by the focusing of his will transform the wretchedness of his daily existence into the glory of his imagined destiny. He could know his will, and more important, do his will. Alan Bullock reminds us that: 'No word was more frequently on Hitler's lips than "Will", and his whole career from 1919 to 1945 is a remarkable achievement of willpower.'[11]

Hitler now agonised over the true meaning of his existence. Perhaps it was not as an artist that men would remember him, but as an architect, one who built cities that men in future centuries would venerate? Certainly men must read his name in history books: might it be as a hero, one who would unite the German peoples? Or perhaps his future greatness was to be sought not in the outer, material world of the detested bourgeoisie but in the inner world of the spirit? He saw himself as a Teutonic Knight on the Quest for the Holy Grail, the glory of which his beloved Wagner had hymned in *Parsival*. As late as 1934 he would suggest: '. . . shall we form an Order, the Brotherhood of Templars round the holy grail of the pure blood?' And again: 'The eternal life granted by the grail is only for the truly pure and noble.'

But there was too much hate in the heart of Hitler for him to be content merely with the truly pure and noble. In any case, could he fulfil his own criterion? If blood was all-important, why was he not a blond, Nordic beast? He forbade the suspicion that his blood was so mixed as to make him deserving of death, but it remained to torment him. How pure was his soul? For there were those frightful sexual urges which completely overwhelmed him, and reduced the perfect knight to an abject object, half-crazed with lust, yet unable to summon the words that would bring him satisfaction from a pure Nordic maiden. Also, there were nightmares from which he awoke sweating and trembling with shame, rage and terror. Always these had the same pattern.

There was a beautiful and blonde German woman, so

superior to his own foul desires. She was chained to something, sometimes a pillar, and completely helpless. And there was a fat, bald, hook-nosed, perspiring and lascivious Jewish butcher, who gloated over the situation, a monstrous sub-human bent upon defiling the girl's German purity. And there was her rescuer, Adolf Hitler, Knight upon the Quest, Defender of the Blood, to whom the woman looked for her deliverance. But this hero was only a sham, a coward, a pathetic imitation of a warrior, and he could only watch in hopeless despair, helpless and disgraced, as the Jewish dragon pawed, clawed and raped the German maiden.

He would wake up screaming. The Jews *must* be destroyed, for only then could Hitler sleep in peace. It was no use Freud telling him that the Jew of his nightmare was but his own suppressed sexuality, for Freud was just another filthy Jewish propagandist. The enemy lay without, and not within the gates of his psyche; Lanz von Liebenfels was right; the Jew must be exterminated.

As for himself, how was he to atone for his sin? Should he redeem himself by destroying the authors of this monstrous blood-pollution? To save his people from Jewry – was this his providential mission? Could it be that he would wield the power before which the strongest men would tremble, the noblest women surrender? Then there would be a reckoning! The proud would bow; the humble would worship; and his enemies, the heretics, and above all the sub-human races would cringe, grovel and die; their blood would for the last time defile the earth, and their bodies be destroyed utterly by the cleansing flames of mighty fires.

He would not be a nobody. No, a thousand times, no! His only asset was his indomitable will: very well, let him work by that will until he became the Superman!

Each day, after he had made the few coppers necessary to secure his continued existence, he visited libraries and read until they closed, endeavouring to concentrate upon the essential and to eliminate the inessential. Unlike the volkisch occultists of his acquaintance, he did not become trapped in a morass of inconsequential symbolism or a maze of myth. Power was his object, and power alone.

From ponderous and verbose writings he extracted scraps of method, not caring whether his sources advocated good or evil, since all that mattered was the will. And, as all do who study occultism with the slightest seriousness, he experimented with the exercises that enhance the faculties and lead to states of transcendent consciousness.

A man with Hitler's simplifying mind must have realised that the essence of all occult disciplines is an eruption of the unconscious brought about by one-pointed concentration of the will, and that this can be achieved by meditation, by drugs, or by ritual. We do not know precisely what exercises he practised; whether or not he employed drugs; whether or not he had a teacher or who that teacher was; how proficient he became; or the nature of his experiences. However, we do know something about the effects of occult exercises in general, and a little about the results upon Hitler's behaviour.

The diligent practice of esoteric disciplines brings about a greatly enhanced control of the brain, and particularly of the faculties of visualisation and concentration. Unsupervised or careless work also produces, with depressing frequency, uncontrolled explosions of the unconscious, egomania, and megalomania. This is notably true for anyone who neither drinks nor eats immoderately, and remarkably true for one who spends much time alone, and who is in a continual condition of mental and emotional tension. Teachers of these matters consequently insist upon self-analysis, self-knowledge and balance before there is any possibility of trying the exercises which activate those parts of the brain that we do not normally use.

If Lanz von Liebenfels, or anyone else did teach Hitler in Vienna, then he was violating all traditions of esoteric teaching. This is the main reason for secrecy in occult lodges that have anything worth learning: not the rational and outdated fear of persecution by the Church but the far more ancient fear that teaching neurotics will result in unbalanced development and the abuse of any psychic powers which might be acquired. We have a first-rate example of this in Hitler. For if we are ignorant on many points of his education, on one point we can at least be certain: that the inner life of Adolf Hitler was transformed beyond his expectations.

A change came over the embittered failure which a 1911 legacy from his aunt does little to explain, for it improved nothing except his appearance. We know that in 1913 he moved to Munich, blaming Vienna's racial contamination for this move, which was actually to avoid service in the despised Austro-Hungarian Army. We know too that although in Munich his material life changed hardly at all from what it had been in Vienna, he never blamed the former city for the things he resented in the latter. It was as though he had convinced himself that it was now only a question of waiting. Oddly enough, he, like other poets and magicians, had become convinced that war was imminent.

Adolf Hitler had arrived at some mysterious knowledge which assured him of a place in the history books, though what its actual nature was, and how he would fulfil his role, were things which in their entirety he did not yet comprehend. It was enough to be certain that though he was still an anonymous face in a crowd, his time would come if only he was patient. He had read that each candidate for initiation is first tried and tested for his fitness by severe ordeals. He had undergone some of them, he thought, and was willing to undergo more, until, baptised by blood and fire, he could step forward to proclaim his mission. It was with a sense of triumph that later he would write:

'Vienna was and remained for me the hardest, though most thorough, school of my life. I had set foot in this town while still half a boy and I left it a man, grown quiet and grave.

'In this period there took shape within me a world picture and a philosophy which became the granite foundation of all my acts. In addition to what I then created, I have had to learn little; and I have had to alter nothing.'[12]

CHAPTER FIVE

Advent of the Daemonic

'Let my servants be few & secret: they shall rule the many and the known.'

The Book of the Law I 10

'After five years of folly and weakness, miscalled politeness, tact, discretion, care for the feeling of others, I am weary of it. I say today: to hell with Christianity, Rationalism, Buddhism, all the lumber of the centuries. I bring you a positive and primaeval fact, Magic by name; and with this I will build me a new Heaven and a new Earth. I want none of your faint approval or faint dispraise; I want blasphemy, murder, rape, revolution, anything, bad or good, but strong.'

Aleister Crowley

If we are to understand any particular time, then we must also endeavour to understand the things that were contrary to the dominant ethos, for therein lie the seeds of change. Therefore, although the ethos of the age at which we are looking was predominantly rationalistic, our attention is also called to an eruption of the daemonic, and it is necessary that this phenomenon be examined.

According to Goethe:

'This Daemonic element manifests itself in all corporeal and incorporeal things, and even expresses itself most distinctly in animals, yet it is primarily in its relation to man that we observe its mysterious workings, which represent a force, if not antagonistic to the moral order, yet running counter to it, so that the one may be regarded as the warp, and the other as the woof.'[1]

53

And Goethe goes on to examine the daemonic in relation to individuals:

'But the most fearful manifestation of the Daemonic is when it is seen predominating in some individual character. During my life I have observed several instances, either closely or at a distance. Such persons are not always the most eminent men, either in intellect or special gifts, and they are seldom distinguished by goodness of heart; a tremendous energy seems to emanate from them, and they exercise a wonderful power over all creatures, and even over the elements; and, indeed, who shall say how much further such influence may extend? All the moral powers combined are no avail against them; in vain does the more enlightened portion of mankind attempt to throw suspicion upon them as dupes or as deceivers – the masses are attracted by them. Seldom or ever do they find their equals among their contemporaries; nothing can vanquish them but the universe itself, with which they have begun the fray; and it is from observation of facts such as these that the strange but tremendous saying must have risen: *Nemo contra Deum nisi Deus ipse*.'[2]

This is the context in which Adolf Hitler must be seen: not that of Mussolini or Stalin, though he had with them many factors in common; but that of the individuals at whom we shall be looking, Rasputin, Gurdjieff, Haushofer, Crowley, all of whom were active at the time that Hitler was educating himself in Vienna.

Grigory Yefimovitch Rasputin is a most misunderstood man, and one who fits admirably Goethe's description of the daemonic. He was a Russian peasant who wandered over Asia in the 1890s, searching for God. It was by no means unusual in the Russia of that time for someone to do so, for the country was very primitive and hence maintained its age-old customs. As Crowley notes:

'Even in the legends of savages we find the same thing universal; somebody who is nobody in particular goes away for a longer or shorter period, and comes back as the "great medicine man"; but nobody ever knows exactly what happened to him.'[3]

This is exactly what happened to Rasputin, who suddenly came to be venerated as a holy man, possessed of curative powers, an inner strength and certainty, an intense magnetism, and the legendary sexual energy which in Central Asia traditionally belongs to yogis and holy men, and which has so excited the lascivious envy of most of his biographers that they have denounced him as a charlatan or as a devil.

In 1905, Rasputin arrived at St Petersburg, and was hailed as a saint by St John of Cronstadt, later to become a bitter enemy. He was soon brought to the attention of the Tsar and Tsarina, who were interested in these matters, and he gained the lasting trust and affection of that unhappy royal couple by curing their son of an attack of haemophilia. By 1910, he had become the nation's most influential adviser, and soon would become the most powerful individual in Russia.

Rasputin is of interest not because he sought to extend his influence, or enjoyed sex, or used his position to enrich his friends, for few do not; but because by virtue of mysterious powers acquired by means of yogic or shamanistic practices, he, a nobody, became for a time the real ruler of a twentieth-century great power. He was hardly the monster of popular fiction: he was a peasant, with the peasant's virtues and the peasant's vices, in whom roared the flames of the daemonic element. Though he had common sense in abundance, the powers of his intellect were minimal, for an eruption of the daemonic cannot bring out of the individual powers which he does not potentially possess. He understood neither the mechanism of the brain which had transformed his life, ascribing it to the God in whom he believed, nor the political situation in which he found himself enmeshed. His main idea about religion was to sin in order to be granted the mystic grace of redemption, an old Christian heresy still common in Russia at that time: his main idea about politics was that the Tsar of All the Russias should be venerated as holy; should resist

55

democracy and govern autocratically, guided by God; and should pay little attention to impertinent and peremptory demands for reform; an idea held too by the majority of simple peasants.

It was Rasputin's powers that brought him to a position of influence: it was Rasputin's limitations that determined the nature of that influence. More than anyone else, he encouraged the Tsar and Tsarina to be obstinate and inflexible, thus contributing, more than anyone else, to the deluge of revolution that would roll over Russia in 1917. Yet Rasputin was also aware that the Romanov dynasty was doomed, prophesying that its demise would fast follow his own. He seems to have made a decision to use his strength to prop up the Tsar and Tsarina, to whom he felt extremely loyal, in the full knowledge that this would mean his own destruction: there followed an attitude of resignation, and Rasputin took to drinking heavily. It does not appear to have struck him that liberal and enlightened reforms might have saved the Romanovs; his fear was war. He felt strongly that war would mean the end for the Russia of the Tsars, and made every effort to avert it in the Balkan crisis of 1912.

At present, we are only in a position to speculate over what it was that happened to Rasputin that had such an effect, but inspection of our next daemonic personage will prove more enlightening in this respect. He was another Russian, George Ivanovitch Gurdjieff, who wandered through Central Asia in search of enlightenment, and who claimed to have received instruction and initiation at the hands of various Hidden Masters or Unknown Supermen, who welcomed him to their Brotherhood. Subsequent descriptions of Gurdjieff recall those of Rasputin: he was possessed of an inner strength and certainty, an intense magnetism, telepathic powers, and a voracious sexual appetite. Interestingly enough, Gurdjieff also became involved in politics, and intrigued at the Russian court.

In the 1880s or 1890s, Gurdjieff became a Tibetan lama under the name of Dorjeff, and a professor of Metaphysics at the Drepung monastery. For a while he shunned politics, and then decided to bring about an alliance between Tibet and Russia, convert the Tsar to Buddhism, use Russian soldiers to defeat any attempt by the British to influence Tibetan affairs, and by virtue of the Tsar being a Tibetan Buddhist, bring Russia increasingly under Tibetan influence. This ambitious and audacious plan was favoured by the Dalai Lama, and a Russo-Tibetan alliance was concluded, but – not surprisingly – the rest did not go smoothly. The Tsar was not converted, the British were provoked into invading Tibet in 1904, Russia did not intervene, and the Dalai Lama and Gurdjieff/Dorjeff were forced to flee the country.

Gurdjieff went to Mongolia, but returned to Tibet after the British had left. The next set of reports have him in Moscow and St Petersburg, where he gave esoteric instruction to a number of pupils, including the celebrated metaphysician, Ouspensky. He taught an unusual cosmology, reminiscent of the writings of Madame Blavatsky; more important, he taught methods of attaining to what some have termed enlightenment. 'My way,' he said, 'is to develop the hidden potentialities of man; a way that is against Nature and against God.' He insisted that Man, as he stands, is 'asleep', and hence no more than a programmed robot: his task is to wake up so that he may know and do his true will (though Gurdjieff did not use this term). The methods to be used were meditation, concentration, and a striving for a permanent awareness in all that one is doing, assisted by the performance of actions with the body so as to focus awareness. One of Gurdjieff's pupils would teach Adolf Hitler: this was Karl Haushofer.

Born in Bavaria in 1869, Haushofer embarked upon a military career. In the course of this, he visited India and the Far East on several occasions, and became an expert on Oriental mysticism. He was with Gurdjieff in Tibet in 1903, 1905, 1906, 1907 and 1908. From 1907–10, he lived mainly in Japan, where he was initiated into an esoteric Buddhist society, The Green Dragon: it is said that one of the tests of initiation in this Order is to activate the germination process of a seed so that it grows into a mature plant in a matter of minutes; it is also said that each member of the Order was sworn to a mission, pledging that he would commit suicide if he failed. It is just possible that Rasputin was also a member of this Society, for its Lodges fringed Russia: how else can one explain his gift to the Tsarina, which was found sewn into her bodice in 1918, of a pair of small, emerald green dragons, the Order's insignia?

Karl Haushofer returned to Germany at some time prior to 1914. Unfortunately there are no documents available which might inform us how, if at all, he had changed. We know only that for no obvious reason, he obtained for himself a university doctorate with a thesis on political geography; also that he possessed remarkable predictive powers which he was to display during the Great War.

The clearest documented example of the daemonic, and how it was evoked, is the case of Aleister Crowley, whom we last saw in 1904. Between 1904 and 1909, Crowley toiled unceasingly at the practice of magic and yoga, much of it conducted in the wastes of Southern China and in the Sahara Desert. He had a number of extraordinary trances, and fortunately has left us with both beautiful descriptions of his experiences and clear instructions as to how these may be achieved:

'It is by freeing the mind from external influences, whether casual or emotional, that it obtains power to see somewhat of the truth of things . . . Let us determine to be masters of our minds.'[4]

Crowley argued that the simplest method was that of one-pointed concentration, the essence of yoga. If this was pursued for a sufficiently long time, the result would be an ecstatic experience:

'For the moment let it suffice to say that this consciousness of the Ego and the non-Ego, the seer and the thing seen, the knower and the thing known, is blotted out.

'There is usually an intense light, an intense sound, and a feeling of such overwhelming bliss that the resources of language have been exhausted again and again in the attempt to describe it.

'It is an absolute knock-out blow to the mind. It is so

vivid and tremendous that those who experience it are in the gravest danger of losing all sense of proportion.'[5]

Crowley remarked that this experience can go hand in hand with the very worst personal defects, and concluded:

'*To sum up*, we assert a secret source of energy which explains the phenomenon of Genius. We do not believe in any supernatural explanations, but insist that this source may be reached by the following out of definite rules, the degree of success depending upon the capacity of the seeker, and not upon the favour of any Divine Being. We assert that the critical phenomenon which determines success is an occurrence in the brain characterised essentially by the uniting of subject and object.'[6]

Something of this sort happened to Adolf Hitler. Both his best and his worst characteristics were monumentally inflated, and he acquired the inner strength and certainty which we have already remarked upon in others. His experience could not have been on the highest level, for, as we shall see, he required further teaching later on in his career. For the present let us remember the intense conviction in himself, the extraordinary personal magnetism, the powers of oratory and of prophecy with which historians have made us familiar.

Not surprisingly, Aleister Crowley fits into the pattern of daemonic individuals too. Even his most hostile biographers remark upon his inner strength and conviction, his intense magnetism, certain odd and inexplicable powers, and his formidable sex-drive which so scandalised his contemporaries. It was in 1909 that this man stumbled upon the missing manuscript of *The Book of the Law*, and became the Book's first convert. For the rest of his life he endured ridicule as he sought to bring about the creation of a new religion for the Age of Horus.

The Book's second convert was not a daemonic personage, but the man who became one of the finest military strategists and most authoritative military historians that England has produced, John Charles Frederick Fuller, then a Captain, later Major-General.

Fuller began his literary career as the author of *The Star in the West*, which hymned the praises of Aleister Crowley, his poetry, his thought, and his religion. Fuller and Crowley were both convinced that a World War was certain, and worked together at preparing the ground for the world which they thought would emerge from it. This conviction was reinforced by an operation of ceremonial magic in 1910, an evocation of Bartzabel, the spirit of Mars, the Roman Horus, at which one Commander Marston RN was present:

'I obtained a great deal of knowledge from the spirit, but the most interesting item is this: Marston, remembering his official duty, asked "Will nation rise up against nation?" followed by more detailed enquiries, on receiving an affirmative answer. We thus learnt that within five years from that date there would be two wars; the storm centre of the first would be Turkey, and that of the second would be Germany, and the result would be the destruction of these two nations.'[7]

In 1911, Crowley and Fuller quarrelled and parted, and though Crowley soon achieved notoriety as 'the Wickedest Man in the World', and Fuller renown and distinction, the latter nevertheless held throughout his life the opinion that the most extraordinary genius he had ever known was Crowley. Few shared this view, especially after Crowley became obsessed by his role as Prophet of the Aeon of Horus. He was not surprised that nine months after *The Book of the Law* was first published, the Balkan Wars erupted, and resulted in the expulsion of Turkey from Europe and a multiplication of international tensions. Nor did it surprise him that nine months after *The Book of the Law* was published a second time, World War broke out in the West.

So much for the daemonic insofar as it manifested in certain individuals. We must turn now to its manifestation in the great mass of human beings, and ask why it was that a World War came about in 1914. There are many explanations to choose from, but none of them quite convincing enough. One is based upon blaming the system of alliances and secret diplomacy which had been going on in Europe since 1871; yet it was precisely this system that had secured an unparalleled period of European peace. Another blames the greed of the capitalist classes, who were apparently possessed by a desire to ruin foreign competition despite the commercial desire for peace which had ruled the nineteenth century: yet there is no evidence at all of a series of sinister capitalist conspiracies. Another explanation blames the militarism of the German Empire, and it is at least true that strange things were happening there.

The intense enthusiasm of Kaiser Wilhelm II for the work of the demon-driven Houston Stewart Chamberlain had led to the latter becoming his monarch's confidential adviser. The Englishman was a frequent guest at the Palace in Potsdam, and the two men became firm friends. By 1912, the position of Chamberlain could be compared to that of Rasputin. 'It was God who sent your book to the German people, and you personally to me,' wrote the Kaiser to Chamberlain. 'My beloved unforgettable teacher and mentor . . .' wrote the Tsarina to Rasputin, while the Tsar declared Rasputin to be a 'very Christ'. This comparison must not be pushed too far. Chamberlain, neurotic and obsessed by demons, had none of the magnetism and inner certainty of Rasputin, being more a medium than a master, while Rasputin was an intellectual infant compared to the Englishman. Moreover, Rasputin desired the peace which might preserve the Romanov dynasty, while Chamberlain desired the war which might place Europe under the heel of the Hohenzollerns. Nevertheless, both men drew their inspiration from the daemonic element within their unconscious. It is certainly very odd that at so critical a point in time, two mystics are to be found advising the monarchs of the Russian and German Empires.

Chamberlain devoted himself to the task of urging the Kaiser onward that he might lead the German people to their destined world supremacy. In forty-three lengthy letters and in private conversations, Chamberlain advised the Kaiser to ignore public opinion, to make Germany strong, and to fulfil a Messianic mission whereby the

61

German race would come to dominate the world.

The Kaiser was not a warmonger. He was a sentimental and emotional man of grandiose ideas, with a gift for bombastic statements and tactless utterances. Impulsive and impetuous, his imagination a stage of Wagnerian dreams, he identified with the role that Chamberlain thrust upon him, as a modern Siegfried, the saviour of his people, a role that Aleister Crowley was later to praise in his absurd pro-German propaganda. 'You wield your pen;' wrote the Kaiser to Chamberlain, 'I my tongue (and) my broad sword.' He became increasingly aggressive in his public declarations on foreign policy, interspersing these bouts of sabre-rattling with protestations of his love of peace. He refused to do anything about the main cause of Anglo-German tension, the growing German Navy. Twice he endeavoured to interfere with French control of Morocco, and succeeded only in ensuring that Great Britain and France drew closer together. Certainly the Kaiser was prepared for war when it came about in 1914, yet it cannot be maintained that he caused it, for he was not an absolute monarch. His ineptitude caused the British to become deeply suspicious of Germany, but it did not cause the First World War.

Nor can we blame German businessmen, for they saw perfectly clearly that the German economy would soon be the strongest in Europe, and that the only event which could prevent this would be a European war. In short, one can discern no hard evidence prior to the summer of 1914 that would enable one to base an explanation for the war upon German guilt.

What *can* explain the outbreak of war? For there is not much evidence, if any, that would suggest that the Great Powers did want a Great War. That most rational of rationalist historians, A. J. P. Taylor, comes much closer to the truth when he writes:

'I would point to one factor which has not perhaps been sufficiently explored. Men's minds seem to have been on edge in the last two or three years before the war in a way they had not been before, as though they had become unconsciously weary of peace and security. You can see it in things remote from international politics – in the artistic movement called futurism, in the militant suffragettes of this country, in the working-class trend towards Syndicalism. Men wanted violence for its own sake; they welcomed war as a relief from materialism. European civilisation was, in fact, breaking down even before war destroyed it.'[8]

Taylor holds the view that it is erroneous to construct explanations for the war which depend upon a chain of events going back to 1878 or earlier. His view is that the First World War was caused by a frightful chain of accidents, mainly on the part of a rather incompetent governing class. With each accident, the prospect of war became increasingly likely, and this prospect was welcomed by the people of Europe as a relief from the dullness of an atrophied way of life. Consideration of the events leading up to the war persuades one that the simplicity of Taylor's explanation has much more to commend it than the ponderous theories of other historians. And what Professor Taylor might refer to as a series of ghastly mistakes, we may term an eruption of the daemonic in the minds of men.

But what actually occurred? It was all most peculiar. On 28 June 1914, the Austrian Archduke Francis Ferdinand went with his wife to Sarajevo to inspect some troops. Sarajevo is in Bosnia, which is inhabited by Serbs, and which Austria-Hungary had annexed in 1908. This made Austria-Hungary the enemy of Serbia, the people of which wanted a Serb state. A secret Serbian nationalist society, the Black Hand, laid plans for assassinating the Archduke. Six fervent Serbian nationalists were therefore waiting for Francis Ferdinand when he arrived in Sarajevo. All six tried to kill him. All six failed.

That could have been the end of the episode. It would have been the end of the episode if the Archduke's chauffeur had not taken a wrong turning, realised his mistake, and stopped the car in front of one of the failed assassins, Gavrilo Princip. Unable to believe his luck,

Princip stepped on to the running-board, fired two shots, and killed the Archduke and his wife. Thus was the First World War ignited.

Austria-Hungary was determined to prove that she was still a Great Power. Here was a golden opportunity to wipe her rival Serbia off the map. She issued an impossible ultimatum to the Serbian government, which had had no knowledge of the assassination plans. Nevertheless, the Serbs complied with most of Austria-Hungary's demands. It was no use, for the Austrians wanted war. In this belligerent attitude, they were supported by Germany and Kaiser Wilhelm, which latter, urged on by Chamberlain, decided that he did not fear war, and was sustained in this view by his belief that the spirit of world historic destiny had already decided the outcome of the war in favour of the German peoples. Backed by the might of the German Empire, Austria-Hungary declared war on 28 July.

So far this was just another Balkan conflict, but now Russia took a hand. As self-proclaimed protector of the Balkan peoples, Russia could not stand idly by and allow the Austrians to dominate the area, seize the Dardanelles, and acquire the power to strangle Russia's economic life. On 30 July, Russia declared a general mobilisation.

One man in Russia could have prevented war, the man who insisted that the Balkans were not worth the life of a single Russian soldier, Grigory Yefimovitch Rasputin. It is by a strange quirk of fate that he was at that time in a hospital bed recovering from an attempted assassination in Pokrovskoe, having been stabbed at the same time that the Austrian Archduke was shot. As Colin Wilson remarks in his *Rasputin*:

'There are fifty degrees of longitude between Sarajevo and Pokrovskoe, which means that eleven o'clock in Sarajevo is about two-fifteen in Pokrovskoe. It is a strange coincidence that two assassins struck at almost exactly the same moment – a coincidence that makes one inclined to doubt the "blindness of history". Ferdinand's death made war probable; Rasputin's injury made it certain, for he was the only man in Russia capable of averting it.'[9]

Rasputin sent the Tsar a telegram, which begged him to avoid war, but this was a poor substitute for intervention in person. It was no use. In the streets of Russia thousands of men were rejoicing at the thought of war, and crying out for blood. Russia had been plagued by discontent, subversion and unrest. Suddenly the populace was united against a common enemy, and it would have taken a far stronger man than Nicholas II to resist the demand for war. Russia mobilised not only against Austria-Hungary, but against her far more dangerous ally, Germany.

And now it was Germany's turn. The country that boasted Europe's finest railways, highest steel production, and most efficient army, possessed, incredible as it may seem, only *one* plan for this eventuality, even though the Generals had foreseen this possibility since 1891, when Russia allied with France. This was the plan of the late Count von Schlieffen, which had been designed to counter the possibility of war on two fronts with France and Russia. Schlieffen thought that it would take the Russians some weeks to mobilise fully, and so the best course was a lightning, pre-emptive strike against France. The invading force would sweep through Belgium, thus evading French defences, encircle Paris and provoke surrender within thirty-six days. An Armistice would then be signed with France, leaving Germany free to fling her entire resources at Russia. Schlieffen therefore contributed, more than any other man, to the outbreak of a European war. How strange a thing is history when its man of destiny is but a rotting corpse!

Germany could not afford to delay while Russia mobilised. Moreover, the German people were also rejoicing at the thought of war. On 31 July, the Kaiser was acclaimed in Berlin by cheering, wild and bloodthirsty crowds. On 1 August, Germany declared war on Russia. The Schlieffen Plan made the next event inevitable. On 3 August, Germany declared war on France. Over one million men poured into the neutral Belgium.

Great Britain could allow neither the violation of Belgian neutrality, which she had guaranteed, nor the possibility of a German victory, which would lead to the

Second Reich dominating the Continent of Europe. Here too crowds were shouting and screaming for battle, and when Germany refused the impossible demand to withdraw from Belgium, Great Britain declared war. Sir Edward Grey, her Foreign Secretary, darkly prophesied: 'The lamps are going out all over Europe. We shall not see them lit again in our lifetime.'

True, for the peoples of Great Britain and of France, of Germany and of Austria-Hungary, of Russia and of Serbia, yelled and screamed for war, for blood, for rape, murder, torture, for anything that would tear apart the putrid fabric of a society that stifled each unconscious impulse. There was a plague of War Fever, and it spread and poisoned all judgement, all reason, all compassion as it released a primaeval urge to fight, to kill, to slaughter. The men of Europe laughed and sang as they flocked to do battle in a War which no one understood. They did not realise that they were drinking to their own damnation, and that the hawk-headed god for whom they killed and died regarded them only with baleful stare and mocking smile.

Chapter Six

How the Old World Died

> 'Now let it be first understood that I am a god
> of War and Vengeance. I shall deal hardly
> with them.'
>
> *The Book of the Law III 3*

1914

The Great War that broke out in the summer of 1914 was to be the most terrible that mankind had ever experienced, yet its participants initially hailed its arrival with joy. They thought in all seriousness that the war would be an affair of great marches and rapid victories, and that it would all be over in time for Christmas. It is instructive to consider the main events of the First World War, since it did not go according to plan for anybody involved. We shall consider these events in a rational manner, and find ourselves drawn to the conclusion that history is never as rational as historians.

At first, the Schlieffen Plan seemed to be working admirably, despite the fact that the German Army's Supreme Commander, Helmuth von Moltke, suffered from an acute lack of confidence. Although the German Armies were marching triumphantly through Belgium, and although a French offensive in Lorraine was crushed with staggeringly high French losses, Moltke kept asking frantically 'Where are the captured guns?'

Nevertheless, the German advance in the West continued remorselessly. The British Expeditionary Force, which had landed in Belgium, found itself hopelessly outnumbered, and was forced into a rapid retreat. By 24 August, the success of the Schlieffen Plan seemed certain as the German Armies swept through northern France and down towards Paris, and it can be argued that a German victory at that point might for a time have saved the fabric of European civilisation.

This was not to be. The Russians had mobilised faster than anyone had anticipated, and were moving against the small German force in East Prussia. Now von Moltke made three fateful decisions. To command the Army on the Eastern Front he brought out of retirement a sixty-seven year old pensionary, General Paul von Hindenburg, who would later become President of the Weimar Republic, and appoint Hitler as his Chancellor. To ensure good generalship, he made the able Erich von Ludendorff his Chief of Staff: this man would become the Military Dictator of Germany in 1917, and support Hitler's attempt to seize power in 1923. And to bolster up the German defence, he transferred some divisions from the Western Front. By 31 August, the Russian offensive had been smashed at Tannenburg, with the loss of 90,000 prisoners. Since this cleared Germany of Russian troops for the duration of the war, Moltke's decisions may well seem to have been astute, but he had reckoned without their effect upon the Western Front.

The dying words of Schlieffen had been to make the right wing strong, for only then could Paris be encircled, but Moltke had weakened it by transferring divisions from the Western right wing to the East. This left him without the strength necessary to take advantage of British and French confusion, and matters were not assisted by the fact that his headquarters were two hundred miles behind the scene of battle. Moltke then allowed General von Kluck to act upon his own initiative, which proved to be another fatal error, since instead of encircling Paris as planned, Kluck wheeled round in front of the city to attack the exposed flank of the retreating French Army. The French then counter-attacked in a last, desperate attempt to save Paris, and on 5 September the Battle of the River Marne commenced. Moltke's reaction was to send a Staff Colonel to the Front, and gave him complete authority. He ordered a temporary retreat from the Marne to the River Aisne for purposes of regrouping. This was the final German error, and it made the Battle of the Marne one of the most decisive in world history. The German advance was halted; Paris was saved; and the French and British Armies recovered their equilibrium.

There followed a race by each side to outflank the other, which stopped at the sea. Both sides then dug trenches, which stretched from the English Channel to Switzerland. Assaults by each side to break this stalemate were cut down mercilessly by machine-gun fire. The Schlieffen Plan had failed, and failed through a concatenation of circumstances which no one had foreseen.

On the Eastern Front, the plan's failure was also glaringly apparent. Although Germany no longer had anything to fear from Russia, the same was not true for Austria-Hungary, whose Armies were defeated by the Russians in Galicia. German troops were now faced with the task of propping up their ally, and the dreaded war on two fronts had become a reality.

Even the most unrealistic of optimists now realised that the war would not be over by Christmas. Indeed, the most moving and pathetic sight of the First World War was probably the fraternisation of English and German soldiers on Christmas Day 1914. This was the last display of humanitarian sentiments by either side, and soon the soldiers would not even know what they were fighting about. The war to end war had barely begun.

1915

Any account of 1915 is bound to add up to depressing reading. One is bewildered equally by the futility of the heroism of the soldiers in the trenches, and by the monumental imbecility of most of their commanders. The French, under General Joffre, clung like limpets to the dogma that the war could only be won by massive offensives on the Western Front. With the British they believed that the way to break through the German trenches was to attack at the enemy's strongest point after an artillery bombardment of at least twenty-four hours: this warned the enemy that an attack was imminent, and churned the ground between the trenches to mud, thus rendering an infantry advance against barbed wire and machine-gun fire completely impossible. The Germans, for their part, insisted that every trench lost must be retaken, which led to bloody and futile battles where the prize was a hundred yards of mud. Allied attacks in Champagne (twice), at Soissons, Neuve-Chapelle, Festubert, Artois and Loos accomplished nothing but pointless slaughter. A German offensive at Ypres introduced soldiers to a new horror, poison gas, but the wind changed, and the assault was halted. Despite the obvious fact that the strategy described was as cretinous as it was murderous, soldiers continued to die in their thousands, and generals continued to stare at the trench-lines and order more offensives with the determined obstinacy of half-wits.

The Central Powers enjoyed a greater degree of success. Serbia was crushed, and an offensive launched against Russia, whose Armies proved to be shamefully ill-equipped. Some divisions possessed only one rifle per three men; some had compasses, but no maps; most had radio transmitters, but found codes so complex that messages were transmitted in Russian, to the delight of German Intelligence. Moreover, Russian Generals, who owed their positions almost entirely to accident of birth, proved uniquely incompetent – to put it charitably. Only Russia's vast expanses of territory saved her in that year, when the Central Powers overran Poland. Tsar Nicholas II, who had made himself Supreme Commander, took the blame for the catastrophe, and revolution inched nearer.

The theatre of war expanded. Turkey entered on the side of the Central Powers in December 1914, and began with a disastrous winter campaign against Russia in the Caucasus Mountains, in which much of her Army froze to death. Italy was induced by a bribe that promised future gains to enter the war on the side of the Allies, and begin a series of futile onslaughts on the mountainous border between her and Austria-Hungary. Great Britain looked for diversionary fronts, and essayed a strike at the Dardanelles Straits, hoping to capture Constantinople and put Turkey out of the war. This campaign was execrably planned and execrably executed. The attack on Gallipoli was eventually terminated without the smallest gain, after 214,000 casualties. An Anglo-French force was sent to Salonika, in neutral Greece, grew to number 600,000 troops, and suffered an illness rate of 110 per cent. This venture and two more, in the Middle East and near the Persian Gulf, cost the British Empire 174,500 men in killed, wounded and dead of disease.

But 1915 did not only demonstrate the ineptitude of Europe's governing classes. For it was not only men who died in that year, but also their values. Everything incompatible with war was sacrificed: freedom, moderation, justice, tolerance, Christianity, humanitarianism and reason. As soldiers died, civilians raged against anyone who failed to display a total commitment to the war effort, and their passions were fed by the slick patriotism and monstrous lies of their overtly propagandist newspapers so that all intelligence was silenced by a torrent of hate.

'Governments and individuals conformed to this rhythm of the tragedy and swayed and staggered forward in helpless violence, slaughtering and squandering on ever-increasing scales, till injuries were wrought to the structure of human society which a century will not efface, and which may conceivably prove fatal to the present civilisation,' wrote Winston Churchill in his *The World Crisis 1915* (1923). D. H. Lawrence was even more succinct: 'It was in 1915,' he wrote, 'that the old world died.'

1916

1915 was only a prologue to the year that followed, that frightful year which John Terraine has termed 'the year of killing'. It was the year of the great offensives, which the Generals hoped would decide the war, and once more the Generals were proved wrong.

The German attack was shifted from the tottering Russians to the Western Front. The Germans hoped to capitalise on the decline in French morale brought about by the failure of her offensives in 1915, and launched a mighty offensive on the French salient at Verdun. The French resisted with magnificent courage and unshakeable resolve, and a hideous battle which gave new meaning to the concept of hell dragged on until 11 July, having started on 21 February. It was a futile struggle, because Verdun had no strategic importance whatsoever. Nevertheless, it was a symbol of French prestige, and for this reason alone could not be abandoned. General Petain, who was in charge at Verdun, became a national hero, to France's subsequent cost, and Verdun remained in French hands. The Germans suffered 281,000 casualties, the French 315,000.

On 5 June, the Russians endeavoured to redeem themselves from defeat by launching an onslaught under General Brusilov. By ignoring preliminary bombardments and like dogmas embraced by other Generals, Brusilov ensured a spectacular advance. His colleagues, however, were so jealous of his success that they delayed sending essential reinforcements. The Germans counter-attacked, and by 17 August, the Russians were virtually back where they started, closer to revolution, and rewarded by over 1,000,000 casualties.

On 1 July, the British launched a major offensive. They now had a vast army of conscripts and a new Commander, Sir Douglas Haig. A seven day artillery bombardment opened the Battle of the Somme, which continued until 18 November. Both sides lost roughly 600,000 men. The British gained a few acres of mud.

Such was the dismal tale of 1916. There is not much to add. Italian attacks continued to fail; Rumania joined the Allies and collapsed within four months; and an indecisive naval engagement was fought at Jutland, which failed to shake British naval supremacy, later a decisive factor. Even the governments of Europe began to sicken of the slaughter, and both sides examined the possibility of peace. But making peace proved to be infinitely more difficult than making war, since neither side could agree on a settlement that would not render the past two and a half years manifestly pointless. On 7 December, Lloyd George succeeded H. H. Asquith as British Prime Minister, and since he had always urged a more vigorous prosecution of the war, he could not possibly advocate a determined approach to the making of peace. There was nothing that anybody could do to stop the war from continuing.

The peoples of Europe, now as weary of blood as earlier they had been enthusiastic, prayed fervently that new men would bring about a new situation. France replaced General Joffre with General Nivelle, who claimed that he possessed the secret of victory. Germany made Hindenburg and Ludendorff her Supreme Commanders. the latter became what amounted to Germany's dictator, and slandered the Jews as slackers and war profiteers, thus breeding the germs of a future myth. Certainly 1917 did bring about a new situation, but again, it was nothing like what anyone had imagined.

1917

It was in 1917 that the world balance of power altered fundamentally, for this most terrible year saw the birth of one of our modern Superpowers, the USSR, and the mobilisation for total war of the other, the USA.

On 29 December 1916, Rasputin was assassinated: this took enough cyanide to kill a room full of people, numerous revolver bullets, and the Little Nevka River. His prophecy that the Romanov dynasty would not long outlive him was soon grimly fulfilled. On 8 March 1917, riots broke out in Petrograd; by 12 March the soldiers had mutinied; and on 15 March, Tsar Nicholas II abdicated. His rule was replaced by that of a provisional government pledged to liberal reforms and continuation of the war.

It did not take the German Government long to make a grave decision. This was to send to Russia in a sealed train one Vladmir Ilyich Ulyanov, better known as Lenin, a Marxist revolutionary then in exile in Switzerland. It was hoped that Lenin, who was committed to a withdrawal from the war, would spark off a further revolution. Lenin failed to seize power, and had to flee to Finland, but he returned after an abortive Russian offensive in the summer, which had left the country completely demoralised. On 7 November, Lenin and Trotsky seized power and set up a communist dictatorship. Four months later, the new regime signed the Treaty of Brest-Litovsk, which took Russia out of the war.

Ludendorff now decided that Great Britain could be starved into submission, and hence advocated unrestricted submarine warfare. Kaiser Wilhelm II agreed. This brought the United States into the war, together with her discovery of a German proposal to Mexico for an alliance against her. On 6 April, President Woodrow Wilson, who had won the 1916 election with the slogan 'he kept us out of the war', declared war on Germany. Immediately the Americans contracted the plague of war fever. To give just one minor example, when a speaker in a Christian Church demanded that the Kaiser, when captured, be boiled alive in oil, 'the entire audience stood on chairs to scream its hysterical approval'.

Madness, however, did not affect the Americans alone. Given the Russian collapse, and the enormous resources of the United States, it is obvious that the Allied strategy should have been to economise their manpower and defend until America could make her presence felt. But this was not obvious to General Nivelle, who wanted to prove that he indeed possessed the secret of victory, nor to Sir Douglas Haig, who seems to have wanted to win the war before the Americans could arrive.

While the Allies were preparing their offensives, the Germans withdrew to a line of especially prepared fortifications, the Hindenburg Line. This left General Nivelle unmoved. On 16 April, the French attacked on the Aisne, guided by an outdated battle plan. In four days, they suffered 187,000 casualties. This finally broke the offensive spirit of the French Army, certainly until 1944, possibly for ever. The troops mutinied, Nivelle was dismissed, and the new Commander, Petain, had to struggle to restore order.

Nor did the British fare any better. The Battle of Arras cost them 158,000 casualties in return for a trench or two. There followed the Battle of Passchendaele, which lasted from 31 July to 20 November. It was a tactically impossible battle, fought on reclaimed swampland, which became a vast bog for the wounded to drown in. British casualties amounted to 380,335 men.

The only British triumph was the battle of Cambrai, in which tanks were successfully employed. The greatest British advance in the war so far took place, but inept infantry generalship resulted in retreat. Nevertheless, the lessons learned at Cambrai would be employed in 1918, to the delight of the Chief General Staff Officer of the new Tank Corps, J. F. C. Fuller, the ex-disciple of Aleister Crowley. It was Fuller too who most neatly summed up the situation at the end of 1917:

'. . . the British were bled white, the French were morally exhausted, the Italians nearly out of the war, and the Americans not yet sufficiently involved to make good a fraction of the losses sustained.'[1]

1918

On 21 March, just after making peace with Communist Russia, Ludendorff flung Germany's entire resources at the Allies in a final bid for victory. Once more the Germans came within sight of Paris. By 2 August, each side had lost roughly 1,000,000 men. The Germans could not make up their losses, but Allied resistance was stiffened by the large numbers of American soldiers who were finally arriving.

The Allies now made their own final effort. The great Battle of Amiens was commenced on 8 August, which Ludendorff termed 'the blackest day of the German Army' and 'the worst experience I had to go through'. Assisted by massed tank formations, the Allies forced retreat upon the Germans. The British fought eight victorious battles in continuous succession, and stormed the Hindenburg Line on 27 September. One day later, Ludendorff advised an immediate armistice.

The German Army was not 'stabbed in the back'; it was defeated in the field. The myth came about because the British naval blockade reduced German civilians to starvation level and provoked both a decline in morale and some anti-war agitation. It is true that Allied soldiers did not reach German soil, but no one knew better than Ludendorff that Germany could hold out no longer. On 5

October, the Germans accepted President Wilson's Fourteen Points as the basis for armistice negotiations. On 9 November, the Kaiser abdicated, and the Weimar Republic was proclaimed. There followed the Treaty of Versailles, which was dictated to Germany by the victorious Powers.

Aftermath

'The influences of the first of the world wars on vanquished and victors were cataclysmic. Most of the Europe of a thousand years was shattered and the balance between its nations destroyed. Three empires were tumbled into the dust. Germany was reduced to economic ruin . . . Russia ceased to be a Christian country and the autocracy of Marx was substituted for the autocracy of the Tsars. The Austro-Hungarian Empire was split into a congeries of squabbling states bereft of economic foundations, and Turkey was almost reduced to her original sultanate of Rum. Nor did the victors emerge much better. France, bled white, was left a demoralised, second-rate power; Great Britain, who before the war had been the banker of the world, ended a debtor country, and for the Pax Britannica was substituted the League of Nations – a sham to replace a reality. The United States was left to pay for the war she had so blindly entered in order to disencumber herself of the consequences she had failed to foresee. Japan, who had played a minor part, alone emerged triumphant. Her empire was extended and the war raised her to a dominant position in the Far East and western Pacific. Such were the sorry products of bankrupt statesmanship.'[2]

(J. F. C. Fuller: *The Decisive Battles of the Western World*)

CHAPTER SEVEN

'What Did You Do in the Great War, Daddy?'

'Ye are against the people, O my chosen!'
The Book of the Law II 25

'We profit from everything. Nothing can stop it. War or no war, it's always the same for us. We always profit.'
George Ivanovitch Gurdjieff

'Creation is not yet at an end, at all events not as far as the creature Man is concerned . . . man has clearly arrived at a turning point . . A new variety of man is beginning to separate out . . . The old type of man will have but a stunted existence. All creative energy will be concentrated in the new one. The two types will rapidly diverge from one another. One will sink to a sub-human race, and the other rise far above the man of today. I might call the two types the man-god and the mass animal . . . Man is becoming God . . Man is God in the making.'
Adolf Hitler

We know what the majority of European men did in the Great War. They killed each other for no objective that could bring them the slightest possible benefit. So badly shaken were they by their experiences, that many subsequently sought security and safety within the certainties of totalitarian ideologies. A long and bloody civil war in Russia was followed by the complete victory of Communism, though its policies had brought hardships unimagined in the days of the Tsars. Chaos and strikes in

Italy were followed by the rise of Mussolini, who denounced liberty as a putrefying corpse and was ecstatically acclaimed by most of his people. No one seemed to know any more what was right and what was wrong, what was good and what was evil. Europe's intellectual leaders offered no leadership, and confessed to the deepest doubts about absolutely everything. Europe's poets were captivated by the despair of T. S. Eliot's *The Waste Land*. Europe's artists proclaimed the end of art. Europe's politicians continued to believe that they were masters of events as they floundered from one crisis to another. Europe's masses just did not know what was going on.

We know what a minority of European men did in the Great War. They sacrificed the lives of millions without understanding either how they had got themselves into this situation, or how they were going to get out of it. They thought that they were mastering events, when it was only too obvious that events were mastering them. They did all they could to arouse hate-filled passions for war, and were forced to give in to the passions they had aroused when the time came to make peace. Of some it may be said that they did their best, but that is a very poor verdict on the European results that were achieved. Very few possessed even the smallest understanding of their time.

Now let us look at what certain odd individuals did in the Great War. It may turn out that they had some inkling of what was happening. Our first witness possessed no conscious comprehension whatever of his time, but his intuition or his imagination was responsible for a most curious event which might light our way. I refer to Arthur Machen, former member of the Golden Dawn, author of tales of the daemonic, who occasionally 'dreamed true'. By 1914, poverty had compelled him to become a reporter for the London *Evening News*. It was wartime, the British had retreated to Mons, the Germans were advancing through Belgium, and the Editor requested from Machen a patriotic short story of the supernatural. Machen reluctantly obliged, and turned in a dismal piece of hack-work entitled 'The Bowmen': St George, in shining armour, and his angels, dressed as the archers of Agincourt, come to the rescue of the British Army. The author was thoroughly ashamed of this tale, and desired only to forget it, but, to his utter stupefaction, scores of soldiers wrote in to the *Evening News* swearing on their honour that they had seen with their own eyes the angels of St George mingling in their ranks at the battle of Mons.

For a brief period, Arthur Machen enjoyed the national fame which his finest work had failed to find. Time and time again, he insisted that 'The Bowmen' was fiction. Nobody believed him. He was wholly at a loss to account for this very odd coincidence, and so are we, unless we choose to believe the suggestion offered by Louis Pauwels and Jacques Bergier:

'Or could it be that hidden forces rose up, in one form or another, summoned by his imagination that had so often been concerned with essential truths and was now, perhaps unconsciously, at work deep down within him?'[1]

It could be, provided we allow, as Machen did, that the world is a much stranger place than is commonly supposed.

We will pass on to two men who, unlike Machen, really did have an effect upon history, Kaiser Wilhelm II and Houston Stewart Chamberlain. The Kaiser was of course toppled by the war he had entered, and he had abdicated in November 1918, fleeing to an estate at Doorn in Holland. There he proceeded to amass a vast collection of books on the occult, his aim being to unravel the conspiracy of certain secret occult Orders which he believed had caused the war, Germany's defeat, and his own humiliation. As for the man to whom he had given the Iron Cross, H. S. Chamberlain, he lingered on, confined to a wheel-chair, broken in spirit.

Those at whom we have so far looked were failures. At the same time they did possess, to a greater or a lesser degree, a faculty for intuitive insights: the problem was that they were, for the most part, incapable of putting them to successful use. We shall now look at those who made these intuitive insights the essence of their lives.

Rasputin was one of the Great War's casualties. He need

not have been assassinated; he could have left St Petersburg at any time; but he had resolved upon linking his destiny to that of his patrons, the Romanovs. After his death, there was a flood of anti-Rasputin propaganda, and he was blamed for almost everything, becoming in time like an ogre created by the mind of a neurotic adolescent girl. His only perceptive biographer, Colin Wilson, has justly remarked that the truth about Rasputin is much more interesting than the legend.

Unfortunately, there are still certain minor mysteries about him which we are unable to elucidate. It is not known for certain whether he was, like Karl Haushofer, a member of the Russian branch of the Green Dragon Society, and hence sworn both to a mission and to suicide in event of failure. And could it have been Rasputin who advised the Tsarina to introduce the Swastika at the Russian court? Badmaiev, a medium and theosophist, who had been brought up in Tibet, where the Swastika is a common symbol, has been advanced as a plausible candidate by Louis Pauwels and Jacques Bergier. Or could it possibly have been Gurdjieff, when he visited the Russian court in the guise of a Tibetan lama and diplomat? This sounds more likely than Rasputin, although Rasputin was often accused, with the Tsarina, of being pro-German.

Mystery also surrounds Rasputin's fellow Russian, G. I. Gurdjieff, who, however, was rather more fortunate. He does not seem to have regarded the Great War as a matter of much importance to him except insofar as it caused him inconvenience. He did not care if millions of sleeping men killed millions of other sleeping men: for him it was much more important if just one man woke up. He occupied his time in teaching pupils and in making money through a variety of schemes. According to Louis Pauwels, he once more dabbled in politics since, 'for services rendered to France during the war, in India and in Asia Minor, he enjoyed the protection of Poincaré who personally authorised his establishment in France.'[2] France, at any rate, is where Gurdjieff went at some time during the Russian civil war, and there he set up his school at Fontainebleau, to which so many eminent writers and intellectuals would go. Some aver that he continued to keep in touch with his former pupil, Karl Haushofer.

The war was good to Haushofer, who achieved the impressive rank of general. He also acquired a high reputation for his uncanny predictive powers. He successfully predicted the dates and times of Allied attacks, the extent of casualties in coming battles, and political events in other countries.

After the war, the General metamorphosed into the Professor. The University was Munich, the subject Political Geography, and the Professor declared his intention of re-educating the entire nation so as to awaken Germany to a fulfillment of its destined greatness.

One of his earliest, and most devoted students, was Rudolf Hess.

Aleister Crowley was also thinking in terms of whole continents in the years 1914–18. He spent them in America after the British Government rejected the offer of his services in 1914, due to his increasingly unsavoury reputation: that, at least, is what he claimed. He also claimed that he had assisted in bringing the USA into the war on the Allied side, by writing deliberately absurd and inflammatory pro-German propaganda. This assertion has been contested, though Crowley was not prosecuted as a traitor when he returned to Britain in 1919. Of three things we can be sure: Crowley's pro-German propaganda was so ludicrous as to be counter-productive to all except humourless Germans, though it hardly brought the United States into the war; the money he received for it preserved him from starvation; and *The Fatherland*, which he edited, was a useful vehicle for serious articles on the religion for which he was the prophet.

For Crowley, a sincere and intelligent man, had despite these qualities become convinced that he was in truth The Beast 666 prophesied in *The Book of Revelation* in *The Bible* and hailed in *The Book of the Law*, who would bring an end to the Christian Age. He welcomed the First World War not only as a vehicle for the destruction of the old aeon, a baptism of blood, but also as the messenger of the freedom which he believed would dawn upon the peoples of the world. The war did not have this latter effect; the people of the world were much too badly frightened to cope with freedom. Crowley thereupon adopted the view that yet another and more destructive world war was inevitable, and would come soon.

After the war, Crowley returned to England, found the climate inhospitable, and set sail for Sicily, where, in Cefalu, he founded the Abbey of Thelema, or Will. This retreat, comparable to that of Gurdjieff at Fontainebleau, was soon savaged by the English press, which regaled its readers with accounts of dreadful and unspecified sexual practices. It was on account of this that Crowley was dubbed 'The Wickedest Man in the World'. It is obvious that for many, the new aeon had not yet dawned.

For Crowley there were compensations. He was elected World Head of the OTO, which gave him tremendous occult influence in Germany, and allowed his manuscripts to circulate among a wider circle of readers. It has been suggested that one of these readers was Adolf Hitler, who was, in the early 1920s, very well known in German occult circles, but it should be stressed that this is pure speculation.

Is it at all significant that Gurdjieff, Haushofer and Crowley were teaching enthusiastically at this time, each one convinced of the importance of his own mission, to wake people up to something? How odd too, that we find Dr Rudolf Steiner setting up an institute to do precisely this at the same time! Why was it so important to wake up? Weren't people aware of their situation?

'We are awake,' said Adolf Hitler to Rauschning, 'let others sleep'. This is a fundamentally different attitude, and based upon a desire for power over others. Was Adolf Hitler 'awake' in the Great War? Certainly he was very different from what he had been in his Vienna days. Like many others, he had rejoiced at the coming of the Great War:

'I am not ashamed to say that, carried away by the enthusiasm of the moment, I sank down on my knees and thanked Heaven out of the fullness of my heart for granting me the good fortune of being permitted to live in such a time.'[3]

He proved himself to be not a casual bohemian but an excellent soldier. He performed a difficult task, that of a messenger between headquarters and front-line trenches, and this made him a constant target for sniper-fire and enemy shells. He was one of the six hundred, out of a regiment of three thousand five hundred, who survived the first Battle of Ypres 1914, and was awarded the Iron Cross, Second Class. He remained at the front throughout the war, save for a brief period in 1916 which he spent in hospital with a leg-wound, fought in the Battle of the Somme and in the 1918 offensive, and was then awarded the Iron Cross, First Class, a decoration conferred only for oustanding valour. Despite this, he never rose above the rank of corporal because, in the opinion of his regimental adjutant, his superiors thought that he would never command respect. This opinion is supported by the recollections of a wartime comrade, who described Hitler sitting

'. . . in the corner of our mess holding his head between his hands in deep contemplation. Suddenly he would leap up and, running about excitedly, say that in spite of our big guns victory would be denied us, for the invisible foes of the German people were a greater danger than the biggest cannon of the enemy.'[4]

Another soldier recalled:

'We all cursed him and found him intolerable. There was this white crow among us that didn't go along with us when we damned the war to hell.'[5]

Hitler's own opinion of himself was of course very different and the wartime letters which he wrote suggest a man of destiny rather than a Vienna dropout. Successive letters stress the miraculous nature of his continued preservation:

'It is an absolute miracle that I was not injured . . . I myself am, through a miracle, still alright . . . Through a miracle I remain well and healthy.'

His conviction that Providence was sparing him for a special mission was thus reinforced, yet that protection seems to have deserted him in the very last month of the war, for he was a victim of a British mustard gas attack.

'A few hours later, my eyes had turned into glowing coals; it had grown dark around me.
'Thus I came to the hospital at Pasewalk, and there I was fated to experience – the greatest villainy of the century.'[6]
This was the capitulation of the German Empire. There is no doubting the shock with which the German defeat affected Hitler. Every atom of German nationalist in him surged to the fore:

'Again everything went black before my eyes; I tottered and groped my way back to the dormitory, threw myself on my bunk, and dug my burning head into my blanket and pillow.
'Since the day when I had stood at my mother's grave, I had not wept . . . And so it had all been in vain. In vain all the sacrifices and privations; in vain the hunger and thirst of months which were often endless; in vain the hours in which, with mortal fear clutching at our hearts, we nevertheless did our duty; and in vain the death of two millions who died . . . Was it for this that the German soldier had stood fast in the sun's heat and in snowstorms, weary from sleepless nights and endless marches? Was it for this that he had lain in the hell of the drumfire and in the fever of gas attacks without wavering . . . And what about those at home – ?
'Miserable and degenerate criminals!'[7]

But Hitler had become rather more than just a German nationalist suffering from intense depression and fearing a return to the hopeless mediocrity of civilian life:

'There followed terrible days and even worse nights – I knew that all was lost. Only fools, liars, and criminals could hope in the mercy of the enemy. In these nights hatred grew in me, hatred for those responsible for this deed.

'In the days that followed, my own fate became known to me.'[8]

How did he become aware of this extraordinary piece of knowledge? In later years he told an aide that as he lay wounded, he received a supernatural vision which ordered him to save Germany. He was at that time, thirty years old, the same age that another Messiah is said to have begun his mission. For this obscure corporal had made a choice which would affect the lives of countless millions:

'I, for my part, decided to go into politics.'[9]

PART TWO

The Rise of Hitler

CHAPTER EIGHT

The Nazis and the Lords of Thule

The political prospects of Adolf Hitler were, at first sight, extremely poor. He had no friends, no money, no job, no employment record, no political experience, and precious few obvious talents. In a stable society, his position would have been hopeless, but post-war Germany was anything but stable. The young Weimar Republic had signed the Treaty of Versailles, and thus had incurred the lasting enmity of all conservatives and nationalists. The Government staggered from crisis to crisis, assaulted by revolts from both the Left and the Right, and saved only by the very half-hearted help of the Army. The people were embittered by the loss of the war, humiliated by the abrupt collapse of German prestige, frustrated by the uncertain conditions of peace, and bewildered by the chaos and street-fighting which they saw all around them. This was especially true in the state of Bavaria, to which Hitler returned in November 1918.

Here, in rapid succession, the Wittelsbach King abdicated; Social Democrats seized power; their leader was assassinated; a Workers' Soviet Republic took control; a right-wing force, backed by the Army, stormed Munich and massacred the left-wing leaders; a moderate but weak Social Democratic government was restored; and this was soon overthrown by the Army, and replaced by a right-wing regime. Small wonder that politics dominated the minds and hearts of the citizens of Bavaria, that there were so many political groups, and that men longed for rapid and effective political solutions.

Reduced in size by the terms of the Versailles Treaty, the Army fought to retain the commanding position it had enjoyed under the Kaisers. It subsidised both private armies of unemployed ex-soldiers and right-wing political parties. It also gave political instruction classes to its troops. Corporal Hitler, who had been retained by the Army and assigned to a job in the Political Department's press and news bureau, attended these classes and displayed considerable enthusiasm. His superiors were impressed by his qualities, especially his anti-semitism, and he was made an education officer, one of whose functions was to discover information about various political groups.

In September 1919, Hitler was sent to investigate a small Munich organisation which called itself the German Workers' Party, a nationalist society which was to meet in the Sterneckerbrau beer cellar. He attended the meeting, and although he agreed with the economic ideas of the speaker, a crank called Gottfried Feder, he found the proceedings dull and the Party unimpressive. He was about to leave when a man stood up, questioned Feder's ideas, and proposed that Bavaria should secede from Germany. Hitler rounded on him furiously, and screamed a torrent of abuse that drove the unfortunate man from the cellar, looking 'like a wet poodle'. The Party's Chairman, one Anton Drexler, promptly approached Hitler, and pressed into his hands his book, *My Political Awakening*. Hitler then returned to his barracks and dismissed the German Workers' Party from his mind as irredeemably feeble and mediocre.

The next day, he read Drexler's book and, to his surprise, agreed with most of it. To his even greater surprise, he also received a postcard which informed him that he had been accepted into the German Workers' Party and invited him to a committee meeting. Despite many misgivings, Hitler decided to accept the invitation, intending to explain his reasons for refusing membership. He has left us his account of this committee meeting, which took place in an uninspiring back room in a shabby Munich tavern:

'In the dim light of a grimy gas lamp four young people sat at a table, among them the author of the little pamphlet, who at once greeted me most joyfully and bade me welcome as a new member of the German Workers' Party.

'Really, I was somewhat taken aback . . . The minutes of the last meeting were read and the secretary was given a vote of confidence. Next came the treasury report – all in all the association possessed seven marks and fifty pfennigs – for which the treasurer received a vote of general confidence. This, too, was entered in the minutes. Then the first chairman read the answers to a letter from Kiel, one from Dusseldorf, and one from Berlin, and everyone expressed approval. Next a report was given on the incoming mail: a letter from Berlin, one from Dusseldorf and one from Kiel, whose arrival seemed to be received with great satisfaction. This growing correspondence was interpreted as the best and most visible sign of the spreading importance of the German Workers' Party, and then – then there was a long deliberation with regard to the answers to be made.

'Terrible, terrible! This was club life of the worst manner and sort. Was I to join this organisation?'[1]

The fact is that Hitler did, 'after two days of agonised pondering and reflection'. He was enrolled as the seventh member of the Party's committee, and he later called this step 'the most decisive resolve of my life'. One cannot understand this extraordinary choice, after all that had gone before, unless one assumes either that Hitler's intuition played a large part in his decision, or that he came upon some information leading him to believe that the German Workers' Party was more important than it seemed, for this was in fact the case.

To discover the roots of the German Workers' Party, we must go back to 1912, when a conference of occultists led to the founding of a magical fraternity, the German Order. The founders included Theodor Fritsch, who edited an anti-semitic periodical, desired to create a nationalistic working class, and who was to be revered after his death by the Nazi press as 'the old Teacher'; Philip Stauff, a disciple of Guido von List; and the new Order's Chancellor, Hermann Pohl, who was also a member of List's Armanen. The Order was soon assailed by internal bickering, and around 1915, Pohl was deprived of his chancellorship, as a result of which he set up another Order, The German Order Walvater of the Holy Grail. He was soon joined by one

Rudolf Glauer, an astrologer and adventurer who practised Sufi meditation, hated Jews, admired the work of List and Liebenfels, and called himself Baron von Sebottendorff, which is how we shall refer to him. Sebottendorff was made Grand Master of the Order's Bavarian Province, and in 1918, with Pohl's approval, he set up another magical fraternity, the Thule Gesellschaft. The symbol of this society was a curved Swastika with a sword and wreath.

The Thule Group, based in Munich, was initially just another volkisch occult society, deriving its name from a pre-historic and legendary Nordic civilisation, its ideology from Blavatsky, List, Liebenfels and Chamberlain, and its ritual from the Wagnerian themes that had dominated previous and similar Orders. In the chaos after the Great War, however, the Thule Society found itself confronted with extraordinary opportunities which it seized to its subsequent benefit. Sebottendorff tirelessly advocated counter-revolution against the Jews and Marxists, who, he claimed, now held total power, and the Thulists became a rallying-point for nationalists, racists, reactionaries, and unemployed and discontented ex-soldiers. This rallying-point was all the more useful in that it was disguised as a society of cranky antiquarians and students of mythology. Thulists played a leading part in assisting the right-wing coup of 1920, which crushed Munich's short-lived Communist government, and this attracted the approval and financial assistance of the Army. The group was also responsible for a consistent output of propaganda, especially in the pages of the paper they had purchased, the *Munchener Beobachter und Sportblatt*, which was to achieve notoriety in later years as the *Völkischer Beobachter*, the Nazi newspaper.

The Thulists in general, and Sebottendorff in particular, were convinced that the minds of the working-classes were being poisoned by Jewish left-wing propaganda, and that an ideological onslaught was essential. It was decided that a 'workers' ring' should be set up to spread the political ideas of Thule, and Karl Harrer, an Order member, was appointed as its head. The workers' ring met with little success, and so, on 5 January 1919, it was amalgamated with another organisation, the Committee of Independent Workers, headed by a locksmith turned railway engineer, Anton Drexler. The product of this amalgamation was the German Workers' Party.

The small organisation that Hitler joined was therefore backed by an increasingly powerful magical Order. As Sebottendorff later claimed, 'Thule members were the people to whom Hitler first turned and who first allied themselves with Hitler.' Hitler could only gain by this alliance. The German Workers' Party was not, therefore, as insignificant as it initially appeared to Hitler. Prior to his advent, it had recruited a powerful ally in the short and stocky Captain Ernst Roehm of the Army's District Command. Roehm was a professional soldier who, in his contempt for civilians and love of loyalty, comradeship, discipline and courage, and his earthy and brutal simplicity, reminds one of a leader of a band of medieval mercenaries. He was respected both by his subordinates and by his superiors; the latter saw in him a ruthless and capable executive, who could play an important part in maintaining the prestige and power of the Army. Roehm used his influence with High Command to channel Army funds to the German Workers' Party, especially after he had met Adolf Hitler. He maintained that from the beginning he had sensed Hitler's fantastic leadership potential.

There was another ally, however, who was to have a more far-reaching effect than Ernst Roehm, the man to whom Hitler paid special tribute in the very last words of his autobiography, *Mein Kampf*:

'. . . I want also to count that man, one of the best, who devoted his life to the awakening of his, our people, in his writings and his thoughts and finally in his deeds.

'DIETRICH ECKART.'[2]

Who was Dietrich Eckart, why was he 'one of the best', what were his writings, thoughts and deeds, and why was Hitler so impressed by him? According to Konrad Heiden, 'Eckart undertook the spiritual formation of Adolf Hitler', and it is hence necessary that we inspect this teacher.

Dietrich Eckart, was an admirer of Schopenauer and Nietzsche and a dedicated occultist. He adopted a Bohemian life-style, and pursued a career as a dramatist, poet and journalist, at first in Berlin, and after the war, in Munich. The products of his pen were of varying quality, ranging from a creditable, if heavily romanticised translation of Ibsen's *Peer Gynt* to competent essays on Norse mythology, to mediocre poetry, to a witty but scurrilous anti-semitic news-sheet, *Auf gut deutsch*.

Eckart also drank heavily and took drugs. It is possible that this included a favourite of many bohemians at that time, the psychedelic peyote, which the pharmacologist Ludwig Lewin had studied as early as 1886, and which Aleister Crowley claimed to have popularised in Europe. Certainly he took morphine, to which he became addicted, and this led to a period in a Berlin lunatic asylum, where, in the manner of the Marquis de Sade, he staged his plays using the inmates as actors.

In 1919, he was living in the artists' quarter of Munich He continued to drink heavily, mixed in high social circles, and loudly proclaimed his views in the city's taverns. These views, unsurprisingly, were fiercely right wing, and it seemed that he wanted Germany to be ruled by a dictator. Heiden quotes a typical Eckart harangue, delivered in the Brennessel wine cellar:

'We need a fellow at the head who can stand the sound of a machine-gun. The rabble need to get fear into their pants. We can't use an officer, because the people don't respect them any more. The best would be a worker who knows how to talk . . . He doesn't need much brains . . . He must be a bachelor, then we'll get the women.'[3]

Eckart believed that he was destined to prepare the way for this leader, and he spoke of this belief to his friends in the Thule Group. There is some doubt as to how active Eckart was in the Thule Gesellschaft, but there is no doubt that he knew Sebottendorff very well, and that the Thulists looked up to him as an adept. He met Hitler at some time during 1919 and the two men with so many interests in common developed an instantaneous rapport. If Hitler had been unaware of the Thule Group and its activities prior to joining the German Workers' Party, he soon learned, and Eckart said of him to the Thulists: 'Here is the one for whom I was but the prophet and forerunner.'

But what could an occultist and a magical order impart to Adolf Hitler? We shall look at the question by considering what magic is and what magical fraternities teach.

Dion Fortune, a twentieth-century magician, has defined magic as 'the science and art of causing changes in consciousness to occur in conformity with will'. Francis King has expanded on this:

'The next great principle of Western magic is the belief that the properly trained human will is, quite literally, capable of anything . . . The motivating power, then, in all magical operations, is the trained will of the magician. All the adjuncts of ceremonial magic – lights, colours, circles, triangles, perfumes – are merely aids to concentrating the will of the magician into a blazing stream of pure energy.'[4]

Whether the magic is white or black depends not on whether sex or drugs are employed as adjuncts, but on how this energy is used. Its proper use is to induce a state of being called variously superconsciousness, the knowledge and conversation of the holy guardian angel, enlightenment, or liberation: black magic consists of using this energy for material gain, or, above all, for the pursuit of power. By this definition, the Thule Group pursued black magic.

Pauwels and Bergier have neatly expressed the beliefs of the Thulists:

'(Thule) . . . was supposed to be an island that disappeared somewhere in the extreme North. Off Greenland? or Labrador? Like Atlantis, Thule was thought to have been the magic centre of a vanished civilisation Eckart and his friends believed that not all the secrets of Thule had perished. Beings intermediate between Man and other intelligent Beings from Beyond, would place at the disposal of the Initiates a reservoir of forces which could be drawn upon to enable Germany to dominate the world again and be the cradle of the coming race of Supermen which would result from mutations of the human species. One day her legions would set out to annihilate everything that had stood in the way of the spiritual destiny of the Earth, and their leaders would be men who knew everything, deriving their strength from the very fountain-head of energy and guided by the Great Ones of the Ancient World. Such were the myths on which the Aryan doctrine of Eckart and Rosenberg was founded and which these "prophets" of a magic form of Socialism had instilled in the mediumistic mind of Hitler.'[5]

The Thule Group was a serious Magical Order: that is to say that its activities did not consist merely of examining the crankier fringes of mythology, acting out meaningless rituals, and dreaming of world conquest. It taught its initiates to practise the magic arts and awaken their own potential. Its teachings included the control of a subtle force, like Lytton's *vril* or the *Kundalini* of the Hindus: the creation of desirable situations through intense and systematic visualisation: and the art of communication with those mysterious Beings we have met before, the Hidden Masters or Unknown Supermen. It is likely that Hitler learned all these techniques, and realised that the one-pointed concentration of the will, a faculty which he already possessed, could have its power greatly enhanced by the force of heightened emotion.

Suddenly, under the tutelage of Eckart, the ex-dropout and ex-corporal began to display extraordinary talents. An occultist would say that magical techniques had aroused his potential; a Jungian psychologist, perhaps, that he had through his practices made the unconscious conscious. At any rate, Hitler proved that he was an excellent organiser and, guided by Roehm and Eckart, he was the moving spirit behind a propaganda campaign that took the obscure Party from the beer cellars to large public meetings. Here, a third talent emerged. Hitler proved to be an orator of genius. On 16 October 1919, he had addressed his first public meeting:

'In a bitter stream of words the dammed-up emotions, the lonely man's suffocated feelings of hatred and impotence, burst out; like an explosion after the restriction and apathy of the years, hallucinatory images and accusations came pouring out; abandoning restraint, he talked till he was sweating and exhausted.'[6]

Wildly acclaimed by his audience, Hitler discovered that he could wield 'the magic power of the spoken word'.

However this was not a case of instant genius, for Hitler had to work hard at perfecting his technique. Minutes of Party meetings inform us that at first, it did need perfecting: 'Herr Hitler then spoke on the subject, but he got into such a rage that people at the back couldn't understand very much.'[7]

But it was not long before Hitler acquired mastery, and Alan Bullock's comments are, in the present context, highly significant:

'His power to bewitch an audience has been likened to the occult arts of the African Medicine-man or the Asiatic Shaman; others have compared it to the sensitivity of a medium, and the magnetism of a hypnotist.'[8]

It is hardly surprising that these performances then so exhausted him that he required several glasses of strong Munich beer before he felt even partially restored to his normal state. His oratory made him the Party's most prominent figure, and at the beginning of 1920, he became head of its propaganda. He insisted upon staging a meeting at the Festsaal, in the Hofbrauhaus, which could seat up to two thousand people. Despite the grave doubts of some of his colleagues, the meeting went ahead and was an astonishing success. He worked tirelessly at publicising the Party, personally typing out and distributing invitations to its meetings. In the summer of 1920, the Party was renamed The National Socialist German Workers' Party to attract both nationalists and proletarians. Hitler's next move was to organise strong-arm squads to preserve order at meetings, pound hecklers to pulp and harass other parties: this was the beginning of the use of 'spiritual terror'.

It was now essential for the growing Nazi Party to distinguish itself from other, similar organisations, and to proclaim itself to be not just a political group, but a quasi-religious movement. Hitler demanded that there be a symbol of Nazism which could be displayed upon innumerable flags. Various designs were submitted, but the one Hitler liked best was that of Dr Friedrich Krohn, a Thulist and former member of the German Order. It was the Swastika.

The red background of the proposed flag symbolised the Party's social ideal; the white disc in the centre symbolised its nationalism; and the black Swastika within the disc depicted 'the struggle for the victory of Aryan man'. There was one thing, however, which Hitler insisted upon altering. Krohn's Swastika was right-handed and span clockwise, which for occultists symbolises light, white magic and creation: Hitler deliberately reversed it to spin anti-clockwise, and hence evoke darkness, black magic and destruction.

As Hitler's star rose in Bavarian politics, Dietrich Eckart introduced him to Munich society. Here he was not as impressive. He was shy, socially awkward, and embarrassing, and either brooded by himself in a corner or silenced the convivial gathering with an impassioned and hate-filled harangue. Strangely enough, this provoked not social ostracism, but patronage from wealthy, middle-aged women, who were as excited over the determined and arrogant young man as their counterparts in the USA were becoming over gangsters. A certain type of woman seems to have found something intensely attractive about this self-proclaimed Messiah with the staring eyes and wild language, sensing, perhaps, his intense sexual frustration, comparable to their own. One of these was Frau Bruckmann, who was also interested in occultism; she invited a practising magician, Alfred Schuler, to give a series of lectures on Guido von List's ideas at her home, some of which were probably heard by Hitler. It was women like Frau Bruckmann who replenished the coffers of the Nazi Party, and enabled it to take over the Thule Group's newspaper and transform it into the infamous *Völkischer Beobachter*: Dietrich Eckart became the Editor.

By the summer of 1921, after a series of intrigues, Adolf Hitler had become the undisputed leader of the Nazi Party. Soon its members were to hail him with the salute of 'Heil Hitler!', the same salute, we may remember, which invoked the Power of Earth, or Soil, in the Order of the Golden Dawn. The Party was becoming increasingly influential, and its Führer increasingly prominent. For this, Eckart must take much of the credit, as Hitler acknowledged in uncharacteristic fashion, and Eckart himself was only too well aware of the fact. As he wrote to a friend in 1923:

'Follow Hitler! He will dance, but it is I who have called the tune. We have given him the means of communication with Them. Do not mourn for me: I shall have influenced history more than any other German.'[9]

CHAPTER NINE

From Ritual to Reality

'Begone! ye mockers; even though ye laugh in
my honour ye shall laugh not long: then when
ye are sad know that I have forsaken you.'
The Book of the Law II 56

'When Hitler spoke to me, he tried to explain
his vocation as the herald of a new humanity
in rational and concrete terms.'
Hermann Rauschning

'Do you understand now the profound meaning of our National-Socialist movement?
Whoever sees in National Socialism nothing
but a political movement doesn't know much
about it.'

Adolf Hitler

There is no denying the appeal which the Nazi Party made
to the hearts and minds of so many Germans. The true
force behind that appeal was the emotion of hatred, and it
was the urge to express it that united the Nazis and made of
them a mass movement of fanatics. Hitler realised only too
well that it is far easier to unite people by appealing to their
dislikes than by appealing to their likes, and so what
Nazism stood for is rather less obvious than what it stood
against. The lack of a clearly defined ideology allowed
those who hated to see in Nazism whatever they wished to
see, and Hitler did not care what they saw as long as they
flocked to follow him.

The early Nazis certainly knew what they hated. They
hated the idea that Germany had been militarily defeated in
the First World War, refused to believe the fact, and
blamed the German collapse upon a fictitious Jewish 'stab

in the back'. They hated the Treaty of Versailles, which had been dictated by the Allies, had reduced Germany to the status of a third-rate power, and had been signed to its shame by the Weimar Republic. They hated the Weimar Republic itself, and thought it was governed by Jews, Marxists, and insipid liberal mediocrities who were pledged to destroy any remaining illusions of German greatness. They hated the boredom of civilian life, governed by bourgeois values to which they could not conform, and with which they could not successfully cope. They hated the internationalism, the intellectualism, and the materialism of the Communists. Above all else, they hated the Jews, whom they blamed for every single one of the ailments which plagued Germany. It was as though the ancient magical rite of primitive tribes, that of transferring the sins of the people to a scapegoat, which is then driven into the wilderness, had been revived in a twentieth-century nation.

In common with the unhappy and discontented throughout history, the Germans looked for a Saviour.

'Where he comes from, no one can say. From a prince's palace, perhaps, or a day labourer's cottage. But everyone knows: He is the Führer, everyone cheers him and thus he will one day announce himself, he for whom all of us are waiting, full of longing, who feel German's present distress deep in our hearts, so that thousands and hundreds of thousands of brains picture him, millions of voices call for him, one single German soul seeks him.'[1]

So wrote one Kurt Hesse in 1922, unaware perhaps, that Adolf Hitler had already become the Führer for several thousands of people.

By the magic arts of his oratory, the power of which lay as much in his delivery as in his words, Hitler expressed the hatred which possessed so many of his countrymen. Now they could hate with a common hate that was ecstatic and exhilarating, and feel with every part of their being that the Führer expressed their innermost aspirations. For nationalists there was the promise of a return to German greatness. For socialists there was a denunciation of finance capitalism shorn of Marxist dialectics. For ex-soldiers there was comradeship, and a call to march once more and win the battle that had been betrayed. For the dispossessed petty bourgeoisie there was a scapegoat to blame for their dispossession. For the proletariat there was an insistence upon fair wages and job security protected from the machinations of grasping employers. For racists there was a consistent barrage of abuse for the Jews, and the exaltation of pure German blood. For occultists there was the hope of their dreams becoming a reality.

We must not make the elementary mistake of dismissing or underrating the importance and influence of occultism, and it will not do to quote Hitler's contempt for the volkisch occultists as conclusive evidence. Hitler despised cranks, and had no use for fools, but then the same is true for Aleister Crowley, who shared his contempt for the general run of occultists. Nor did Hitler want his pursuit of political power to be impeded by public knowledge of his esoteric interests, for that would only invite ridicule. Nevertheless, his Nazi movement drew its inner strength from the daemonic element; as Hermann Rauschning aptly remarked: 'Its deepest roots are hidden in secret places.'

The ideas contained in Nazism were, as we have seen, derived from the writings of mystics and magicians like Blavatsky, Chamberlain, List and Liebenfels. The Nazi Party was a creation of a magical Order, the Thule Gesellschaft. The Führer himself was a magician, having undergone a mystical experience in Vienna, and received instruction at the hands of the Thulist adept, Dietrich Eckart. And throughout the early 1920s, this marriage between magic and politics continued harmoniously.

Bearing this in mind, we shall consider the fate of the man whom the Nazis treated as if he were their greatest foe. He was neither a Jew nor a Bolshevik, nor even a politician. He was an occultist, Dr Rudolf Steiner.

Steiner was an Austrian, born in 1861. After a brilliant school career, he went to the University of Vienna, where he distinguished himself in both arts and sciences. At the age of twenty-nine, he began work in the Goethe Archives, and soon acquired an impressive reputation. Shortly after, he began a regular regime of meditation. In 1899 he was invited to speak to a branch of Madame Blavatsky's Theosophical Society, which he then joined, becoming in time the General Secretary for Germany. He also joined the Ordo Templi Orientis, which taught sex-magic, though there is no evidence that Steiner practised this technique and he did not remain a member for long. In 1909, Steiner also broke with the theosophists, and formed his own Anthroposophical Society, which still flourishes.

Steiner's prime aim was to help humanity. He believed that the human mind is an instrument of incalculably vast potential and that we can develop it to our lasting benefit. He himself became a fine painter and sculptor; he discovered fertilisers which do not harm the soil and metals that affect metabolism; he also pioneered a radically different system of education, which has resulted in the establishment of numerous Steiner schools.

In addition to the stress he laid on inner development, Steiner was convinced of the existence of supernatural forces, teaching that some are good and others evil. He believed that evil was at work in the world, heralding the coming of a daemonic age, and working through magical sodalities. This was the man whose destruction the Nazis resolved upon. Despite the fact that Steiner was not concerned with politics, armed gangs of Nazi thugs broke up his meetings and threatened his followers with death. Steiner was forced to flee to Switzerland. This was not enough for Hitler and Eckart, and Nazi vengeance pursued the founder of anthroposophy as if he was a major threat. In 1924, the Nazis burned down the Rudolf Steiner centre at Dornach, and Steiner died of grief a year later.

It is instructive to compare the fate of another mystic, Houston Stewart Chamberlain. He met Hitler in Bayreuth in 1923. So deep was the impression made by the Nazi leader on the English mystic that he wrote him a letter the following day:

'You have mighty things to do . . . My faith in Germanism had not wavered an instant though my hope – I confess – was at a low ebb. With one stroke you have transformed the state of my soul. That in the hour of her deepest need Germany gives birth to a Hitler proves her vitality; as do the influences that emanate from him; for these two things – personality and influence – belong together . . . May God protect you!'[2]

Chamberlain joined the Nazi Party, and occasionally wrote for its publications. One of his articles had a familiar ring about it when it hailed Hitler as the saviour destined by God to lead the German people.

For their part, the Nazis revered Chamberlain as a prophet and sage. The *Völkischer Beobachter* devoted much space to extolling Chamberlain's genius, and affirmed that his *Foundations of the Nineteenth Century* was 'the gospel of the Nazi movement'. When Chamberlain went to his death in January 1927, he was convinced that Hitler would fulfill the destiny he had foreseen.

Hitler had been introduced to Chamberlain by another peculiar character, Alfred Rosenberg, who had arrived in Munich in 1919, a penniless refugee from Bolshevik Russia. He soon made contact with Dietrich Eckart, then at the centre of right-wing political intrigue, and raised his status by showing him a document in his possession entitled *The Protocols of the Learned Elders of Zion*. This purported to be a record of the proceedings of the World Zionist Congress of 1897, at which the Jews had allegedly laid plans for world domination. Needless to say, it was a forgery composed by a Russian writer named Nilus at the instigation of the Tsarist secret police, who hoped to discredit the Jews and hence enable the launching of another pogrom. This, however, was not the version of Rosenberg, who asserted that 'a mysterious stranger' had entered his home, 'laid the book on the table and silently vanished'.

As Francis King rightly points out, the Nazis reacted in one of three ways to the *Protocols*: they believed them; they wanted to believe them and so smothered all doubts as to their authenticity; or they did not care whether they were true or false as long as other people believed them, the attitude finally taken by Hitler. Even today, some people, most notably the former Marshal Amin of Uganda, still insist that this wretched document is precisely what it claims to be.

Hitler saw staggering propaganda potential in the *Protocols*, and Rosenberg's rise in the Nazi movement was consequently swift. His importance has been both overestimated and underrated: Lewis Spence argued that Rosenberg was the satanic genius behind the Nazi movement; by contrast, Joachim C. Fest saw him as being almost entirely ineffectual save within his own imagination. The truth of the matter is that Rosenberg had a strong influence upon Hitler's ideas and on the Nazi movement during the 1920s, but was subsequently cast aside in favour of more ruthless and determined rivals. He posed as an intellectual when his Führer had no use for intellectuals; he demanded a rigid adherence to what he conceived of as being Nazi ideology when his Führer was interested only in power and insisting that 'the ideas behind our programme do not oblige us to behave like fools'; and by 1940, he was reduced to political impotence.

This was definitely not the case in the early days of the Nazi Party, particularly since Rosenberg was patronised by Dietrich Eckart, who introduced him to Hitler. The latter was so impressed that he could still recall their first meeting in a letter he wrote to Rosenberg in 1943. Rosenberg was even more struck by Hitler, and became a fervent Nazi. Guided by Eckart, he began to write feverishly for the Nazi press:

'In . . . all his subsequent writings, he revealed himself as a man of profound half-culture, acquainted with countless apocryphal sources and theories and all the cranky tract literature of pathological nationalist fanaticism . . . His growing literary output, which brought him the overvalued status of chief ideologist of the NSDAP, culminated in *The Myth of the Twentieth Century* in 1930 – according to one contemporary bibliography "the most important book of National Socialism next to Adolf Hitler's *Mein Kampf*" . . . After the grandiose opening, "Today world history must be written afresh", it interprets history in terms of race conflict, inspired by Houston Stewart Chamberlain, Gobineau and their followers, but also by a misconstrued Nietzsche.'[3]

Rosenberg wanted nothing less than a completely new religion. This he had in common with Chamberlain, but he went further and proposed its principle constituents:

'Today (he wrote) a *new* faith is stirring: the myth of blood, the faith that along with blood we are defending the divine nature of man as a whole. The belief, incarnate with the most lucid knowledge, that Nordic blood represents that mystery which has replaced and overcome the old sacraments.'[4]

He insisted that he was a rationalist, despite his exaltation of 'blood consciousness'. In his guise as a reasoning intellectual, he denounced German neo-paganism with the cry 'Wotan is dead', and attacked astrology and Christianity as foul superstitions. To him, his religion of the blood was eminently reasonable since it was, he thought, based upon the obvious facts of life.

The most fundamental principle of Rosenberg's thought, however, was the certainty of the true religious experience. He argued that this mystical ecstasy, which 'has always been outside space and time and non-casual, that is non-materialistic, non-historical and non-rational', granted one a clear comprehension of the universe and of one's own place in it. From the medieval mystic Meister Eckart, he derived the belief that in this experience, the soul meets God 'at the ground of one's being', and he went on to assert that the ground of one's being is the blood. From this proposition he leapt to another, that since one can meet God in one's blood, and since blood is the basis of race, therefore 'races are God's thoughts'. By this stage, logic was being edged out by emotion, for since Rosenberg went on to lambast the Jews, one can only conclude that if he was right, some of God's thoughts must be intensely impure.

He ignored this deduction. He was much more interested in establishing a national 'religion of the blood', in which he wanted to celebrate with joyful rites the truths of the human condition which he had discovered. He thought he was being perfectly rational when he demanded that the religion be based not upon dogmatic creeds, alleged historical events and hollow ceremonies, like Christianity, but upon the experiential certainty of the mystical experience.

Hitler agreed with Rosenberg's ideas, and his recorded monologues display the extent of his intellectual indebtedness:

'The religions are all alike, no matter what they call themselves. They have no future – certainly none for the Germans . . . Whether it is the Old Testament or the New it's all the same old Jewish swindle . . . One is either a German or a Christian. You cannot be both . . . We need free men who feel and know that God is in themselves . . . The Ten Commandments have lost their validity . . . Our peasants have not forgotten their true religion. It still lives . . . The peasant will be told what the Church has destroyed for him: the whole secret knowledge of nature, of the divine, the shapeless, the daemonic . . . We shall wash off the Christian veneer and bring out a religion peculiar to our race . . . through the peasantry we shall really be able to destroy Christianity because there is in them a true religion rooted in nature and blood.'[5]

He allowed Rosenberg to draw up articles for a future National Reich Church. These included a determination to 'exterminate irrevocably' the 'strange and foreign' Christian faith, and a demand for the suppression of the Bible and its replacement by the 'holy book', *Mein Kampf*.

'On the day of its foundation (the last article stated), the Christian cross must be removed from all churches,

107

cathedrals and chapels and it must be superseded by the only unconquerable symbol, the Swastika.'[6]

If Germany had won the Second World War, this would probably have occurred, for although Rosenberg was no longer significant, Christianity had another and much more powerful enemy in Martin Bormann, who flatly declared: 'National Socialism and Christianity are irreconcilable'.

Rosenberg's influence upon Hitler can also be seen in Dietrich Eckart's posthumous pamphlet, *Bolshevism from Moses to Lenin: A Dialogue between Adolf Hitler and Myself*. The ideas attributed therein to Hitler were so obviously borrowed from Rosenberg, that when the Führer came to power in 1933, he ordered the suppression of all copies.

While Rosenberg was formulating his ideas and enjoying his influence, another occultist found his way to Nazism. This was Rudolf Hess, a moody young neurotic, whose faith in himself had been crushed by an overbearing father. Hess was a depressed and introverted student at Munich University who had become emotionally dependent upon the lecturer in Geo-Politics, Professor Karl Haushofer. The Professor was not especially impressed by his adoring pupil:

'He was one student among others, not particularly gifted, of slow intellectual grasp and dull in his work. He was very dependent on emotions and passionately liked to pursue fantastic ideas. He was only influenced by arguments of no importance at the very limits of human knowledge and superstition; he also believed in the influence of the stars on his personal and political life ... I was always disconcerted by the expression of his clear eyes, which had something somnambulistic about it.'[7]

Although Hess always would look up to Haushofer, he found a new master in 1921, Adolf Hitler. He went to hear Hitler speak, and underwent the ecstasy of a religious conversion. His wife described his subsequent attachment to Hitler as 'magical'. Like Rosenberg, Hess wanted to found a new religion, but the central idea of which he was the prophet was far simpler than Rosenberg's muddled marriage of reason and mysticism. Hess's religion replaced God with Hitler. 'Hitler is simply pure reason incarnate,' he declared. Another public speech, made in 1934, proclaimed the Führer's infallibility:

'With pride we see that one man remains beyond all criticism, that is the Führer. This is because everyone feels and knows: he is always right, and he always will be right. The National Socialism of all of us is anchored in uncritical loyalty, in the surrender to the Führer that does not ask for the why in individual cases, in the silent execution of his orders. We believe that the Führer is obeying a higher call to fashion German history. There can be no criticism of this belief.'[8]

Just as Hitler was possessed by an overpowering need to rule, so was Hess possessed by an overpowering need to serve. He surrendered his will entirely to his Führer. Even in the dock at Nuremberg, with the Third Reich a mass of rubble, he reiterated the tenets of his faith:

'It was granted me for many years of my life to live and work under the greatest son whom my nation has produced in the thousand years of its history . . . I regret nothing. If I were standing once more at the beginning I should act once again as I did then.'[9]

Hess was sentenced to life imprisonment. He is still behind bars. He is still unrepentant.

The total devotion of Rudolf Hess won him the affection of Adolf Hitler, who made him his personal adjutant, and later, Deputy Leader of the Nazi Party. Hess was, with Goebbels, the High Priest of Hitler's messianic cult, and so faithfully did he perform his duties that the Führer tolerated the interests which in others he would have condemned. For Hess was devoted to the occult sciences in a manner that was so irrational, it surpassed the most muddled excesses of the volkisch occultists. He was obsessed by astrology, by clairvoyance of every variety, and by fringe medicine of every description. For six years he sought after magical potions which would enable his wife and he to produce an heir. When they finally succeeded, Hess made each Gauleiter send him earth from every part of Germany. He wanted to perform a rite involving the placing of German soil beneath the baby's cradle.

The personality of Hess seems a far cry from that of another leading Nazi who pushed his way to prominence at around the same time, Hermann Goering. So it was, but there were certain peculiar resemblances. On the face of it, though, there was nothing of the depressed introvert about the former air ace and war hero of the famous Richthofen Squadron. Unlike many other Nazis, Goering had coped quite successfully with peacetime conditions, working as a show flier and pilot in Denmark and Sweden. There he fell in love with the Baroness Karin von Foch-Kantzow, took her back to Germany, and married her in Munich in 1922. A fervent German nationalist, Goering felt oppressed by the insipidity of the Weimar Republic, took an interest in politics and, partly influenced by his wife, became a Nazi. 'I joined the Party because I was a revolutionary, not because of any ideological nonsense,' he later declared, and most historians have seen in him the enemy of mysticism and ideas of any description. Vain, cunning and brutal, Goering united in himself the superficial charm of the gentleman adventurer, the rough joviality of the boon companion, and the cold-blooded ruthlessness of the successful gangster. He adored art, and despised 'culture'; he was a loving husband and father, yet he created the Gestapo. Yet he saw no contradictions in his own personality. 'I am what I have always been,' he insisted, 'the last Renaissance man . . .' Hitler concurred. In later years, when rivals complained about Goering's ostentation and outrageous excesses, he thrust their claims aside with a brusque 'Let him be, he's a Renaissance man!'

This was the key to Goering's character. Not only did Goering have the love of display, the artistic refinement, the overwhelming desire for wealth and power, and the complete amorality of the great Renaissance princes, he shared too their lack of faith in any fixed system of beliefs, and their bursts of interest in unorthodox and esoteric

110

Horus: the Egyptian God of War.

Aleister Crowley (1875-1947): Prophet of the Age of Horus.

Adolf Hitler: an idealised portrait of the Aryan Messiah.

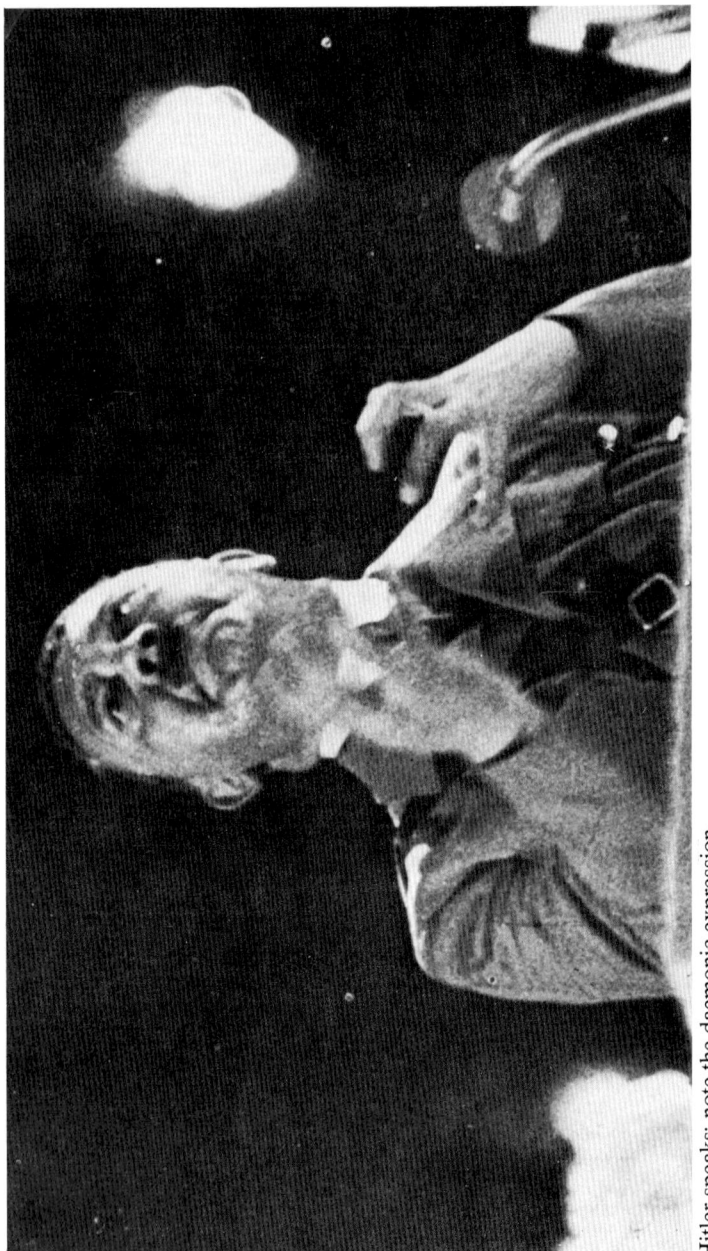

Hitler speaks; note the daemonic expression

A Nuremburg Rally – or ritual for invoking the God of War that any practising magician would approve of.

Heinrich Himmler: Reichsfuehrer S.S. and dedicated occultist.

Hermann Goering gives the Nazi salute – and magical gesture of Earth from the Golden Dawn Order.

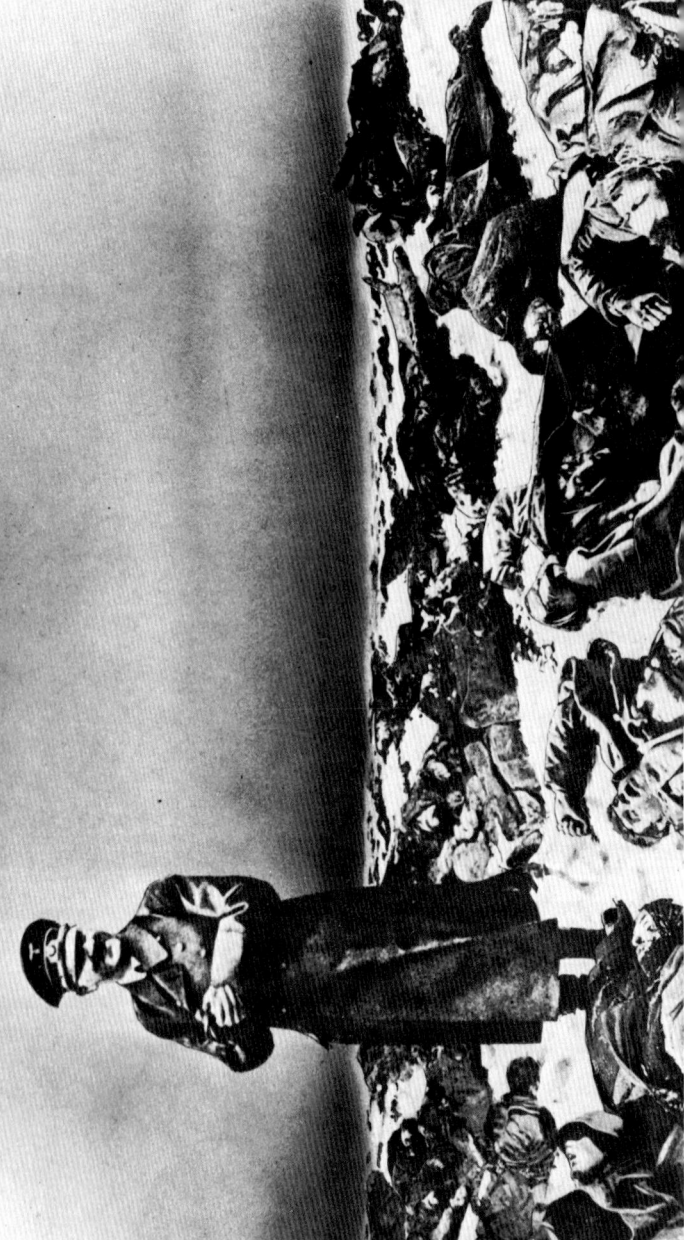

ideas. He was never an occultist, but he took more than just a passing interest in occultism. In Scandinavia he had joined a group dedicated to Nordic racial supremacy and Aryan mysticism, the Edelweiss Society. Later on, he joined the German Luminous Lodge or *Vril* Society. And he was to take seriously the Hollow Earth doctrine of Peter Bender, as we shall see in due course.

Such were the speculations entertained by the mind of Hermann Goering. He never took them to the absurd lengths that Rudolf Hess did, though he did imitate awkwardly Hess's worship of the Führer, nor did he have time for the wearisome philosophising of Rosenberg, but occult ideology nevertheless made an impression upon his psyche.

Goering's real value at this time was to lend to the Nazi movement an aura of respectability. An even bigger asset for the Nazis was the support of another war hero, General Erich von Ludendorff. More responsible than any other man for America's entry into the war, for Russia's collapse into Bolshevism, and for Germany's military defeat, Ludendorff nevertheless insisted that the army had been stabbed in the back by Jews and Marxists, and was delighted to find his claims echoed by the Nazis. A man of startling political naïvety, Ludendorff was also attracted by the neo-paganism which the Nazis displayed, for he too wanted to abolish Christianity, and thought that Germany could recover its greatness if the worship of Wotan was revived. When Ernst Roehm introduced Ludendorff to Hitler, the old General was most impressed, and soon he was appearing in uniform to inspect the Nazi para-military formations, the Sturmabteilung, or Brownshirts Ludendorff was no more a practising occultist than Goering, but he shared Goering's tolerance of and interest in esoteric ideas, seeing in Hitler a German mystic Messiah. These two men did much to increase support for Nazism among the wealthier classes, and they counterbalanced the influence of thugs and perverts like Julius Streicher.

Streicher was a Thulist who in 1922 had brought his Nuremberg branch of the Thule-inspired German Socialist Party over to Hitler. In his *Ostara* style newspaper, *Die*

Sturmer, he published anti-semitic pornography of the most nauseating kind. Even certain Nazis were appalled by Streicher's foul pen, foul mouth, foul habits, and fouler manners, but Hitler held him for a while in very high esteem. The main reason for this may well have been that in the pages of *Die Sturmer*, Streicher expressed Hitler's secret sexual fantasies. Such were the collection of men who emerged at the forefront of the Nazi movement, and who hailed as their saviour the little man with the comic moustache, the staring eyes, the loud, hoarse voice, the jerky and over-emphatic gestures, and the feminine strut, whose slender arm always wielded a heavy riding-whip made from hippopotamus hide.

By the autumn of 1923. Hitler had become convinced that the strength of the Nazi Party and its allies would soon enable a sudden seizure of power. He was sustained in this over-confident and erroneous belief by the conditions which then prevailed in Germany. As a result of Germany's failure to pay her instalment of the £6,600,000,000 in reparations demanded by the Allies, the French had occupied her industrial heartland, the Ruhr. Catastrophic inflation ensued: soon one needed a barrow full of million mark notes just to purchase a bowl of soup. In Bavaria there was a political crisis. Its exact nature does not concern us. Suffice to say that on 8 November, Hitler resolved upon action.

The story of the 'beer hall putsch' is too well known to bear repeating. It was amateurishly planned and incompetently executed. It culminated in a march of around 3000 armed men on Munich, led by Hitler and Ludendorff, on 9 November. This 'March on Munich' was easily dispelled by a few rifle volleys fired by a small detachment of policemen. Hitler, Streicher, Hess and Goering fled ignominiously; the latter badly wounded; Ludendorff contemptuously gave himself up on the spot; sixteen Nazis died; the Brownshirts were dissolved; the *Völkischer Beobachter* was suppressed; the Nazi Party was banned; and Hitler was finally arrested. It was a most dismal fiasco.

This should have been the end of Nazism. All that Hitler had worked for now lay in ruins. Even the movement's spiritual founder, Dietrich Eckart, was no longer able to give words of consolation and encouragement, for he had died. Hitler had nothing to look forward to except a trial for treason.

But the Führer, amazingly enough, still had boundless faith in his own mission. His inner certainties had been confirmed by his followers, and also by the horoscope cast for his nativity by an astrologer called Frau Elsbeth Ebertin, who wrote:

'His constellations show that this man is to be taken very seriously indeed; he is destined to play a Führer-role in future battles. The man I have in mind . . . is fated to sacrifice himself for the German nation and to face up to all circumstances with audacity and courage.'[10]

Contrary to all rational opinion, Hitler felt that it was not the end, either for himself or for National Socialism, and events were to prove him correct. He decided to use his trial as a splendid opportunity for propaganda, which would be reported throughout the world, and hence enable him to found a legend. This was a plan that required the most brazen effrontery, but Hitler carried it through, transforming the prisoner's dock in which he stood into an orator's podium. He treated his prosecutors with contempt, refuting their arguments and asserting the patriotic nature of his mission:

'The man who is born to become a dictator is not compelled. He wills it. He is not driven forward but drives himself. There is nothing immodest about this. Is it presumptuous of a man with the high forehead of a thinker to ponder through the nights till he gives the world an invention? The man who feels called upon to govern a people has no right to say, "If you want me or summon me, I will co-operate." No! It is his duty to step forward.'[11]

By the time that the judges were ready to pass sentence, Hitler had obtained complete psychological ascendancy over the courtroom, and in his final speech he openly defied the Law:

113

'For it is not you, gentlemen, who pass judgement on us. That judgement is spoken by the eternal court of history. What judgement you will hand down I know . . . You may pronounce us guilty a thousand times over, but the goddess of the eternal court of history will smile and tear to tatters the brief of the state prosecutor and the sentence of this court. For she acquits us.'[12]

CHAPTER TEN

Triumph of the Vril

'These are dead, these fellows; they feel not.
We are not for the poor and sad: the lords of
the earth are our kinsfolk.

Is a God to live in a dog? No! but the highest
are of us. They shall rejoice, our chosen: who
sorroweth is not of us.'

The Book of the Law II 18–19

'We are often abused for being the enemies of
the mind and spirit. Well, that is what we are,
but in a far deeper sense than bourgeois
science, in its idiotic pride, could ever
imagine.'

Adolf Hitler

It was fortunate for Hitler that his judges had strong right-wing sympathies. They sentenced him to a mere five years imprisonment in Landsberg Fortress, knowing full well that he would not serve out his sentence. Hitler was released after nine months of extremely comfortable detention. He had become a national figure, a rallying-point for the discontented throughout the whole of Germany. He had turned the disaster of the beer hall putsch into a triumph.

It was the autumn of 1923. Dietrich Eckart was dying. Now he gave utterance to a prayer of fundamental importance, addressed to the black meteorite he owned, which he called his 'Mecca Stone'. He prayed that after his death, The Thule Gesellschaft would continue to flourish and would perform its appointed task of changing the world.

The prayer was answered, though not in the exact manner hoped for by Eckart. After his death, the Thule

Group went into decline, but what Thule represented nevertheless continued to flourish, and did change the world. This was due mainly to Eckart's protégé and pupil, Adolf Hitler, but a share of the credit must also go to that extraordinary friend of Eckart's to whom he sent a manuscript just before he died, Karl Haushofer.

We have seen how Haushofer was taught by Gurdjieff in Tibet, and by the Green Dragon Society in Japan, how his predictive powers brought him esteem as a general, and how his formidable intellect won him renown as a professor. He never made the mistake of openly attributing his success to his occultism. Like Hitler, he was shrewd enough to realise that a passion for the esoteric usually invites ridicule and he hid the true nature of his interests beneath a cloak of cold-blooded rationalism, which has taken in more than one historian.

Like Crowley and Hitler, Haushofer despised the majority of occultists as ineffectual and self-important cranks who succeeded only in bringing the entire subject into deserved disrepute. We have seen how unimpressed he was by Rudolf Hess. Initially too, he was equally unimpressed by Hess's god, the ranting Adolf Hitler. Even so, Hess, or probably Dietrich Eckart's manuscript, persuaded the Professor to attend Hitler's trial for treason. The Nazi leader's magnificent courtroom performance exercised a profound effect upon Haushofer and caused him to revise his opinion. When Hess begged him to visit Hitler in Landsberg Fortress, Haushofer complied. As Joachim C. Fest remarks:

'Acting as intermediary between Haushofer and Hitler was the most important and virtually the only personal contribution Rudolf Hess made towards the birth and shaping of National Socialism.'[1]

Unfortunately, Fest does not enlighten us as to the nature of Haushofer's influence, which was both exoteric and esoteric.

It is best to deal first with the exoteric aspect. Dietrich Eckart had instructed Hitler in the art of propaganda; Haushofer broadened the scope of his vision and taught him Geo-Politics. The Professor was obsessed by the concept of lebensraum, or living-space. A fierce believer in Nordic supremacy and Jewish degeneracy, he thought that the Aryan race had originated in Central Asia, and urged the conquest of this area. Hence, in *Mein Kampf*, we find a constant reiteration of the importance of *lebensraum*, and in Chapter 14, a discussion of land and sea power, security and living area and the place of geography in military strategy that could have come straight out of Haushofer.

Haushofer's exoteric influence upon Hitler has often been remarked upon, but the nature of his esoteric influence is not so well known. We do not know for certain if he remained in contact with Gurdjieff, then domiciled in Paris, though this is rumoured to be the case. There may well be some substance to this rumour for, according to Gurdjieff's leading English disciple, J. G. Bennett, Gurdjieff took an extraordinary interest in the Third Reich and declared that the events it precipitated were of profound significance for humanity. But whether or not Gurdjieff kept in touch, his former pupil certainly provoked another eruption of the daemonic in the mind of Adolf Hitler.

Hitler's first experience of magic had been in Vienna: the climax was a mystical experience which was probably self-induced, though the methods employed may have owed something to Lanz von Liebenfels; from it dates Hitler's inner strength and certainty. The second was provoked by Dietrich Eckart and the Thule Society; from it dates Hitler's mastery of 'the magic power of the spoken word', the mediumship of his oratory, his flair for propaganda, and probably his intense personal magnetism. Now let us look at the results of his third experience, under the guidance of Karl Haushofer.

Firstly, Hitler developed greater self-control. He learned that greatest of secrets, how to wait. He never again made the mistake of trying to seize power by armed revolution. He no longer felt the need to be seen with a riding-whip. The exhaustion brought on by his oratory could now be remedied with a cup of sweet tea rather than copious draughts of strong beer, and he gave up alcohol altogether, a practice recommended by all Eastern teachers of yoga Secondly, Hitler developed the predictive powers which we have noticed in Haushofer, and which we shall in time be examining. Thirdly, he gained instruction in various Tibetan occult teachings which had a profound effect upon him.

In Vienna, Hitler had learned from books and from German volkisch occultists. The Thule Group of Eckart and Sebottendorff taught him a system of magic based upon a marriage between volkisch occultism and the teachings of Arab magicians picked up in the Middle East and North Africa. Now Haushofer introduced him to a new combination: the wisdom of Gurdjieff, derived from Sufi mystics and Tibetan lamas, and the Zen mysticism of the Japanese Green Dragon Society. These teachings stressed the existence of certain centres of power, or *chakras*, in the human body which correspond to the endocrine glands of Western science. In most human beings, these chakras are dormant, but they can be activated by dint of yogic or magical exercises and bring to the practitioner some rather unusual powers, most notably that of being able to impose one's will upon others. The student is usually taught to resist this temptation, but Haushofer had little interest in ethics. The most important of these centres, according to the systems he was teaching, is that which corresponds to the pineal gland, between and behind the eyebrows. When activated, it confers super-human powers and magical vision. It is known by some as the Ajna Chakra, by some as the Third Eye, and by some as the Cyclops Eye.

This is all very interesting, but is there the slightest scrap of evidence to show that Hitler even knew of its existence? As it happens, there is. 'Hitler was always talking about this Cyclops Eye,' recalled a baffled Hermann Rauschning. 'Hitler was fascinated by these ideas and loved to immerse himself in them.'

Evidently, Haushofer did nothing to diminish Hitler's belief in the imminence of the Superman's advent; very probably, he encouraged it, for he had been to Tibet, which

Blavatsky and Gurdjieff had declared to be the home of the Unknown Superman.

It must at this point be stressed, for it is usually forgotten or ignored, that whatever powers Hitler did acquire were wholly independent of the intellect. Esoteric prowess has little to do with intellectual distinction, though these do occasionally unite in one individual. Haushofer was one of these, and Aleister Crowley was another; the latter even forced his students to develop their intellects so as to prevent bigotry and fanaticism. This, however, is uncommon. Indeed, the poverty of Hitler's intellect is there for all to deplore in the autobiography he dictated to Hess while in prison, *Mein Kampf*.

Mein Kampf is probably the worst 'holy book' ever written. Some of it was blatantly untruthful, but, as its author might say, 'this was not the worst of it'. The style is awkward, clumsy, and quite intolerably tedious. The content is much of the time devoid of the slightest interest or originality. It is a succession of rambling, banal, and intensely wearisome monologues by a thoroughly third-rate mind. Apparently the book still sells in Arabic translation, but those who are foolish enough to purchase it must most deeply regret their gullibility. The only occasions when the book becomes readable are when the author succeeds in expressing his emotions in one or two compressed paragraphs, or when he summarises the views of Dietrich Eckart on propaganda, or Karl Haushofer on German foreign policy; here there are insights of genius which authors have often quoted. Unfortunately, these insights do not occur very often, and most of the book's 629 pages lack the smallest redeeming value.

'How could a man so ignorant, so enslaved by stupid dogmas, have achieved such practical success?'[2] asks a bewildered A. J. P. Taylor, and many others have echoed him. The fact is that Hitler depended not upon his conscious intellect but upon the powers of his unleashed unconscious, supplemented by the cunning and knowledge of mens' weaknesses which he had learned in Vienna, and by an ability to concentrate upon one aim to the exclusion of everything else. This fact has been noted by many who observed him, for example, Herman Rauschning:

'One cannot help thinking of him as a medium. For most of the time mediums are ordinary, insignificant people. Suddenly they are endowed with what seem to be supernatural powers which set them apart from the rest of humanity . . . The medium is possessed. Once the crisis is past, they fall back again into mediocrity. It was in this way, beyond any doubt, that Hitler was possessed by forces outside himself – almost demoniacal forces of which the individual named Hitler was only the temporary vehicle. The mixture of the banal and the supernatural created that insupportable duality of which one was conscious in his presence . . . It was like looking at a bizarre face whose expression seems to reflect an unbalanced state of mind coupled with a disquieting impression of hidden power.'[3]

Today it is fashionable to talk of supernatural forces in terms of the unknown powers of the unconscious, though it does not matter where these powers are: what matters is that they exist, can be used, and were used with incalculable effect by a man as banal as Adolf Hitler.

When he emerged from prison, where he had lived comfortably with the faithful Rudolf Hess and enjoyed the company of visitors like Karl Haushofer, the Nazi Party had split into a number of bickering groups. This was exactly what Hitler had wanted; he had put Rosenberg in charge because he knew that this would be the result. He did not want to risk the possibility of anyone usurping his position of supremacy. Now he was able to set about the task of re-uniting the fragmented movement as its acclaimed and undisputed leader.

His new strategy was much more intelligent than previously. No longer did he preach a violent seizure of the reins of power. He advocated instead a campaign of patient propaganda which would result in a democratic victory at the polls. He insisted that it was essential to win over the nation's powerful vested interests. He devoted his energies to transforming the National Socialist German Workers'

Party from a provincial Bavarian grouping into a significant national movement.

It was hard uphill work. The Weimar Republic had recovered from the crisis of 1923, and had taken steps to reestablish itself as the permanent constitutional form of German Government. Guided by its exceedingly able Foreign Minister, Stresemann, it secured large American loans, solved the problem of inflation, negotiated a new Reparations agreement with the Allies, and took credit for the benefits of a period of general world prosperity. It must have been very difficult to persuade Germans of the importance of the Nazi message, and yet, very slowly, Party membership grew. Probably we can attribute this growth to German students, who were not impressed by mere material prosperity, and yearned for something more exciting and idealistic. This hypothesis is borne out by the election figures of 1930, which reveal that $2\frac{1}{2}$ million of the 4 million new voters voted for the Nazi Party. For the young, the movement possessed the wayout and slightly scandalous appeal of today's rock stars.

While the Nazis battled grimly onward in the political arena, they were fed by a new influx of power from the world of the daemonic. The Luminous Lodge or Vril Society was founded in Berlin. Its leading light was Karl Haushofer. Members included Alfred Rosenberg, Dr Theodor Morrel, later the Führer's doctor, Heinrich Himmler, Hermann Goering, and Hitler himself. We have met the concept of the *vril* before, in Bulwer Lytton, and his *The Coming Race* was thought by initiates to be a work of supreme importance. The Vril Society was first heard of outside Germany when the rocket expert, Willi Ley, fled from his country in 1933, and informed those who were willing to listen that the Lodge took Lytton's book literally:

'He added with a smile that the disciples believed they had secret knowledge that would enable them to change their race and become the equals of the men hidden in the bowels of the earth. Methods of concentration, a whole system of internal gymnastics by which they would be

121

transformed. They began their exercises by staring fixedly at an apple cut in half . . .'[4]

Perhaps, like Japan's Green Dragon Society, they were endeavouring to make the seeds germinate, but this was just a minor diversion. The main aim of the Vril Society was to make further researches into the origins and nature of the Aryan Race and discover how to reactivate the vril force, which, it was held, slumbered in the blood, but when awakened would produce the Superman.

The investigations of the Lodge were under the guidance of Haushofer, and it is only to be expected that much time was spent in the study of Tibetan secret teachings. Soon the initiates came to believe that they had formed an alliance with mysterious Tibetan lodges situated in Agarthi and Schamballah, of which we shall be hearing more, and with an Unknown Superman and Master, the King of Fear. No one knows who this King of Fear was, though J. H. Brennan has suggested Gurdjieff. Nor do we know if Hitler ever met the King of Fear, though certain of his remarks do imply this:

"'The new man is living amongst us now! He is here!' exclaimed Hitler triumphantly. 'Isn't that enough for you? I will tell you a secret. I have seen the new man. He is intrepid and cruel. I was afraid of him.'

"'In uttering these words," added Rauschning, "Hitler was trembling in a kind of ecstasy."'[5]

Initiates kept in touch with the Unknown Master both with electronic transmitters and, rather more bafflingly, by means of a 'game' played with a Tibetan pack of cards like the Western Tarot. Were they essaying telepathic communication? And could it have been with Gurdjieff, whose telepathic skills have frequently been described by his pupils? No one seems to know. Louis Pauwels informs us that the 'game' was played regularly between 1928 and 1941, and that Joseph Stalin seems to have been aware of the Nazi preoccupation with the occult, declaring in council that it was 'inconceivable that, in the twentieth century, heads of States should indulge in such devilries' Though we cannot make much of the fact, it is curious to note that Stalin had been a fellow-student of Gurdjieff's in the Seminary at Alexandropol.[6]

Whatever the identity of the King of Fear, the Nazis certainly took an extraordinary interest in Tibet. According to Pauwels and Bergier, as soon as funds were available, they mounted a series of expeditions to that distant land, which followed one another in rapid succession until 1943. Nor was this interest one-sided. A colony of Tibetan lamas settled in Munich and Berlin in 1926. One of them, known as 'the man with the green gloves', was said to 'possess the keys to the kingdom of Agarthi'. He had predictive powers, for he used to forecast successfully the number of Nazi deputies elected to the Reichstag. It is said that Hitler consulted him regularly. And when the Russians took Berlin in 1945, they found to their astonishment one thousand Tibetan corpses in German army uniforms.

Some Germans, especially intellectuals, found the Nazis attractive precisely because of the daemonic element. Ernst Junger expressed this attitude in 1932:

'One of the best means of preparation for a new and bolder life is to be found in the annihilation of the values of the free-floating and autocratic spirit, in the destruction of the standards which the bourgeois age has laboured to impart to man ... The best answer to the high treason of the spirit against life is high treason of the spirit against the spirit, and to be a part of this blasting operation is one of the great and cruel pleasures of our time.'[7]

Another example of this type of intellectual, then very common throughout Germany, was Hans Heinz Ewers, whose tales of horror, *In Terror* and *The Mandragore* anticipated the malefic sadism of the Nazi regime. Ewers was under no illusions regarding the Nazis. He joined them because he saw in their movement 'the strongest expression of the Powers of Darkness'. His main contribution was the Sturmabteilung hymn, the *Horst Wessel Lied*.

The destined leader of the Aryan peoples, however, obviously had things other than the Vril Society with which to occupy his mind, in particular the increasing strength of his vehicle, the Nazi Party. He agreed with the opinion of the astrologer, Elsbeth Ebertin, that his trial had not only given 'this movement inner strength, but outer strength, a massive impetus to the pendulum of world history'. One does not know if he also agreed with Frau Ebertin's description of him as 'on the platform like a man possessed, like a medium, the unconscious tool of higher powers': Hitler did not hold astrologers in high regard except when their conclusions pleased him. He had many cutting things to say about astrology as a predictive science, and preferred to rely on his own intuition. Now his intuition told him that Germany's prosperity would not last, and he could afford to feel pleased with his slow but steady political progress. The reconstituted SA was also attracting recruits, and two more willing and capable executives of his will had come to his attention, Joseph Goebbels and Heinrich Himmler.

Goebels was a frustrated and cynical club-footed intellectual who, like so many of his breed, had come to despise the intellect and exalt the passion of violence for its own sake. This in itself does not make him very interesting, but he possessed too a genius for propaganda that was superior to Hitler's own, and a talent for oratory that was second only to the Führer's. Originally something of a Socialist – and in a Communist country he would have remained so – Dr Goebbels was finally mesmerised by Hitler, and like so many others, he came to worship him. It no longer mattered if Hitler was interested in occultism and like pursuits, for which Goebbels felt nothing but contempt; all that mattered was that he had found faith once more in a god.

In time, Goebbels came to usurp the role of Rudolf Hess as Hitler's High Priest, devoting every particle of his propagandist skills to persuading others to abandon all reason and lie at the feet of the divine being whom he praised. His rise had really commenced in 1926, when Hitler made him Gauleiter of the small party organisation in Communist dominated Berlin. 'Beware you dogs,' wrote Goebbels. 'When the Devil is loose in me you will not curb him again,' and he made good his promise, becoming within months the city's most feared demagogue. He organised demonstrations, printed propaganda, mass meetings and street brawls, convinced that 'history is made in the street'. He had absolutely no regard for truth whatsoever, and did not care how much bad publicity he received provided there was plenty of it. By 1932, the Nazis ruled the streets of Berlin, and Goebbels was ready to become master of his nation's propaganda and public enlightenment.

Heinrich Himmler was not as intelligent, as colourful or as talented as Joseph Goebbels. As a man, he was distinguished only by a disturbing mediocrity. He relied for his advancement upon an unquestioning loyalty to Hitler, an uncritical devotion to Nazism, and unexciting but thoroughly conscientious bureaucratic skills. A chicken farmer by profession, his polite but pedantic manner reminded observers of an elementary schoolteacher. Although he had joined the Nazis in 1923, even they paid little attention to the dutiful little nonentity. Eventually, Hitler found him a job, Commander of a very small organisation known as the SS. This was then the body-guard of the Nazi elite, and subordinate to the SA, and only Himmler seems to have regarded his task as something other than a backwater for a devoted subordinate.

His mild manner belied his ambition; more important from his own point of view, his meticulous attention to the smallest details impressed Adolf Hitler. Within four years of his appointment, Himmler had persuaded Hitler to allow him to increase the strength of the SS to 30,000 men, though it was still nominally subordinate to the SA. Even this was not nearly enough for Himmler and his assistant, the ruthless Reinhard Heydrich, and the two men tirelessly schemed that they might succeed in three aims: the SS would become not only an independent Nazi Praetorian Guard; not only the controllers of all police forces throughout Germany; but also the most powerful magical Order that the world has ever known. For Heinrich Himmler was, as we shall see, a completely dedicated occultist.

The years from 1924–9 were therefore years of consolidation in which the Nazi movement laid the foundations for future conquest. They were also happy years insofar as Hitler's personal life was concerned. He found himself a lovely home at Berchtesgaden, on the Obersalzberg in the Bavarian Alps, which became his haven for solitude, rest and relaxation. 'Yes, there are so many links between Obersalzberg and me,' he later reminisced. 'So many things were born there . . . I spent there the finest hours of my life . . . It is here that all my great projects were conceived and ripened. I had hours of leisure in those days, and how many charming friends!'

Some of those friends were women, whose company he enjoyed, especially if they were beautiful. 'What lovely women there are in the world!' he once exlaimed dreamily, though he admired female bodies rather more than female minds, and paid no attention at all to the first-rate advice of one of them, whose words Hermann Rauschning has recorded:

'My Führer, don't touch black magic. As yet both white and black are open to you. But once you've embarked on black magic it will dominate your destiny. It will hold you captive. Don't choose the quick and easy successes. There lies before you the power over a realm of pure spirits. Do not allow yourself to be led away from your true path by earthbound spirits, who will rob you of your creative power.'[8]

For Hitler, women were just exquisite toys that brought one pleasure, though his own particular taste in pleasure was a little unusual. Although he was in a position to enjoy the bodies of beautiful women, there is no evidence that he did so, for his sexual inclinations formed something of a barrier.

For a long period, Hitler continued his adolescent practice of looking at women, admiring women, but not touching women. He was attracted by the tall and stately Erna Hanfstaengl, and the authoritative Winifred Wagner, daughter-in-law of the composer, but it was not until 1928 that he finally embarked on an affair. The girl was his niece, Geli Raubal, and their relationship was odd, quite aside from considerations of age or incestuousness. On the one hand, Hitler dominated her completely, installing her in a luxurious Munich apartment, but forbidding her to see other men, to leave him, or to pursue a career as an opera singer: on the other hand, he begged the young, blonde, attractive and vivacious girl to enslave and humiliate him. He wrote her a letter which expressed his masochistic desires. She must have co-operated only in order to please him, for the letter was left lying around, and fell into the hands of the landlady's son. Others saw copies, to their subsequent regret, for in 1934, all suspected of knowledge of its contents were hunted down and killed.

It is understandable that Geli Raubal was unable to endure her situation after a while. She wanted to pursue a career; Hitler became insanely jealous; their sex-life she probably did not find especially satisfying; and a series of violent quarrels brought her close to a nervous breakdown. The morning after a furious row on 17 September 1931, she was found shot dead. The Coroner's verdict was suicide, and despite the rumours that hinted at the possibility of murder by Hitler or Himmler, there is no evidence to contradict the court's findings.

Hitler was inconsolable for months. He threatened suicide and wept at her grave. Pictures of Geli were hung in the Obersalzberg villa, and subsequently in the Berlin Chancellery; on each anniversary of her birth and death, fresh flowers were placed before these shrines. He always spoke of her in tones of reverence, and this was to be his sole adult experience of anything that could remotely be called love. His relationship with Eva Braun was by comparison just a pale substitute.

It was fortunate for Hitler's sanity, though hardly for the world, that by 1931 there were considerations of immense importance to take his mind of his tragedy. In 1929 there had occurred the event which terminated Germany's economic boom and once more reduced its citizens to penury, to the delight of the Nazis. This was the Wall Street Crash, the effects of which spread throughout the world as banks and businesses collapsed in quick succession. By 1930, 3,000,000 Germans were unemployed, and the figure was growing. Misery was almost universal. Unemployed workers were joined by the middle classes, who had lost their savings when the banks had crashed. Men, women and children huddled together in long lines for free bread and soup.

Two messianic parties stood to gain from the Depression they had prayed for, the Communists and the Nazis. In the elections of 1930, the Communists polled over $4\frac{1}{2}$ million votes and gained 77 seats in the Reichstag. The Nazis did even better, for their vote rose from 800,000 to 6,409,600, which increased their parliamentary representation from 12 to 107 seats. The Weimar Republic tumbled into another period of chaos. In all industrial cities, Communist demonstrations defied the police, and were in turn defied by the Nazi SA. Hitler made up a quarrel he had previously instigated with his old comrade, Ernst Roehm, and recalled him from training the Bolivian Army to take charge of the SA. With Roehm in charge, SA membership grew from 100,000 to 300,000 in just one year.

The Brownshirts enjoyed nothing more than marching, drinking, singing old Army songs and beating up Jews, unless it was battling in the streets with the Communists. Hitler did not care if Roehm and his circle were avowed pederasts, or if the SA men were no more than criminals, louts and psychopaths. The SA was serving its purpose in demonstrating the Goverment's inability to maintain order, and its own ability to contain Communism.

This was not lost on wealthy industrialists like Thyssen and Voegler. Deeply conservative, but lacking in moral principles, they saw in Hitler a man they could use to combat the Red Threat. Goering, a man of their own class, hastened to reassure them that the 'Socialism' in 'National Socialism' was not to be taken too seriously,and after a secret meeting at the Industry Club, Dusseldorf, the men of the Ruhr agreed to help Hitler. Money flooded in to the Nazi treasury, and influential political parties like the right-wing Nationalists allied themselves with the demonic little orator. Whilst Goering continued to court established institutions, Goebbels used spectacular light and sound displays to inflame the masses with the burning conviction that Hitler was their only hope. The Führer himself had never spoken better as he screamed the rage, shame and frustration that ate at the souls of millions.

The elections of July 1932 saw the Nazis emerge as the country's largest single party, with 13,745,000 votes and 230 seats, but they still lacked an overall majority. President Hindenberg vowed he would never appoint 'the Bohemian corporal' as his Chancellor, and gave the reins of government to a 'Cabinet of Barons'. The Nazis were within sight of victory, but could not quite grasp it, and their consequent violence and ill-temper caused a loss of 2,000,000 votes in the next election, held in November. Many predicted that they had passed their peak.

Hitler managed to hold his disappointed followers together. He was still in a relatively strong position. Unemployment had reached 6,000,000; the Communists were still a threat; and the SA were now 2,000,000 strong. Moving with considerable cunning and adroitness, he took part in a complex series of political intrigues, allowing his conservative rivals to believe they could use him for their own shady ends. Both the story and the result are well known. On 30 January 1933, President Hindenburg obeyed his advisers and appointed Adolf Hitler as Chancellor of Germany.

Few people in the world knew what Hitler's real aims and passions were. Fewer still knew or cared about his experience of the occult, and the teachings of Karl Haushofer, which would soon be put into practice. Although Rudolf Hess has formally stated that Haushofer was indeed the secret Master, the latter himself probably did not realise the magnitude of his contribution to history, and if he did, he has nowhere stated the fact. However, we will find it best expressed in the poetry of his son, Albrecht.

Originally a fanatical Nazi, Albrecht Haushofer turned against the Führer, and was involved in the 1944 Army plot to murder him. He was arrested, and shot by the SS at Moabit prison. After his death, a curious poem was found on his body:

THE FATHER

A proround legend of the East
Tells us that the spirits of the power of evil
Are held captive in the Marine night,
Sealed by the prudent hand of God.
Until fate, once in a thousand years
Accords a single fisherman the power
To break the chains of the prisoners.
If he doesn't at once throw back his catch
                    into the sea.
For my father, destiny had spoken.
His will had lost the strength
To push the demon back into its jail.
My father broke the seal,
He did not feel the Devil's breath,
He let the demon loose on the world."[9]

CHAPTER ELEVEN

Subjugation of a Nation

'Them that seek to entrap thee, to overthrow
thee, them attack without pity or quarter; &
destroy them utterly. Swift as a trodden
serpent turn and strike! Be thou yet deadlier
than he! Drag down their souls to awful
torment: laugh at their fear: spit upon them!'
The Book of the Law III 42

'I had to encourage 'national' feelings for
reasons of expediency; but I was already
aware that the "nation" idea could only have
a temporary value. The day will come when
even here in Germany what is known as
"nationalism" will practically have ceased to
exist. What will take its place in the world will
be a universal society of masters and overlords.'
Adolf Hitler

Hitler was now Chancellor of Germany, but his position
remained precarious. Theoretically, he was still subject to
the President, to the voting in a Reichstag in which he
lacked an overall majority, to the decisions of the courts,
and to the result of any future election. If his power was to
be permanent, it was essential that appropriate measures be
taken with all possible speed. The Nazis therefore
dedicated themselves to a ruthless consolidation of the
victory they had achieved. Their aim was simple: total
power over every aspect of German life.

They were greatly assisted by the Reichstag Fire of 27
February 1933, so much so that many think the Nazis to
have been responsible for the conflagration. Whoever the
real culprit was, the Nazis chose to blame the Communists,
and using the fire as evidence for their claim that the Reich

was in danger, they smashed the left, which would never again be a threat to them. On 23 March, the Reichstag reconvened in the Berlin Opera House, where Hitler demanded full emergency powers, which would enable him to rule by decree. With the exceptions of the Communists, who had been arrested, and the Social Democrats, who opposed the motion to their subsequent agony, the Reichstag deputies cheerfully vested all their powers in a dictator.

This was only the beginning. One by one, all German institutions surrendered to the National Socialists. The judiciary was Nazified, and no longer would decisions of the courts carry any weight against those of the Government. The trade unions were disbanded, their funds stolen, and their members made subject to a Labour Front under a drunken Nazi fanatic, Robert Ley. The onslaught on the mind revealed itself on 10 May, when students joyfully burned all books proscribed by the new regime, including the works of Shaw, Wells, Brecht, and Hermann Hesse: culture was henceforth to be regulated by Dr Goebbels. In Prussia, Hermann Goering founded the Gestapo, and purged the state government of all elements hostile to Nazism. Elsewhere, Himmler and Heydrich extended their influence until almost every police organisation was within their control. Nazi Party officials took over large areas of administration previously run by an impartial civil service. German citizens had to choose between acclaiming their leaders with the overblown language of Goebbels's Propaganda Ministry, or facing the terror of the unleashed Sturmabteilung.

Despite these successes, two rival organisations possessed the power to undermine Hitler's position, the SA itself, and the Army. For the SA, the Nazi revolution was proceeding much too slowly. It was not enough for them to trample upon the faces of Jews, and torture their enemies in hastily improvised concentration camps. Even when Goering used them as auxiliary police units and empowered them to maim and kill anyone they chose, this did not leave them satisfied. With their leader, Ernst Roehm, they demanded a Second Revolution, in which the power

132

they had fought for would be transferred into their grasping hands. Like victorious medieval mercenaries, they desired to loot the nation they had captured. They had victory, but where were the spoils? And Roehm insisted upon nothing less than for the SA to replace the Army and become a state within a state. 'The grey rock,' he proclaimed, 'must be submerged beneath the brown flood.'

Obviously, the Army regarded the SA as a threat to its position of privilege. Its generals had no intention of being submerged by the brown flood of Ernst Roehm. They despised the SA as scum, and when the Brownshirts became impatient and proceeded to cause havoc throughout Germany, they informed Hitler that if the SA remained uncurbed, President Hindenburg would declare Martial Law.

Hitler was now placed in a serious dilemma. A tactical blunder would provoke either his own dismissal or even a civil war. His sympathies lay with his old comrades, and he knew that the Generals regarded Nazism with distrust, and himself as a distasteful upstart corporal. He knew too that the SA numbered 3,000,000 men compared with the Army's paltry 100,000. Yet he could not afford to be sentimental and unrealistic. The Army did have the support of Hindenburg and the respect of the German people. Although it was numerically small, Hitler was far too experienced a soldier not to recognise that the Army held the key to future German expansion, while the SA was just a brawling and undisciplined street-rabble. The demands of the latter for a social revolution were a thorough nuisance; their behaviour was bringing his government into national and international disrepute; Roehm had become too powerful for comfort; and Himmler and Goering, jealous of their rival, were advocating his removal.

After months of indecision, Hitler finally reached a solution that was as brilliant as it was treacherous. He consented to the Army's demands on condition that they gave him their full support, and having secured the whole-hearted backing of one institution, he proceeded to use

Himmler's SS to break the power of the other. On 30 June 1934, SS men executed the bloody 'Night of the Long Knives', in which all leading SA men, including Roehm, and numerous other prominent threats to the regime, were ruthlessly butchered. The black-shirted murderers were rewarded; the SS became an autonomous organisation, above the Party; and, as Joachim Gunthe wrote soon after: 'The vital idea which inspired the SA was replaced on 30 June 1934, by an idea that was purely Satanic – the SS.'

But the man who gained most from the purge was Adolf Hitler. When President Hindenburg died in the August of 1934, the Generals compelled every Army officer to take an oath of unconditional obedience to the 'Führer of the German Reich and nation, Adolf Hitler, the Supreme Commander of the Wehrmacht.' Within a short period of time, leading Generals would be disgraced by Nazi plots, and no one in the land would dare to whisper against the man in whose hands all power was concentrated.

Nothing remained safe from Nazi terror. The independence formerly enjoyed by the various German states was abolished. Persecution of the Jews became systematic and Government-backed with the odious Nuremberg Laws of 1936, which took away all rights of citizenship and barred them from professions. German men and women jeered and howled with derision as Jews were publicly humiliated, laughed when their businesses were smashed and ruined, ignored the sudden disappearances of Jews of their acquaintance, cheered when their leaders mocked the helpless, gloated over the tormenting of Jewish children, and later expected others to believe that they were ignorant of the regime's racism. Why should they have cared about the fate of the Jews? They were the Master Race, their leaders told them, in a Third Reich that would endure for one thousand years.

They offered little resistance to totalitarianism. They believed, or chose to believe, the slogans of Goebbels, and all feared the arbitrary powers of the Gestapo, now under Himmler and Heydrich. Many welcomed the abolition of individual responsibility for one's actions; for some it is easier to obey than to accept the dangers of freedom. Workers now had job security, a health service, cheap holiday schemes; if freedom meant starvation, then slavery was preferable. Besides which, there was an exhilaration in losing oneself in a screaming crowd, and experiencing an ecstasy of self-abandonment, which made all deprivations seem worthwhile.

The Nazis now had what they wanted, total power. Hermann Goering controlled the economy, and cowed both workers and industrialists. Joseph Goebbels controlled the mind, censoring all news, and arbitrating over all matters of culture and the arts. Heinrich Himmler controlled the criminal, political, and secret police forces, against which the courts offered no protection. Every district had its Gauleiter, every block on every street its informer. Heydrich kept files on each and every individual who showed the slightest sign of deviation from the norm. Those who failed to demonstrate their complete allegiance to the Nazis were thrown into concentration camps and treated with a sadism that was emotionless, methodical and thorough, its aim nothing less than to reduce human beings to the level of grovelling zombies. Despite all this, the Germans were prouder of their country than they had ever been before. In the words of Tacitus: 'There have never been better slaves, never worse masters.'

In the manner of all totalitarian regimes, the National Socialists sought to mould the minds of youth. Here, Hitler was at his clearest about his aims:

'The youth learns nothing else than to think German, to act German, and if these boys enter our organisation at the age of ten and there often get and feel a breath of fresh air for the first time, then four years later they come from the Jungvolk into the Hitler Youth, and we keep them there for another four years, and then we certainly don't give them back into the hands of the originators of our old classes and estates, but take them straight into the party, into the Labour Front, the SA or the SS, the NSKK, and so on. And if they are there for another two years or a year and a half and still haven't become complete National Socialists, then they go into the Labour Service and are polished for another six or seven months, all with a symbol, the German spade. And any class consciousness or pride or status that may be left here and there is taken over by the Wehrmacht for further treatment for two years, and when they come back after two, three or four years, we take them straight into the SA, SS, and so on again, so that they shall in no case suffer a relapse, and they don't get free again as long as they live. And if anyone says to me, yes, but there will always be a few left over: National Socialism is not at the end of its days but only at the beginning!'[1]

In response, the youth of Germany flocked to follow the Führer. They were joined by millions of women, whom the Nazis said were fit only for Church, children and kitchen. At first too, they had for company the intellectuals in their droves, who proclaimed their worship of the openly avowed 'enemies of mind and spirit', and who joyfully humbled themselves when Hitler declared: 'I don't want any intellectuals.' With the exception of the hopeless mediocrities who could create in accordance with Goebbels's decrees, the love-affair between the intellectuals and the Nazis was not to be a lasting one: and many artists and writers who had initially hailed Hitler with such enthusiasm found themselves forbidden to pursue their vocation. National Socialism wanted the total man, and only those who could give all of themselves to the State, without reserving the slightest right to criticise or judge, could afford to feel secure.

The intellectuals had imagined that Nazism would bring with it a frenzied, pagan freedom. They found that this freedom was only for the very few, and that for the vast majority, Nazism was just a conspiracy of mediocre minds against all expression of the individual human spirit. A similar, and probably more profound disillusionment affected the occultists, who, after all, had some excuse for believing that the Nazis would regard them with considerable favour

They were wrong. In the spring of 1934, Berlin's police

chief banned all forms of fortune-telling. There followed a confiscation of occult books throughout Germany, and many booksellers of the esoteric were 'persuaded' to sell something else. Freemasonry was exposed and eliminated. Even Sebottendorff, founder of the Thule Gesellschaft, discovered to his astonishment that he was now persona non grata. His book, *Bevor Hitler kam*, and his lecture both of which revealed the occult origins of Nazism and the influence of the Thulists, led to his arrest and imprisonment; all his writings were suppressed; the Thule Group was dissolved, and former membership of it and of the German Order was made a disqualification for holding office. He was eventually released only on condition that he left the Reich and promised to keep silent about the Nazis' occult connections.

After a brief period of tolerance for groups which were pro-Nazi, the persecution was renewed in 1937. Virtually every single occult fraternity was banned, its publications seized, its leaders often imprisoned. Astrologers especially were harassed and murdered. A long list of prohibited societies was compiled by the SS: it included the Theosophical Society, all groups derived from Rudolf Steiner or the Golden Dawn, Aleister Crowley's OTO, and even the Order of New Templars, whose leader, Lanz von Liebenfels, was forbidden to write for publication. To be a magician became as dangerous as to be a Jew.

There were many reasons for this occult purge, which reveals Hitler's considerable concern with esoteric matters rather than, as some allege, his lack of interest. Firstly, no totalitarian regime can tolerate secret societies. Secondly, as leader of a European nation, Hitler wanted to demonstrate the respectability of Nazism, and could not permit rumours about his magical preoccupations which would damage both his national and his international prestige. Thirdly, as a magician, he appreciated the danger of allowing other magicians to work independently of his own will. Fourthly, he insisted that magic was only for the Nazi élite, and hence could be practised only by an Order with a total commitment to him and to his desires, the SS. As we shall see in due course, the SS swallowed any Orders which could be of use to it, and by 1939 was the sole magical organisation in the land.

Hitler was plain enough about his occult policy to Rauschning, in the course of a monologue on Freemasonry:

'All the supposed abominations, the skeletons and death's heads, the coffins and the mysteries, are mere bogeys for children. But there is one dangerous element, and that is the element I have copied from them. They form a sort of priestly nobility. They have developed an esoteric doctrine not merely formulated, but imparted through the symbols and mysteries in degrees of initiation. The hierarchical organisation and the initiation through symbolic rites, that is to say, without bothering the brain but by working on the imagination through magic and the symbols of a cult, all this is the dangerous element, and the element I have taken over. Don't you see that our party must be of this character . . . ? An Order, that is what it has to be – an Order, the hierarchical Order of a secular priesthood . . . Ourselves or the Freemasons or the Church – there is room for one of the three and no more . . . We are the strongest of the three and shall get rid of the other two.'[2]

He was equally plain, for the most part, when he spoke of the character of what it was that would replace 'the other two':

'I will tell you a secret,' said Hitler to Rauschning; 'I am founding an Order.' He spoke of the Burgs where the first initiation would take place, saying: 'It is from there that the second stage will emerge – the stage of the Man-God, when Man will be the measure and centre of the world. The Man-God, that splendid Being, will be an object of worship . . . But there are other stages about which I am not permitted to speak . . .'[3]

One wonders who it was that withheld permission.

In other words, Hitler's policy was to make the world of magic serve him as totally as did every other German institution. This meant an end to *volkisch* occultism, and its replacement by a faith which to Hitler was entirely clear and truthful for those with eyes to see. This he enunciated in no uncertain terms at the Reich Party Congress of 1938:

'At the pinnacle of our programme stands not mysterious premonition, but clear knowledge and hence open avowal. But woe if the movement or the state, through the insinuation of obscure mystical elements, should give unclear orders. And it is enough if this lack of clarity is contained merely in words. There is already a danger if orders are given for the setting up of so-called cult-places, because this alone will give birth to the necessity subsequently to devise so-called cult games and cult rituals. *Our* cult is exclusively cultivation of that which is natural and hence willed by God.'[4]

There was to be, in other words, absolutely no deviation from the first principle of magic, the one-pointed concentration of the will upon the desire, which, for magicians, is entirely 'natural and hence willed by God'. Any deviation from this would lead to a lack of clarity, a profusion of crazy cults, and the nation ultimately failing to respond to his will as one man.

Whatever else the Führer might have been, he was not a fool. Like all successful magicians, he realised that it is essential first to define one's will, and then to find the means appropriate for fulfilling it: no magician worth his salt believes that one can make a car go by means of meditation and prayer. His means were to be the resources of the German people, hence his first task was to unite them behind him, and to prepare them for any sacrifice that might be necessary. This task was accomplished through a combination of propaganda and terror, and through an economic policy based upon German rearmament, which solved the problem of unemployment. Rearmament led on automatically to the second goal, a war which Hitler believed to be inevitable. Hitler wanted war in order to make Germany great once more, and found an Empire which would contain all Germans within its borders: he would then expand to the East and secure lebensraum for his people, which would enable the Germans to exploit natural economic resources and cheap slave-labour, and make the Third Reich the most powerful Empire that the world had ever known.

This, however, was only the half-way stage. The Third Reich would not be just another empire: it would be an entirely new kind of civilisation, with new values and new men. The Jews, polluters of the blood, would be exterminated. Other inferior races would be used as slaves. Germans would enjoy unprecedented material comforts in exchange for the surrender of all freedom in uncritical allegiance to National Socialism. Above the ordinary Germans would be the hierarchy of Party members, and above them, the Nazi élite. From the finest of their youth would be bred the heroes and demi-gods who would come to bestride the Earth.

Thus would the way be cleared for what, according to Dr Achille Delmas, was Hitler's ultimate aim:

'... to perform an act of creation, a divine operation, the goal of a biological mutation which would result in an unprecendented exaltation of the human race and the "apparition of a new race of heroes and demi-gods and god-men".'[5]

Such were the dreams of the mystic from the Vienna gutter who had risen to control the destiny of a great European nation. As he so aptly remarked: 'What luck for the rulers that men do not think,' and as Baldur von Schirach exclaimed on behalf of the Germans, with equal aptness: 'We simply believed.' The Germans never asked Hitler where he was leading them just as long as he was leading: they gave away their freedom, and were afterwards amazed when the victorious allies raised questions of responsibility. For them it was sufficient to be part of an ecstatic crowd at a torchlit rally and experience the Führer's proclamation of the nation's innermost hopes, dreams and dreads. In the words of the American writer, William Shirer, who witnessed this all through the 1930s:

'Today, as far as the vast majority of his fellow-countrymen are concerned, he has reached a pinnacle never before achieved by a German ruler. He has become – even before his death – a myth, a legend, almost a god, with that quality of divinity which the Japanese people ascribe to their Emperor.'[6]

One does not know what is more extraordinary: the bewitchment of the German nation; the phenomenon of Hitler himself; or the inability of most to recognise the sources of the Führer's powers. Yet the signs are plain for all to see in the work of historians of unimpeachable integrity like Alan Bullock and Hugh Trevor-Roper. 'Until the last days of his life,' writes Bullock, 'he retained an uncanny gift of personal magnetism which defies analysis, but which many who met him have described . . . This was connected with the curious powers of his eyes, which are persistently said to have some sort of hypnotic quality.'[7] Professor Trevor-Roper concurs: 'Hitler had the eyes of a hypnotist which seduced the wits and affections of all who yielded to their power.'[8] One does not acquire such power by accident! Someone who believes that, will believe anything. One acquires it by patient training. Hence the above descriptions are ludicrous if applied to Mussolini or Stalin, but perfect if applied to men such as Rasputin, Gurdjieff or Crowley, with whom, we insist again, Hitler must be classed: all four men possessed to a remarkable degree this intense personal magnetism, which, in all four cases, was associated with their 'hypnotic' eyes.

One has to be inflexibly dogmatic and unscientific to deny the proposition that the human brain is capable of doing extraordinary things, in face of all the evidence, and indeed, the current intellectual fashion is to accept the existence of ESP powers as long as we can talk about them in terms of the brain or the unconscious. As long as our terms are sufficiently 'modern', we are on safe ground: yoga we can label *Psychocybernetics*, and magic, *Applied Mind Dynamics*, and this almost makes them respectable. Unfortunately, in considering Adolf Hitler, we are also forced to consider the possibility that the world of spirits and demons may have some objective existence, or at least, that Hitler thought it did. Time and time again we come upon the phrase used to describe him, 'the unconscious tool of higher powers'. We may add to the testimony of witnesses we have quoted earlier the words of the French Ambassador, Francois-Poncet: 'He entered into a sort of mediumistic trance; the expression of his face was ecstatic,'[9] and of another Frenchman, Bouchez:

'I looked into his eyes – the eyes of a medium in a trance ... Sometimes there seemed to be a sort of ectoplasm; the speaker's body seemed to be inhabited by something ... Afterwards he shrank again to insignificance, looking small and even vulgar. He seemed exhausted, his batteries run down.'[10]

Finally, Hermann Rauschning relates a curious tale, which reminds one of the Unknown Supermen of Mathers and Crowley:

'A person close to Hitler told me that he wakes up in the night screaming and in convulsions. He calls for help, and appears to be half paralysed. He is seized with a panic that makes him tremble until the bed shakes. He utters confused and unintelligible sounds, gasping, as if on the point of suffocation. The same person described to me one of these fits, with details that I would refuse to believe had I not complete confidence in my informant.

'Hitler was standing up in his room, swaying, and looking all round him as if he were lost. "It's he, it's he," he groaned; "he's come for me!" His lips were white; he was sweating profusely. Suddenly he uttered a string of meaningless figures, then words and scraps of sentences. It was terrifying. He used strange expressions strung together in bizarre disorder. Then he relapsed again into silence, but his lips still continued to move. He was then given a friction and something to drink. Then suddenly he screamed: "There! there! Over in the corner! He is there!" – all the time stamping with his feet and shouting. To quieten him he was assured that nothing extraordinary had happened, and finally he gradually calmed down. After that he slept for a long time and became normal again.'[11]

Is it possible that this was one of the mysterious beings which forbade him to speak about further stages in evolution? Hitler's behaviour invites one to compare the remarks of Mathers. The 'string of meaningless figures, then words and scraps of sentences . . . the strange expressions strung together in bizarre disorder' all sound remarkably like the arcane languages and 'barbarous names of evocation' used by ceremonial magicians to control their consciousness. The reader may learn with relief that there is another, more rational, explanation; overbreathing. Oxygen intoxication is probably the simplest method of getting into a trance; it has been suggested that Hitler used this method in his oratory, hence his shouting; and it is certainly possible that an exercise of this sort produced hallucinations.

We cannot resolve the question of whether spirit beings have an existence independent of the human brain, or whether they are personalised components of the unconscious mind, and we leave the reader to judge. From the above, however, it is clear that the Führer thought in terms of an objective world of spirit beings. Admittedly it is hard to accept that such obsessions nourished one of the twentieth century's most prominent political figures, and yet he said himself, when talking of the destiny of the human race: 'Politics are only a practical and fragmentary aspect of this destiny.'

The world of magic will not leave us alone when we turn to examine the phenomena that have fascinated so many people, the Nuremberg Rallies, where its techniques were used with a precision that leaves one gasping. Francis King has taken a close look at them, and has seen much more than mere vulgar propaganda:

'Hitler's public appearances, particularly those associated with the Nazi Party's Nuremberg Rallies, were excellent examples of this sort of magical ceremony. The fanfares, military marches and Wagnerian music all emphasised the idea of German military glory. The massed Swastika banners in black, white and red filled the consciousness of the participants in the Rally with

National Socialist ideology. The ballet-like precision of the movements of the uniformed Party members, all acting in unison, evoked from the unconscious the principles of war and violence which the ancients symbolised as Mars. And the prime ritual of the Rallies – Hitler clasping to other Nazi banners the "blood banner" carried in the Munich putsch of 1923 – was a quasi-magical ceremony designed to link up the minds of living Nazis with the archetypal images symbolised by the dead National Socialist heroes of the past.

'The religio-magical aspects of the Rallies were emphasised by the fact that their high points were reached after dusk and took place in a "Cathedral of Light" – an open space surrounded by pillars of light coming from electric searchlights pointed upwards to the sky.

'If a modern ritual magician of the utmost expertise had designed a ritual intended to "invoke Mars" he could not have come up with anything more effective than the ceremonies used at Nuremberg.'[12]

Mars was the Roman equivalent of the Egyptian Horus, whose Age is alleged to have begun in 1904. One cannot resist speculating whether Hitler had had some kind of intercourse with the beings described by Aleister Crowley . . .

At any rate, two things are certain: European statesmen were to prove as blind, if not more so, than they had been from 1914–18; and Hitler was bent upon a war which he knew would be many times as destructive as that which he had fought in. There was no indecision about this: 'I go the way that Providence dictates with the assurance of a sleepwalker.' Whether or not Hitler knew of Horus, he was only too happy to serve the god. Years before the World War he said to Hermann Rauschning:

'We must be prepared for the hardest struggle that a nation has ever had to face. Only through this test of endurance can we become ripe for the dominion to which we are called. It will be my duty to carry on this war regardless of losses. The sacrifice of lives will be immense. We all of us know what world war means. As a people we shall be forged to the hardness of steel. All that is weakly will fall from us. But the forged central block will last forever. I have no fear of annihilation . . . Cities will become heaps of ruins; noble monuments of architecture will disappear forever. This time our sacred soil will not be spared. But I am not afraid of this.'[13]

PART THREE

Hitler and Horus

CHAPTER TWELVE

The Conquest of an Empire

'Worship me with fire and blood; worship me
with swords and with spears. Let the woman
be girt with a sword before me: let blood flow
to my name. Trample down the Heathen: be
upon them, o warrior, I will give you of their
flesh to eat.'

The Book of the Law III 11

'The idea of treating wars as anything other
than the harshest means of settling questions
of very existence is ridiculous. Every war costs
blood, and the smell of blood arouses in man
all the instincts which have lain within us since
the beginning of the world: deeds of violence,
the intoxication of murder, and many other
things. Everything else is empty babble.'

Adolf Hitler

The values of Western civilisation continued to crumble
after the hammer-blows of the First World War. There was
a brief respite in the world economic boom of 1925–9,
which induced in the naïve a temporary return to the belief
in progress, but once the 1930s were under way, it was
obvious that conditions had worsened to an extent
undreamed of by the most feverish pessimist of far-off
1889. Never had there been such tyranny over the
individual human spirit. Never had suffering been so
widespread: nor was this suffering dictated by the natural
enemies of man, hunger, thirst, and the rages of the
elements, but by his alleged benefactors, the men who
governed.

We have seen what happened in Germany. It is arguable
that the plight of man was even worse in the Soviet Union.

Stalin's drive to industrialise had produced horrors unseen in the most frightful days of the British and French industrial revolutions. For this, Stalin had at least the excuse of economic necessity, but there can be no excuse whatever for his purges, which began with the elimination of his political rivals, and ended with the extermination of millions of innocents. The Soviet Union, whose birth had been welcomed by men of good will the world over, was now little more than a vast and gloomy prison-camp, ruled by a cunning, astute, and utterly unscrupulous paranoiac.

With the possible exception of Hitler's Third Reich, nothing could be worse, but this was cold comfort to the people of the world. The USA, self-proclaimed 'land of the free', staggered beneath the weight of a Depression in which millions were brought to the verge of starvation, and the resulting lack of American investment crippled the economies of Europe. Economic collapse brought with it the inevitable political repercussions. With the notable exception of Czechoslovakia, every Eastern European state succumbed to dictatorship. In the West, Italy continued to place its faith in an egomaniac, Benito Mussolini. Spain exploded into civil war. France was torn by internal dissensions which left her dispirited and enfeebled. Great Britain elected a National Government which governed with a complacency which was as startling as its ineptitude.

The notion of freedom most found quite terrifying. The intelligentsia, especially, hymned the praises of tyranny. If one had any claim to be regarded as a serious intellectual, it was necessary to become a slavish sycophant of the nearest available megalomaniac. One exception, Bertrand Russell, was for a while ostracised for mildly criticising Soviet Russia. The Webbs sang the praises of Stalin, as did the younger generation of poets. Bernard Shaw praised not only Stalin, but also Mussolini, and insisted that the only disturbing aspect of Adolf Hitler was his anti-semitism. Indeed, Hitler had quite a number of foreign admirers, including the leader of a curious Christian movement, Moral Re-Armament, who revealed his own ideology in an hysterical worship of Nazi Germany, though this admiration was not just confined to imbeciles. Lloyd George was one of the first to extol the achievements of Hitler, and though he had sense enough to change his mind, many prominent politicians did not. All through the 1930s, three watchwords ruled the world: Security, Fear and Cowardice; the watchwords of the slave.

Winston Churchill later called the Second World War 'the unnecessary war'. It was. Had men in time resurrected the pagan values of adventure, bravery and courage, the Second World War would not have happened, and the Third Reich would soon have fallen. This, however, was much too much to ask for in what we may term the Era of the Slaves. Men of vision, men of character, men of strength, were either killed or ignored. Such was the world of appeasement, in which, to paraphrase Churchill, 'the bravest of the brave' were led by 'the vilest of the vile'.

In considering this period, three factors must be borne in mind. The first two are the iron resolve of Germany's messianic dictator and the abject spinelessness of Britain and France: the third is the patent fact that the old world was on its last legs, refused to admit it, and thus prepared the way for a Second World War more frightful than the First.

Hitler never made any secret of his determination to tear up the Treaty of Versailles, and the formerly victorious Allies proceeded to assist him in the manner of obsequious butlers. When he withdrew from the League of Nations and its sponsored Disarmament Conference, no one offered anything other than old-maidish expressions of concern. When, in March 1935, Hitler announced the recommencement of German rearmament in direct defiance of the Versailles settlement, British leaders, assisted by *The Times* and *Daily Mail*, almost outdid Goebbels in their pro-German propaganda. The British even allowed Hitler to rebuild the German Navy in an agreement from which their allies, the French, were excluded.

There was one man with the resolve to oppose Hitler, Benito Mussolini, who at first termed Hitler 'a mad little clown'. In 1934, he had forced Hitler to abandon an attempt to seize Austria by a show of force, and thus demonstrated to Britain and France that Germany dared not oppose the military resources of a power as weak as Italy. British and French leaders ignored the lesson, though they did join with the Duce in an anti-German alliance, the Stresa Front. This was broken up in 1936, when Mussolini invaded Abyssinia: the League of Nations half-heartedly imposed economic sanctions; Britain and France soon broke them, but succeeded only in offending Mussolini and causing him to seek the possibility of an alliance with Hitler. Hitler was only too pleased to join forces with the Duce. Together they helped the fascist General Franco win the Spanish Civil War: Britain and France responded by condemning their aid without assisting the Spanish Republican Government, and once more demonstrated both their feebleness and their incompetence.

France, torn asunder as it was by internal strife, no longer dared to act without the backing of Britain, and Britain no longer dared to act decisively. Its Prime Minister, Stanley Baldwin, cared only for the support of the electorate. Like Harold Wilson in our own time, he believed that if problems were ignored, they might go away: unflappable, pipe in mouth, an adept politician, an adroit public relations man, he assured the electorate that there was nothing to worry about, and the nation was only too happy to believe him.

France and Britain, therefore, the main props of a discredited League of Nations, the supposed guarantors of the Versailles Treaty, which had ended 'the war to end war', had neither values nor vision, neither things to defend nor the resolve to defend whatever they might be. By contrast, the Führer of the Third Reich knew only too well what he wanted, and believed only too obviously in the destined success of his own world historic role, and his people were united behind him. Compared to the alleged Great Powers, his military strength was negligible, but with his will as his weapon, he was soon to expose the complete decadence of the democracies. Already he had defied them over re-armament, and he was soon to exploit their political ineptitude to an extent unparalleled in European history. What Hitler had accomplished in Germany, he would, with less trouble, achieve on a far grander scale in Europe.

In March 1936, Hitler embarked upon an adventure which all experts, even in Germany, thought to be completely insane: the military reoccupation of the Rhineland in flagrant defiance of the Versailles Treaty. From every rational point of view, the move had absolutely no chance of success. The French Army was the strongest in Europe; the Germans even had orders to withdraw at the slightest sign of French resistance. 'Considering the situation we were in, the French covering army could have blown us to pieces,' averred General Jodl.

'A retreat on our part would have spelled collapse,' admitted Adolf Hitler. Yet in spite of these factors, the German occupation was unopposed; the experts were wrong; the Führer was right. He had exercised the predictive powers taught him by Haushofer: he looked ahead; he saw nothing; and nothing was done.

In March 1938, Hitler again disregarded the advice of his country's foremost diplomatic and military experts when he seized Austria, this time with the consent of Mussolini. This was an even more fundamental breach of the Versailles Treaty, but Hitler's intuition was correct once more. He looked ahead; he saw nothing; and nothing was done.

By this time, Britain had a new Prime Minister, Neville Chamberlain, who, it was promised, would take a more active interest in foreign policy than Baldwin. He did, advocating a fawning subservience to the German dictator's whims in the forlorn hope that peace might somehow be the result. 'A man who might have made a good Lord Mayor of Birmingham in a lean year,' Lloyd George termed him, and he amply justified this remark, uniting in his character an ignorance of all matters of history and foreign policy, a self-righteous arrogance, and a determinedly wilful blindness. Destiny had indeed thrown up a suitable mediocrity to expose the extent of Great Britain's lamentable decline.

Shortly after his Austrian triumph, Hitler embarked

upon a fantastic gamble. He demanded the incorporation of the Czechoslovakian Sudetenland into the Reich on the grounds that Germans lived there. The odds against him were astronomical. Czechoslovakia, which resisted his demands, was not only a fierce ally of the Western democracies, but it also possessed a large, well-trained, and well-equipped Army and magnificent defensive fortifications on the Czech-German border. The German Generals later admitted that it would have been an almost impossible task to breach them: moreover, France had guaranteed Czechoslovakia; and there was absolutely no hope of Germany winning a war on two fronts even if Britain did nothing. Given these facts, Hitler's demands were imbecilic. Even so, the Führer once more looked into the future; once more he saw nothing; and once more, nothing was done.

It was Neville Chamberlain who ensured Hitler's triumph. He restrained the French, and flew to see Hitler at Berchtesgaden, his aim being to avoid war no matter what the consequences. Doubtless he meant well, but the consequences in human suffering of his extraordinary actions rob this excuse of all validity. He knew what was happening to the Jews in Germany and Austria: he knew too that the Führer, known behind his back as 'Carpet Eater', was by English standards evil and insane. Despite this, Hitler's ravings convinced the British Prime Minister that the Nazi leader was a man of his word. He persuaded his Cabinet to accept Hitler's demands, whereupon Hitler immediately increased them at a second meeting in Godesberg. Chamberlain scuttled back to Britain, rather like a seedy insurance salesman representing a collapsing insurance company, desperate to sell to Parliament his policy of appeasement. Despite his efforts, war seemed likely, but in September 1938, there was a final international congress in Munich. The Czechs were not even represented. Chamberlain gave Hitler everything he wanted. Daladier, the French Premier, returned to his country broken in spirit. The Czechs learned that the Sudetenland, including their fortifications, had been given to the Third Reich. Chamberlain returned to Britain, where he pretended to be a statesman, and proclaimed: 'Peace in our time.'

The astuteness of Hitler and the foolishness of Chamberlain soon became glaringly apparent, even to the latter. In March 1939, Hitler seized Bohemia and Moravia: Czechoslovakia was now raped and finished with. As Hitler intuitively knew in advance, nothing was done. Chamberlain finally realised that he had been tricked, and endeavoured to make up for it by offering discredited British guarantees to any nation which desired them: one of these was Poland. The obvious course was a defensive alliance between France, Britain and Russia, a course of action which had aroused the enthusiasm of Stalin. But Chamberlain's pursuit of such an agreement was so completely half-hearted that the Russian dictator sought other methods of safeguarding his country from German aggression. Hitler seized his opportunity, and his Foreign Minister, Ribbentrop, brought about a pact between Nazi Germany and Communist Russia in spite of their incompatible ideologies. British ineptitude had plumbed new depths.

In contrast, Hitler's triumphs had been sensational. Both the League of Nations and the Versailles Settlement were now fit subject-matter for jokes. Almost all Germans were now within the boundaries of the Third Reich. The democracies were discredited. Eastern Europe was falling under German economic domination. And, as he set down plainly in *Mein Kampf*, German expansion to the East would continue. His next target was Poland, and he no longer had to worry about the USSR. When the Poles resisted Hitler's demands, he found an excuse for declaring war, and on 1 September 1939, German troops poured into Poland. Once again Hitler had looked ahead; he had seen nothing; and, in a certain sense, nothing was done.

This is perhaps a surprising statement. After all, in September 1939, Britain and France finally declared war on Germany. Hitler was utterly astonished. 'If we lose this war, then God help us,' commented Goering. And yet, although the Führer had blundered, his prophetic foresight had not entirely misled him, for although they declared war, the Allies did do nothing. Poland was crushed in a lightning campaign while Allied soldiers sat behind the French Maginot Line singing songs and broadcasting futile propaganda. It would have been extremely easy to have smashed through the small German force which opposed them, and seize the industrial heartland of the Ruhr, but the Allies did not. Their leaders were obviously determined to prove themselves as inept in matters of war as earlier they had been in matters of peace, and no one can dispute their success.

This display was not confined to politicians. French and British Generals were also bent upon losing the war in the fastest possible time, to judge by their actions. The French, remembering the disastrous dogma of the offensive which had cost them so dearly in the last war, decided to remain behind the 'impregnable' Maginot Line until the Germans attacked. As for the British, they obstinately refused to learn from their finest strategist, J. F. C. Fuller, or from the German success in Poland.

This catalogue of German rapacity and Allied stupidity is almost beyond belief. One may well ask whether there was anyone with any awareness of what was occurring. There were such men, but they were not listened to. Churchill was one of them, but he had had to wait until the onset of war before he was offered a post in the Cabinet. Another was G. I. Gurdjieff, who visited Berlin all through the 1930s, and who seems to have known of the impending catastrophe. Aleister Crowley was another, but people paid even less attention to him than they did to Gurdjieff.

Crowley had visited the Third Reich on a number of occasions, but was under no illusions as to its nature. He believed, correctly, that Hitler was a magician bent upon changing the nature of civilisation and of man: he was probably in error, though, when he stated that Hitler had read *The Book of the Law* and followed many of its precepts quite consciously; the truth is more likely to be that Hitler unconsciously expressed the more disturbing of its doctrines, for both Crowley and Hitler drew their inspiration from the daemonic. We have seen how Crowley became convinced that another world war was imminent, and a pamphlet which he wrote in the later 1930s is certainly of interest:

'The MASTER THERION (Crowley) . . . has . . . undertaken the Work of a Magus to establish the word of His Law on the whole of mankind. He will succeed . . . As long as the Book of the Law was in manuscript, it could only affect the small group amongst whom it was circulated. It had to be put into action by publishing it.

'THE FIRST PUBLICATION, *nine months before* the outbreak of the Balkan War, which broke up the Near East . . .

'THE SECOND PUBLICATION, *nine months before* the outbreak of the World War which broke up the West . .

'THE THIRD PUBLICATION, *nine months before* the outbreak of the Sino-Japanese War which is breaking up the Far East.

'THE FOURTH PUBLICATION, 6.22 a.m. 22 December 1937 *nine months before* the Betrayal (Munich) which stripped Britain of the last rags of honour, prestige and security, and will break up civilisation . . .

'The world is stricken today by an epidemic of madness. On every side we are confronted by evidence of insanity which is sweeping across the earth like a pestilence.

'Murder and terror in Soviet Russia; concentration camps and persecution in Germany; war fever and blood lust in Italy and Japan; civil war in Spain; economic crisis in USA; recurrent strikes and labour discontent in France – there is no corner of the Globe untouched!

'What is the cause?

'The old standards of human conduct, the ancient religions which have served humanity for thousands of years, have broken down . . .

'A universal law for all nations, classes and races is here. It is the Charter of Universal Freedom . . .'[1]

Thus spake Crowley, but few bothered to listen.

Crowley's former disciple, J. F. C. Fuller, was no longer listening either, but most would argue that he had a greater effect upon the Second World War than either Aleister Crowley or *The Book of the Law*. The activities of the architect of the 1917 Cambrai battle do deserve brief

157

mention. After the First World War, Fuller wrote *Tanks in the Great War* (1920), *The Reformation of War* (1923), and *Field Regulations III* (1932) which were immensely influential in the subsequent conduct of war. He advocated the use of massed formations of tanks for a swift and unstoppable armoured offensive, what the Germans were to call *Blitzkrieg*. The Czechs and the Soviets learned from his writings, but they had their greatest effect in Germany. So great was his influence upon the military strategy of the Third Reich, that he was the only foreigner at Hitler's first manoeuvres in 1935, and one of the two Englishmen invited to the Führer's fiftieth birthday celebrations in 1939. While the Germans expressed further appreciation by adopting Fuller's ideas regarding tank warfare, and adding to them the use of dive-bombers, the British High Command chose to ignore them. Though Fuller was made a Major General in 1930, his frustration resulted in his resignation in 1933. He thereupon devoted the rest of his life to the writing of history, and only his strong sympathy for Fascism soured an otherwise laudable subsequent career.

The Allies were to pay heavily for their stupidity. In the spring of 1940, Hitler turned his attention to the West, and successfully occupied Denmark and Norway. The one hopeful result of this from the British point of view, was the fall of Neville Chamberlain, and his replacement by the man whose sense of personal destiny was almost as strong as the Führer's, Winston Churchill. Even so, given the unimaginative pedantry of the French High Command, this appointment came too late to affect the early course of the war.

Hitler's powers of prediction – for he prophesied the exact date of the entry of his troops into Paris – were once more superior to the expertise of his generals when the Blitzkrieg was finally unleashed against the waiting Allies. Holland and Belgium both collapsed within three weeks. The Maginot line, termed by Fuller 'the tombstone of France' was breached and the French Army suffered a series of defeats in which the morale of its soldiers proved to be as feeble as the spirit of its leaders. The British were driven back to Dunkirk, from which they escaped on account of German miscalculations, but had to abandon their equipment. By June, the French were beaten and begging for an Armistice. The swiftness of the German victory was astonishing, and Goebbels promptly acclaimed Hitler as the greatest general of all time.

There followed peace proposals to Britain. There is every reason to believe that these were genuine. As he stated in *Mein Kampf*, Hitler wanted the British Empire to continue, and could gain little from its downfall. His obsession was lebensraum in the East, and he had not desired a war in the West: it was at least technically true that it had been forced upon him. Yet he had succeeded where Schlieffen's Plan had failed, and was now free to fling Germany's might at Russia whenever he chose. He had concluded an Armistice with France, and Britain was to him of no more import than a mosquito. It made no sense, to his mind, for England to refuse his terms.

It was unfortunate for Hitler that the British had at last been inspired by stirring leadership, and were determined to fight to the bitter end. He was enraged by Churchill's defiance, and contemplated the prospect of an invasion of the little island, the sole country in the world which still defied him. Yet this invasion was not as easy as it superficially seemed. Although the German Army was now overwhelmingly superior to the British, the difficulty consisted in transporting it across the Channel and keeping it supplied in face of the stronger British Navy. The only possible solution was the attainment of German air superiority, which would enable the Luftwaffe to rid the Channel of English warships, and the result was the Battle of Britain. The magnificent courage of the Royal Air Force saved the British Isles. For the first time, Goering's Luftwaffe was defeated. The invasion of Britain was postponed.

The result of the Battle of Britain, and Hitler's lack of real enthusiasm for the project, are very probably adequate explanations for the absence of a German invasion, but there is another, more bizarre explanation. It was first put forward by an odd character, Gerald B. Gardner, who had hired Aleister Crowley to compose a set of rituals for a reconstituted witchcraft religion. As a result of Gardner's book, *Witchcraft Today* (1954), dozens of witchcraft covens sprang up, all claiming an ancient lineage, many of which still exist today. Here is Gardner's explanation:

'Witches cast spells to stop Hitler landing after France fell. They met, raised the great cone of power and directed the thought at Hitler's brain: "You cannot cross the sea. You cannot cross the sea. Not able to come. Not able to come" ... I am not saying that they stopped Hitler. All I say is that I saw a very interesting ceremony performed with the intention of putting a certain idea into his mind and this was repeated several times afterwards; and though all the invasion barges were ready, the fact was that Hitler never even tried to come. The witches told me that their great-grandfathers had tried to project the same idea into Boney's (Napoleon Bonaparte) mind.'[2]

This story is true insofar as the facts are concerned. In 1970, Francis King presented evidence which showed conclusively that this ritual was performed by a coven of Hampshire witches which predated the Gardner revival of witchcraft. The oldest and weakest member of this coven deliberately failed to grease his body to keep out the cold, so that he would sacrifice his life during the ceremony and add to its power. Whether the theory is true or not is, of course, an entirely different matter.

Despite his public avowals, Hitler lost interest in invading England. Instead, he contented himself with a campaign of night-bombing, intended to reduce British cities to rubble and destroy morale, and with a U-boat war in the Atlantic against British merchant shipping, hoping, as had Ludendorff, to starve the British into submission. Although both strategies caused enormous suffering and profound concern in the British Government, neither succeeded.

On land, Hitler hoped that the Italians, who had entered the war when a German victory seemed certain, would put to rout the smallish British force in North Africa. The Italians met with disaster, and with another catastrophe in

Greece. German forces were rushed to both these areas, and by the late spring of 1941, Greece and Crete were under German occupation, and Rommel had advanced to within a few miles of the Egyptian border and was threatening Suez, and hence Britain's hold on Middle Eastern oil and trade routes to India and the Far East. There seemed little point in bothering with Britain, whose prestige had sunk to an all-time low, and Hitler decided to leave the English for later. This was a grave strategic blunder, for had Rommel been given the reinforcements and equipment he desired, he could have taken Suez and forced Britain to negotiate an armistice. Hitler failed to see this, so obsessed was he by lebensraum, and came to regard the North African front as a side-show.

Hitler's objective, as it always had been, was the conquest of Russia, and the fact that Germany had a treaty with the Soviet Union was to him entirely meaningless. He was convinced that his invincible Army and his own military genius would enable him to subjugate the USSR before the winter of 1941. After all, his conquests up to now were without historical parallel. He had overrun Poland in twenty-seven days, Denmark in one, Norway in twenty-three, Holland in five, Belgium in eighteen, France in thirty-nine, and, just recently, Greece in twenty-one days, Crete in eleven, and Yugoslaiva in twelve. Hungary and Bulgaria had become German satellites. He believed more than ever before in his own infallibility.

In June 1941, Operation Barbarossa commenced, without a declaration of war. Soon the two most disgusting tyrannies that man has ever known would be locked together in the bloodiest war of all time on a front that stretched from Leningrad to the Black Sea. The German successes were again quite extraordinary. By the middle of July, German tanks were just over two hundred miles from Moscow, having advanced nearly five hundred and fifty miles. By early October, the Ukraine was almost entirely in German hands, Leningrad was under seige, and Russian losses of men and equipment were staggeringly high. 'Russia is now virtually defeated,' announced the Führer.

Nothing, it seemed, could possibly prevent the victory of

Adolf Hitler, former Vienna drop-out, now ruler of an empire that extended from the Norwegian Arctic coastline to the sands of the Libyan desert, from the Atlantic Ocean to the outer suburbs of Moscow. Behind his victorious Armies marched the standard bearers of National Socialist civilisation, welcomed by the Russians as liberators, though this illusion would not last long. The SS sallied forth, eager to create the new civilisation dreamed of by their Führer. By dint of his initially unaided will, Adolf Hitler had brought about what looked like the decisive turning-point in the destiny of mankind. 'We are moving,' he remarked, 'towards a sunny, really tolerant outlook; man shall be in the position to develop the faculties given to him by God.'

We shall be inspecting the truth of the above remarks. We shall be looking at the basics of National Socialist civilisation and the values that ruled the Third Reich. We shall therefore end this chapter with Nazi Germany at the height of her success and with her defeat inconceivable, before we look further at what her leaders wanted for man. As a foretaste, we shall leave the reader with some remarks by the rulers of the Master Race.

'As for the ridiculous hundred million Slavs, we will mould the best of them to the shape that suits us, and we will isolate the rest of them in their own pig-sties; and anyone who talks about cherishing the local inhabitant and civilising him, goes straight off to a concentration camp.' — *Adolf Hitler*

'This year between twenty and thirty million persons will die of hunger in Russia. Perhaps it is well that it should be so, for certain nations must be decimated . . . In the camps for Russian prisoners they have begun to eat each other.' — *Hermann Goering*

'Whether or not 10,000 Russian women collapse from exhaustion while digging a tank ditch interests me only in so far as the tank ditch is completed for Germany.' — *Heinrich Himmler*

'A time of brutality approaches of which we ourselves can have absolutely no conception, indeed we are already in the middle of it . . . We shall only reach our goal if we have enough courage to destroy, laughingly to shatter what we once held holy, such as tradition, upbringing, friendship and human love.' — *Joseph Goebbels*

'The Slavs are to work for us. In so far as we do not need them, they may die . . . We are the masters, we come first.' — *Martin Bormann*

'In the course of this Final Solution of the European Jewish problem, approximately eleven million Jews are involved.' — *Reinhard Heydrich*

'If I wished to order that one should hang up posters about every seven Poles shot, there would not be enough forests in Poland with which to make the paper for these posters.' — *Hans Frank*

'The men I want around me are those who, like myself, see in force the motive element in history, and who act accordingly . . . Those who see in National Socialism nothing more than a political movement know scarcely anything of it . . . It is even more than a religion: it is the will to create mankind anew.' — *Adolf Hitler*[3]

CHAPTER THIRTEEN

Theory of the New Order

'Mercy be off: damn them who pity! Kill and torture; spare not; be upon them!

'That stele they shall call the Abomination of Desolation; count well its name, & it shall be to you as 718.

'Why? Because of the fall of Because, that he is not there again.'

The Book of the Law III 18–20

'Close your hearts to pity. Act brutally. Eighty million people must obtain what is their right. Their existence must be made secure. The strongest man is right. The greatest harshness.'

Adolf Hitler

'There is a Nordic and National Socialist Science which is opposed to Judaeo-Liberal Science.'

Adolf Hitler

The unparalleled horrors of National Socialism have been documented in detail, and it is clear that they were as much a part of Nazi theory as of practice. What has not been so fully explored is the philosophy behind these horrors, and so we shall be looking at certain of the beliefs of the Nazi leaders. These beliefs, many of which we have already expounded, were so bizarre that it is tempting to regard them as abhorrent but unimportant eccentricities. This would be erroneous, for not only did they form the basis of what Hitler was trying to create, but they also had an important effect upon decisions taken during the course of the Second World War. We shall begin by noting this effect upon the Deputy Leader of the Nazi Party, Rudolf Hess.

After Goering, then the recognised Number Two, Hess was heir-apparent to Hitler. Yet, as we have seen, 'he was convinced the stars ruled human destiny, had diagrams worked out for him by an old soothsayer, and devoted himself earnestly to the tortuous efforts of the practitioners of terrestrial radiation, animal magnetism, pendulum diagnosis, and the various means of foretelling the future.'[1] It was due to obsessions of this nature that Hess, dissatisfied too with his increasingly minor role in wartime Germany, climbed into a Messerschmitt on 10 May 1941 and flew to Scotland, 'his pockets . . . filled with medicaments and drugs, mostly of a homeopathic nature, among them an elixir supposed to have been brought back from Tibet by Sven Hedin'.[2] His mission, unknown to any of the astonished Nazi leaders, was nothing less than to bring about peace between England and Germany, and it had been suggested to him by the magician, Karl Haushofer. Haushofer had had a predictive dream in which he had seen Hess 'striding through the tapestried halls of English castles, bringing peace between the two great Nordic nations'.[3]

The predictive powers of Haushofer had failed him, for Hess's mission brought him nothing but misfortune. He met the Duke of Hamilton, but failed to impress him, and was handed over to the British authorities, who ignored his proposals, and treated him as a prisoner of war. Shut up in a cell, Hess relapsed into a twilight world of persecution mania, suicide attempts, and bouts of amnesia.

It is interesting to note that shortly after the incarceration of Hess, an odd idea was mooted by a young intelligence officer who went on to create the greatest hero-myth of the 1960s, Ian Fleming. The future author of the James Bond stories advocated an interrogation of Hess by another occultist, Aleister Crowley. The latter was then occupying his time by writing patriotic poetry and creating 'magical signs' which he thought would help win the war: he was the author of *THUMBS UP! A pentagram – a pentacle to win the war* (1941) in which he advocated the use of this 'Sign of Khem', and he claimed to have originated the use of the 'V' sign, or 'Sign of Apophis and Typhon', which was employed with such excellent effect by Churchill. As we know, these gestures were frequently used by the British without their magical origin being known, and if the idea of using them did not originate with Crowley, it would be fascinating to know who did first have the idea. Was it this which brought Crowley to Ian Fleming's attention? It is more likely that it was the ageing magician's general notoriety. Unfortunately, however, Fleming's suggestion was vetoed, and Crowley and Hess never did meet, to the chagrin of the unorthodox historian.[4]

Back in Germany, the sudden flight of Hess had caused immense consternation. Hitler was 'in tears and looked ten years older', though he soon recovered sufficiently to declare: 'He is crazy: if he comes back, shoot him on sight.' Martin Bormann, who detested occultists, replaced Hess as controller of the Nazi Party, and the Gestapo was unleashed upon the few astrologers, mystics and occultists outside the SS, who, it was thought, might have influenced Hess's action. One of those arrested was Karl Haushofer.

Although he was eventually released, this demonstrates Haushofer's lack of personal influence on the Führer by 1941. Hitler no longer had any time for men with independent minds and the Professor was of no more use to him. He lived on, encouraging from the sidelines the movement he had played so significant a part in spawning. Its ultimate failure would break him. On 14 March 1946, he would kill his wife and commit suicide with full Japanese ceremonial.

Haushofer's teachings, however, continued to dominate Nazi thinking, and the influence of his esoteric ideas was not, it must be stressed, confined to obvious cranks like Rudolf Hess. Indeed, the very fundamentals of National Socialist ideology were derived from occultism, and this included the world of science. Hard though it is to accept, the Nazi leaders had formed a picture of the world that flatly contradicted the one accepted by our own civilisation. They not only rejected 'Jewish ideas' like the

Einsteinian Theory of Relativity; they embraced the cosmology of a figure almost as influential as Haushofer, Hans Horbiger.

Horbiger, who was born in Austria in 1860, was a successful businessman who had transformed himself into a white-bearded prophet of the truths about the universe which he himself had discovered. The origin of his teachings may be traced back to a mystical experience. One day, he witnessed the explosion produced by molten metal falling upon frozen mud: thus was born the World Ice Theory. During the 1920s, Horbiger bombarded scientists with his own propaganda:

'While Hitler is cleaning up politics, Hans Horbiger will sweep out of the way the bogus sciences. The doctrine of eternal ice will be a sign of the regeneration of the German people. Beware! Come over to our side before it is too late!'[5]

Horbiger died in 1931, but his campaign had been so successful that leading Nazis like Himmler and Rosenberg, and millions of other Germans, accepted his views as being the one true explanation of the universe: even after 1945, there remained half a million Horbigerians. So strong was the support of Heinrich Himmler, who announced that he was 'taking the World Ice Theory under his protection', that Rosenberg felt compelled to inform his fellow Nazis that one did not *have* to follow Horbiger in order to be a good National Socialist.

What was the World Ice Theory? It has been stated in over eight hundred pages in *The Glacial Cosmogony of Horbiger* by one Philip Fauth, whom the Nazis appointed a Professor by special decree in 1939. We shall endeavour to summarise the essentials in more merciful form.

Firstly, the origin of the universe: Horbiger taught that thousands of millions of years ago, a super-star collided somewhere in space with an accumulation of cosmic ice. Eventually there was a vast explosion. Blocks of ice were hurled into space; these are the planets and moons of our solar system. The only exception is the earth, which is the scene of an eternal struggle between ice and fire. Around the solar system is an immense band of ice, which orthodox astronomers falsely call the Milky Way. Each planet circles the source of fire, the sun, in a spiral which slowly decreases, owing to the force of gravitation. Each planet will eventually fall on to its nearest neighbour, and the final mass of ice will again unite with the fire at the centre of the solar system, bringing the old system to an end, causing a great explosion, and hence creating a new beginning. The universe is thus the eternal conflict between attraction and repulsion, ice and fire, which ensures its birth, death and resurrection.

Secondly, the earth itself, meeting-point of ice and fire: Horbiger taught that it had already attracted three moons, and that the one we see at present is the fourth, which, of course, is made of ice. Like its predecessors, this moon will eventually collide with our planet, and then it will be the turn of Mars. All of earth's history is the result of the forces exerted by its successive moons, and can be divided into four distinct geological epochs: at the end of each epoch, the cosmic forces are at their strongest, due to the closeness of the moon, and the result has been beings of gigantic size.

The first epoch culminated in the age of giant vegetation and insects: the second in the dinosaurs, the giant mammals, and the first human beings, a race of giants, as mentioned in Genesis 6.4, who ruled the earth some 15,000,000 years ago: the third was the mythical Golden Age, that of Lemuria, Atlantis and Thule, destroyed by the cataclysm of the third moon falling on the Earth 150,000 years ago; the fourth age is our own.

According to Horbiger, the beginning of this age was marked by battles between the giants who had survived the third, and the men of the fourth, as recorded in mythologies. Other giants taught men to found the ancient civilisations of South America, Egypt, Mesopotamia, India and China. Eventually the giants died out, and man declined into the drabness of Judaeo-Christian civilisation, where he forgot his glorious heritage. But this is only temporary. Affected by the cosmic rays of a moon which is spiralling imperceptibly closer, man will awaken to a realisation of his place in a living universe, mutations will transform his existence, and demi-gods and giants will again arise in our midst. Horbiger averred that an 'uprush of fire' was imminent, that great initiates would co-operate once more with the cosmos and its struggle between ice and fire, that Supermen would once more walk the earth's surface, and that before them the slave-men would tremble and obey.

These doctrines conformed with the legends of primitive peoples and the mythologies of the ancients, with the visions of Nietzsche and of Wagner. They had many similarities too with the teachings of Gurdjieff and Madame Blavatsky, though it is hard to see how the Nazis could have reconciled Blavatsky's Five Root Races with Horbiger's Four Lunar Epochs. However, like Hitler, Horbiger used to say that to bother about coherence was a deadly vice. National Socialist philosophy consisted not of a series of logically argued and consistent theses, but of a bundle of theories arrived at by intuitive means. 'You put your trust in equations but not in me!' fumed Horbiger. 'How long will it be before you understand that mathematics are nothing but lies and are completely useless?'[6]

A cameo of Hitler's remarks, drawn from his *Table Talk*, displays his agreement with the teachings of Horbiger:

'I'm quite inclined to accept the cosmic theories of Horbiger. It's not impossible, in fact, that 10,000 years before our era there was a clash between the earth and the moon that gave the moon its present orbit. It's also possible that the earth attracted to itself the atmosphere of the moon and that this radically altered the conditions of life on our planet... It seems to me that these questions will be capable of solution on the day when a man will intuitively establish the connection between these facts, thus teaching exact science the path to follow ... It was a great step forward in the days of Ptolemy to say that the earth was a sphere and that the stars circulated around it. Since then there has been continual progress ... Copernicus first. Copernicus, in his turn, has been largely left behind and things will always be so. In our time, Horbiger has made another step forward ... The real question is whether the earth came from the sun or whether it has a tendency to approach it. For me there is no doubt that planetary satellites are attracted by the planets, just as the latter are attracted by a fixed point, the sun. Since there is no such thing as a vacuum it is possible that the planets' speed of rotation and movement may grow slower. Thus it is not impossible, for example, that Mars may become one day a satellite of earth ... I shall construct ... an observatory in which will be represented the three great cosmological conceptions of history – those of Ptolemy, Copernicus and Horbiger.'[7]

Horbiger's theories taken with those of a commentator, Edgar Daque, confirmed Hitler's own belief in the imminence of the transformation of man. As Hermann Rauschning had noted some time before the war:

'A savant of Munich (probably Daque) . . . had also written some curious stuff about the prehistoric world, about myths and visions of early man, about forms of perception and supernatural powers. There was the median eye, the organ of magic perception of the Infinite, now reduced to a rudimentary pineal glad. Speculations of this sort fascinated Hitler, and he would sometimes be entirely wrapped up in them. He saw his own remarkable career as a confirmation of hidden powers . . . Humanity, he proclaimed, was in the process of a vast metamorphosis. A process of change that had lasted for literally thousands of years was approaching its completion. Man's solar period was coming to an end. The coming age was revealing itself in the first great human figures of a new type. Just as ... the world has continually to renew itself, the old order perishing with its gods . . . so must man now, apparently, turn back in order to attain a higher stage.'[8]

Hitler thought that the only true species of man, the species with potential for evolution, is Aryan man. He followed Blavatsky in believing that the Aryans had originated through a mutation in the latter days of Atlantis. Shortly before the catastrophic floods which submerged that fabulous civilisation, Manu, the last of the Atlantean

Supermen, had led the Aryans across Europe and Asia to the Gobi Desert, and thence to the mountains of Tibet. The descendants of these Aryans subsequently colonised the world and created civilisation anew, but were poisoned by the creed of Judeao-Christianity and by race-pollution, and lost their magical faculties, which it was the task of the Führer to reawaken. Not all the Aryans had allowed their faculties to atrophy, however: some had stayed in Tibet and their descendants had retained the ancient wisdom; these were the present day Hidden Masters and Unknown Supermen, who preserved the secrets of Initiation. The Führer's task, however, was a greater one than that of preservation: it was that of co-operating with the evolution spoken of by Horbiger to bring about the New Age of the Aryan Superman.

Insofar as the Jews were concerned, Hitler added the ideas of Horbiger to the beliefs he already held. They were an envious, degenerate race, born through a sudden mutation after the fall of the third moon when creative power was at a low ebb. Since the Jews were not part of humanity, it was not a crime to exterminate them. Thus did the darkest, maddest hinterlands of occultism result in the greatest atrocity in the history of humankind.

But the extermination of the Jewish race was not the only result of esoteric theories. Another example is the part played by the theories of Horbiger in the planning of the campaign against the Soviet Union. Hitler was usually most attentive to the equipment of his troops, but the only additions to their outfits for the Russian campaign were a scarf, and a pair of woollen gloves. The usual explanation given for this staggering blunder, which affected the entire course of the Second World War, is that Hitler thought that by the winter, Russia would be conquered, and his troops in winter quarters. This explanation cannot be correct as Francis King has demonstrated. The Führer's *War Directive 37* (10 October 1941) refers to the 'final capture of Murmansk, the Fisherman's Peninsula and the Murmansk railway next year': Hitler certainly thought that the Russian Army would be crippled by December 1941, but, as his directive shows, he envisaged fighting in 1942.[9] As for winter quarters, it is difficult to envisage where he thought these would be, for he had ordered the total destruction of places of shelter such as Leningrad. The real reason for the inadequacy of his soldiers' equipment is to be sought in the pronouncements of the disciples of Horbiger.

Horbiger had insisted that his theory enabled one to predict the weather all over the planet months and even years in advance. Consequently, Heinrich Himmler had employed devoted Horbigerians in the meterological section of the SS Ahnenerbe department. These confidently declared that the Russian winter of 1941–2 would be relatively mild. Hitler believed them, and hence saw no need for his soldiers to be provided with winter clothing.

The results of this decision were disastrous for Germany. The first snow fell in early October. By early November, temperatures had fallen below zero. Lubricating oil froze and jammed the German guns. German synthetic fuel separated into two component parts. Dressed in light summer uniforms, lacking warm headgear, winter boots, protective clothing, or goggles to prevent snow blindness, thousands of soldiers dropped from frostbite or died of exposure while performing their natural functions. In December the temperature dropped to minus forty degrees Centigrade, and the Red Army launched an all-out counter attack. Obsessed by the desire to capture Moscow, Hitler forbade retreat, and ignored the conditions in which his troops were fighting, but Moscow remained in Russian hands, and the Red Army steadily pushed back the German troops. When General Guderian insisted upon the necessity for a tactical retreat Hitler retorted: 'As to the cold, *I* will see to that. Attack.' Did Hitler believe that as the earth's chief representative of fire, he could command the ice? Whatever he thought, whatever he desired, his Armies could not hold out against the Russians, and suffered before Moscow their first defeat of the war. Thus did a mystical theory lead, by spring 1942, to 1,168,000 German casualties, excluding the sick.

Hitler and his strange beliefs must therefore take the blame for the losses suffered by the hitherto invincible Armies of the Third Reich. On the other hand, they must take the credit for ensuring that the defeat did not turn into a catastrophic rout. Guided once more by his intuition, the Führer overruled his High Command, and flew in the face of all the established principles of military science by refusing to allow any tactical withdrawals. He insisted that his troops had to fight wherever they stood without yielding an inch of ground. Costly though this strategy was, it prevented the melting away of his Armies in the frozen Russian wastes, which had been the fate of the Grand Army of Napoleon. Unfortunately for his soldiers, the Führer would subsequently insist upon a repetition of this strategy for the duration of the war, no matter how inappropriate the circumstances, and so what originally prevented disaster ultimately invoked total defeat.

But for the present, the Russian front had been saved, and Hitler was still convinced that victory would be his. It was during this period, however, that Hitler developed to the full those traits of character which would make victory impossible. Alan Bullock's theory cannot be faulted: that Hitler came to believe completely in his own infallibility. Previously, the Führer's decisions, though prompted by his intuition and predictive powers, had been based upon calculations, albeit those of a gambler: now he adopted the view that whatever he did was right, simply because he did it, and no one dared check, criticise or question his insistence upon his own omnipotence. Previously, he had used facts, albeit in an extraordinary way; now he simply refused to accept the existence of facts that displeased him. An occultist would say that he fell victim to the occupational disease of black magicians; total megalomania coupled with an inability to recognise the realities around him.

When the Japanese bombed Pearl Harbour, Hitler did not wait until he had received a Japanese pledge to make war also on Russia: he immediately declared war on the United States of America. This declaration was almost casual, and completely ignored the fact that America's resources were vastly in excess of those of the Third Reich. But by now Hitler was no longer living in a world in which unpleasant facts had any importance. Convinced that he was the representative of Providence, he was, in Brasillach's words, prepared to 'sacrifice the happiness of the whole human race, his own and that of his fellow-countrymen included, if ordered to do so by the mysterious Force whose commands he obeyed.'[10] The magical approach which had brought him so much success, he was now to parody, and in this lay the seeds of his downfall.

Hitler was not the only man to believe in his own infallibility: it was shared by his subordinates and by the entire German nation, with a handful of exceptions. So strong was his personal magnetism that the Generals who entered his headquarters with an iron determination to apprise him of the true facts of the military situation, left with the conviction that the Führer knew better. All doubts vanished, moreover, in the spring of 1942, when the German offensive against Russia was renewed with startling success.

It is incredible that in a nation which conquered Europe we should find the beliefs which we have been describing, but such was the case. Furthermore, the leading Nazis seriously considered another cosmological conception which made that of Hans Horbiger seem rational and scientific by comparison: this was the hollow earth doctrine of Peter Bender.

The origins of this curious dogma are outside the scope of this book. Suffice to say that Bender, a First World War fighter pilot and friend of Goering, had through his reading of bizarre books and pamphlets, become converted to the hollow earth doctrine, and emerged as its principal proponent. Bender proclaimed that the earth is hollow. Furthermore, *we are living inside it*, like insects on the inside of a goldfish bowl. Outside this womb-like structure there stretches eternal rock. Within the globe is 'the phantom universe', a dark blue sphere of dense gas, around which revolve points of light, the stars. The sun, which is a ball of red hot rock about a hundred miles in diameter, and the planets also revolve around this blue sphere within our globe. Night and day are the result of the sun's revolutions around 'the phantom universe', which latter we mistake for infinite space. 'An infinite universe is a Jewish abstraction,' insisted Peter Bender. 'A finite, rounded universe is a thoroughly Aryan conception.'

Needless to say, the advocates of Horbiger's World Ice Theory fought a bitter ideological battle with Bender and his disciples. Once Hitler himself was asked to decide between these incompatible theories, and the answer he gave supplies a peculiar illustration of the workings of his mind: 'Our conception of the world need not be coherent. They may both be right.'[11]

Hermann Goering took the hollow earth doctrine seriously, and it was probably through his advocacy that Bender's theory was finally put to the test. In April 1942, a secret expedition was dispatched to the island of Ruegen in the Baltic with the full approval of Hitler, Himmler and Goering. Although the Third Reich required every available atom of equipment and manpower, the expedition was supplied with a large budget and German's finest infra-red ray detectors, and led by an expert on infra-red rays, Dr Heinz Fisher, a puzzled and sceptical scientist. This infra-red ray detector, which performed the same functions as radar, was then aimed at the sky at an angle of forty-five degrees, in which position it remained for several days. The aims of this expedition were firstly to prove Bender's theory to be true, and secondly to apply it to the winning of the war. The Benderites had asserted that if the detector was aimed at the sky at a forty-five degree angle, images would be obtained of distant parts of the globe on the inside surface of the hollow earth; it would therefore be easy to obtain the exact position of the British fleet. Needless to say, the detector screen remained blank, and no such information was obtained. Hitler did not appreciate the humorous side of this fiasco, and so, despite the protestations of Goering, Bender was flung into a concentration camp, along with most of his supporters, where he died.

Even this did not put a stop to the attempts of the Nazis to make military use of esoteric doctrines. It was also in 1942 that a new occult fad captured the minds of Germany's masters; radiesthesia, or the use of pendulums. This was employed by the fervently pro-Nazi German

Navy when the British began to destroy increasing numbers of U-boats. A Pendulum Institute under a Captain Hans Roeder was established within the confines of Berlin's Naval Research Institute. Month after month, clairvoyants and psychics sat with their pendulums swinging over charts of the Atlantic, endeavouring by this method to divine the whereabouts of British convoys. The results eventually proved unimpressive, and yet another group of occultists experienced the concentration camp.

It was not out of wilful crankiness that leading Nazis embraced these intuitively derived doctrines. Their motives were rather more profound. First and foremost, Hitler knew that the creation of a new civilisation requires also the adoption of a new way of looking at the world: the reader is invited to imagine the effect which a sincere acceptance of Horbiger's theories would have upon him and his outlook. Secondly, esoteric doctrines had served Hitler so well in the past, that he had reason to believe that they would continue to do so in the future. Thirdly, we are not looking at a world like our own, but at a society which had emerged from an embracing of the daemonic and which had deliberately rejected a rational, logical and humanist world outlook. Finally, the Führer was a pragmatist, prepared to use anything that would assist his success; to a pragmatist, a theory is true if it works; as Hitler said, 'And in the last analysis, success is what matters.'

Had the Third Reich won the war, the beliefs we have looked at would have been taught, in a modified form, to every German schoolchild. Its society would have differed from our own as vastly as we differ from the ancient Aztecs. Its sciences, its philosophy and its psychology would have possessed hardly any points of contact with ours. As for its social structure, here is Hitler's description:

'We do not want to do away with inequalities between men, but, on the contrary, to increase them and make them into a principle protected by impenetrable barriers. What will the social order of the future be like? Comrades, I will tell you: there will be a class of overlords, and after them the rank and file of Party Members in hierarchical order, and then the great mass of anonymous followers, servants and workers in perpetuity, and beneath them, again all the conquered foreign races, the modern slaves. And over and above all these there will reign a new and exalted nobility of whom I cannot speak . . . But of all these plans, the ordinary militant members will know nothing . . .'[12]

The 'ordinary militant members' had one duty – to obey. The grandiose visions and plans of the Führer were no business of theirs. Their job was to carry out orders without the slightest hesitation, or else face annihilation at the hands of their colleagues in the New Order. As Robert Ley, head of the Labour Front, proclaimed in his *The Way to the Order Castle*:

'He who fails or actually betrays the party and its Führer, he who is unable to master the baseness in himself, the Order will destroy. He from whom the party removes the brown shirt – this each one of us must know and recognise – will not thereby merely be deprived of an office, but he personally, together with his family, his wife, and his children, will be destroyed. These are the harsh and implacable laws of an Order.'[13]

When, therefore, the German Army recommenced its Russian offensive and secured by the summer a series of spectacular victories that brought it to the southern reaches of the Volga River on the borders of Central Asia, it was not just fighting for the victory of a nation, but for the triumph of a civilisation radically different from anything that man had yet envisaged. Its exact nature concerned neither the soldiers who died for it, nor the civilians who screamed their worship of its prophet. The Germans as such did not interest Hitler. They were just an instrument for the fulfilment of his providential mission. He did not care how many died as long as he succeeded in his world historic role of inaugurating a new epoch in man's history with the establishment of an invincible empire from which the Superman would spring.

And we must turn now to the Nazi élite, the group which was most intimately acquainted with the occult side of Nazism, the organisation responsible for the transformation of society, the supreme representatives of National Socialism, the magical Order of the SS. 'I know that there are many people in Germany who feel sick when they see this black tunic; we can understand that,' said the Reichsführer of the SS, Heinrich Himmler. But the German people feared the SS because it was this organisation which ran the Security Service and the Gestapo; they were unaware for the most part of the real nature of the society which the SS were endeavouring to create. Not for nothing did Adolf Hitler speak to his intimates of his 'quite special secret pleasure of seeing how the people around us fail to realise what is happening to them.'

CHAPTER FOURTEEN

Practice of the New Order

'We have nothing with the outcast and unfit:
let them die in their misery. For they feel not.
Compassion is the vice of kings: stamp down
the wretched and the weak: this is the law of
the strong: this is our law and the joy of the
world.'

The Book of the Law II 21

'One principle must be absolute for the SS
man: we must be honest, decent, loyal, and
comradely to members of our own blood and
to no one else. What happens to the Russians,
what happens to the Czechs, is a matter of
utter indifference to me. Such good blood of
our own kind as there may be among the
nations we shall acquire for ourselves, if
necessary by taking away the children and
bringing them up among us. Whether the
other peoples live in comfort or perish of
hunger interests me only in so far as we need
them as slaves for our culture; apart from that
it does not interest me.'

Heinrich Himmler

In the spring of 1942, when the reinforced German Army
was unleashed upon the Caucasus, three SS mountaineers
climbed the sacred hill of the Aryan race, Mount Elbruz.
Their mission was to plant upon its summit the Swastika
flag, and bless it according to the magical rites of the SS.
This mission was successfully accomplished. Henceforth, it
was believed, victory would be guaranteed to Germany.

It was within the confines of the SS that Nazism found its
most concentrated and essential expression, for this Order

fulfilled almost every one of the ideals which obsessed Adolf Hitler. The man responsible for implementing Hitler's dreams was the most sinister figure of the Third Reich after Hitler himself, Heinrich Himmler, Reichsführer SS, who, like Hitler, united in his personality that curious combination of the banal and the daemonic which we have noticed in other leading Nazis. A perfect bureaucrat, devoid of all traces of emotion, Himmler's grand passion was nevertheless the occult.

We have seen how Himmler took the World Ice Theory 'under his protection', but this was merely one of the bizarre beliefs which his mind harboured. Hermann Rauschning has recalled how Himmler acted on another occasion, when he became converted to the racial theories of the occultist Hermann Wirth:

'Himmler called me to account about a professor who lectured on prehistoric times both at Danzig and at Konigsberg. This man, he said, had been criticising current ideas about the origin of the Teutons and the age of their civilisation, and had condemned these ideas from allegedly scientific points of view. At that time a sensation had been created by an exceedingly silly book, a manifest forgery, the *Uralinda Chronicle*. The book traced back the history of the Teutons to an infinitely remote period; and it proved once more that the original German-Teuton race was the true creator of European civilisation. The professor had treated this book with proper severity, and Himmler wanted me to dispose once and for all of this scientific mischief-making. He himself would put the fear of God into the professors of Konigsberg and Breslau; I was to do the same in Danzig.'[1]

Small wonder that Himmer struck General Heinz Guderian as being like a man from another planet, for his mind worked in a way which was in total contradiction to the rational-humanist outlook. He was, for example, convinced of the truth of astrology, and employed his own astrologer, Wilhelm Wulff, though he shared Hitler's conviction that studies of this nature were only for the élite:

'We cannot permit any astrologers to follow their calling except those who are working for us. In the National Socialist state astrology must remain a privilegium singulorum. It is not for the broad masses.'[2]

He also believed wholeheartedly in fringe medicine, especially herbalism, on account of which herb gardens were attached to the concentration camps.

In common with the vast majority of occultists, Himmler accepted the theory of reincarnation. At a speech made in Dachau in 1936, he informed high-ranking SS officers that they had all met before, in previous lives, and that after their present lives had ended, they would meet again. Himmler thought that he himself was the reincarnation of a ninth-century personality, King Heinrich the Fowler, whom he also claimed as a distant ancestor. He revered the memory of the first of the Saxon kings, who had defeated a Polish invasion from the east, and he referred to his tomb in Quedlinburg Cathedral as 'a sacred spot' to which we Germans make pilgrimage'. In 1936, on the thousandth anniversary of King Heinrich's death, he swore a solemn oath to continue the Saxon monarch's 'civilising mission in the East'. On each subsequent anniversary, Himmler descended into the crypt and spent the night in meditation by the tomb, communing with the spirit of the dead king.

It is difficult to see how Himmler could believe both that he was the reincarnation of King Heinrich I, and that he could communicate with his spirit, but this contradiction does not appear to have troubled him. Perhaps he thought that he communed with an 'inner soul' like the Hindu *atman*, which had inhabited the king's body and now inhabited himself; or else he did not feel the need for his beliefs to be coherent. Certainly he accepted the spirit world as a reality. To his masseur, Felix Kersten, he boasted of his ability to call up spirits and converse with them. One of these spirits was that of King Heinrich I, with whom Himmler held long night-time conversations.

Such were the deepest beliefs of one of the most dreaded figures of the twentieth century, who by 1942 was the second most powerful individual in the Third Reich. Given this, it is hardly surprising that Himmler chose to base the SS upon esoteric principles. Just as Nazism was represented by a magical sign, the Swastika, so did the SS have its own occult banner, the double 'S' or *sig* rune, which looks like two small lightning flashes: like Guido von List, Himmler was convinced of the profound significance of runes. This sign signified the élite nature of the SS, and its role as the vanguard of the New Order.

The SS was structured like a religious rather than a political organisation. In order to join in the first place, one had to satisfy stringent racial requirements, which demanded Nordic blood, and to pass a rigorous physical examination. Ideally, thought Himmler, all important posts should be filled by men with pure Nordic blood, and he even hoped that within 120 years, the entire German race would be of this type. After all, it was from this stock that the Superman would be bred, as Lanz von Liebenfels had long ago foreseen.

If the candidate passed, he then had to undergo a lengthy period of testing and training, rather like a potential Jesuit; part of this training was in the mystical significance of runes. He would only be allowed to assume the black SS uniform (though without the collar patches) on the anniversary of Hitler's 1923 putsch which first followed his acceptance. He received a provisional SS identity card on the next anniversary of Hitler's appointment as Chancellor. On the following anniversary of Hitler's birthday, he took part in a neo-pagan ceremony in which he swore 'obedience unto death' to Adolf Hitler: this entitled him to a full SS identity card and to collar patches on his uniform, but still not to full membership. Next, on the ensuing 1 October, came an examination in a catechism which contained the fundamentals of SS religious and political doctrines, part of which ran 'We believe in God, we believe in Germany which He created in His world and in the Führer, Adolf Hitler, whom He has sent us.' After a period of service in both the Labour Corps and the Army, the successful candidate was at long last initiated into the

Order, and received the coveted SS dagger in commemoration.

Many SS men then entered the Waffen SS, the Order's own Army. These were the men whom training had turned into killing machines. As Himmler said of the preliminary schooling, 'pupils learn how to kill and how to die', and he summed up their training in the command: 'Believe, obey, fight; that's all.' Others, more intelligent, entered the Security Service or the Gestapo. Most of the more promising candidates, however, entered the Death's Head SS, the group responsible for the concentration and extermination camps. For these men, the camps possessed a significance over and above the trivial sufferings of the prisoners: the camps were their university, where they stripped from themselves all remaining traces of compassion or morality. When SS Captain Josef Kramer was asked at Nuremberg what his feelings were when he gassed eighty inmates of Auschwitz, he replied: 'I had no feelings. That . . . was the way I was trained.' The moral point of view of Captain Kramer echoed that of Himmler:

'I shall speak to you here with all frankness of a very serious subject . . . I mean the evacuation of the Jews, the extermination of the Jewish people . . . Most of you know what it means to see a hundred corpses lying together, five hundred or a thousand. To have gone through this and yet – apart from a few exceptions, examples of human weakness – to have remained decent, this has made us hard. This is a glorious page in our history that has never been written and never shall be written.'[3]

The Death's Head SS were given further training in the Burgs, in which they learned that 'the only living being that exists is the cosmos or universe. Everything else and all other beings, including Man, are only the various forms, which have been multiplied through the ages, of the living universe.' SS men were instructed in their glorious mission, to create a New Age, a New World, a New Man, in cooperation with the evolution of the cosmos, and they swore vows which proclaimed their allegiance to an 'irreversible superhuman destiny'. Pauwels and Bergier have commented upon this latter ceremony:

'Those who know do not talk; there is no description in existence of the initiatory ceremony in the Burgs but it is known that such a ceremony took place. It was called *the ceremony of the Stifling Air* the allusion being to the extraordinarily tense atmosphere which prevailed until the vows had been pronounced. Some occultists, such as Lewis Spence, believe that the ceremony included a Black Mass in the purest Satanic tradition. On the other hand, Willi Frieschauer, in his study of Himmler, interprets the *Stifling Air* as the moment when the participants were overcome by complete stupor.'[4]

The concept of *Stifling Air* reminds one of the respiratory difficulties experienced by Mathers and Hitler when in contact with the Secret Chiefs, and there is no doubt that this was a full-blooded magical ceremony. We do not know, however, whether this ritual was at all similar to *The Ceremony of the Stifling Air* allegedly practised by the medieval Knights Templar, or to that celebrated today by the Church of Satan in San Francisco; the latter can be found in *The Satanic Rituals* by the Master of the modern Church of Satan, Anton Szandor LaVey.

Above the high-ranking initiates of the Death's Head Order sat the Grand Council of Knights. There were thirteen of them, the number of a witch's coven, and each one had achieved the rank of SS General or higher. At their head was the Grand Master, Heinrich Himmler, whose personality proclaimed the peculiar union of the banal with the daemonic, the key to the mystery of National Socialism. This was the man who could in all seriousness declare:

'He (Hitler) rose up out of our deepest need, when the German people had come to a dead end. He is one of those brilliant figures which always appear in the Germanic world when it has reached a final crisis in body, mind and soul. Goethe was one such figure in the intellectual sphere, Bismarck in the political – the Führer in the political, cultural, and military combined. It has been ordained by the Karma of the Germanic world that he should wage war against the East and save the Germanic peoples – a figure of the greatest brilliance has become incarnate in his person.'[5]

And simultaneously he could switch his mind from these profound considerations to a lecture on the importance of porridge, delivered in a memorandum to the mothers in the SS stud farms:

'I want them to be told that Englishmen, and particularly English Lords and Ladies are virtually brought up on this kind of food . . . To consume it is considered most correct . . . the mothers in our homes should get used to porridge and be taught to feed their children on it. Heil Hitler!'[6]

Should it then astonish us to hear Schellenberg's description of one impromptu meeting of the Grand Council of Knights?

'I witnessed for the first time some of the rather strange practices resorted to by Himmler through his inclinations towards mysticism. He assembled twelve of his most trusted SS leaders in a room . . . and ordered them all to concentrate their minds on exerting a suggestive influence . . . I happened to come into the room by accident, and to see these twelve SS leaders sitting in a circle, all sunk in deep and silent contemplation, was indeed a remarkable sight . . . each (Knight) had to devote himself to a ritual of spiritual exercises aimed mainly at concentration, the equivalent of prayer, before discussing the higher policy of the SS.'[7]

The vast majority of the Order's inner rites were performed in the ancient castle of Wewelsberg in Westphalia. Himmler had chosen this location because he believed in an ancient prophecy which announced: 'a gigantic storm which would appear out of the east to overwhelm the German peoples if not confronted and turned back in the region of Birkenwald in Westphalia.' An ascetic and parsimonious man in his private life. Himmler nevertheless proceeded to lavish 13,000,000 marks on restoring the castle and decorating it to his bizarre requirements. Every room was luxuriously furnished by the finest craftsmen in a different style, and every chamber was dedicated to a hero of the German race: the Frederick Barbarossa suite was permanently reserved for Hitler (who, surprisingly, never visited). Francis King informs us of the nature of the other rooms:

'The centre of the castle was the great banqueting hall, furnished with a gigantic table around which were placed large wooden chairs – almost thrones – upholstered with pigskin and with the name of the rightful occupant inscribed on silver plates. In these chairs Himmler and his favourite subordinates would sit both for conferences concerned with mundane matters and for group meditation – long hours of silence in which the participants were supposed to strengthen their ties with the "Race Soul". Besides Himmler himself, never more than twelve SS men were allowed to sit down at the table; the reasons for this are not clear, but it is possible that he was either blasphemously parodying the Last Supper or seeing himself symbolising the sun surrounded by the twelve signs of the zodiac.

'Above the banqueting hall were Himmler's own rooms. Here were housed his library and his weapon collection . . .

'Below the hall was the crypt, 'the realm of the dead', in which twelve unoccupied pedestals were placed around a stone hollow. On the death of each of Himmler's chosen twelve his coat-of-arms was to be burned, and the ashes placed in an urn on one of the pedestals, there to be venerated by future generations of the SS clan.'[8]

This castle was the nerve centre of the Black Order, where its most sacred and secret rites were performed by its greatest initiates. For the broad mass of SS men, there was a compulsory pagan religion based upon these rites which was derived from the occultism of List and Liebenfels. The SS celebrated the festivals of the Nordic pagans, the high point of their religious year being the favourite festival of occultists, the Summer Solstice: Christmas was frowned upon unless celebrated in a Nordic manner. Pagan rites replaced the Christian ceremonies of baptism and marriage, which latter was thought by Himmler to be 'the Satanic work of the Roman Catholic Church'. The Christian ideal of monogamous marriage was also deplored. Himmler laid plans for polygamous marriages which SS war heroes would be able to enjoy; he even authorised the establishment of human stud farms, as advocated by Liebenfels, and the SS became the godparents of the children born there.

By 1941, the SS had virtually become an independent state within the Third Reich. SS men were not subject to any jurisdiction other than their own courts: they were forbidden to converse with non-initiates unless circumstances made this essential: and when criticised at meetings, they would simply walk out. 'A veil of secrecy descended over the activities of the SS,' writes Heinz Hohne. 'No one, not even a member of the party or an SA man, was allowed to know what the SS was doing; Himmler's Order began to withdraw into a twilight of mystery.'⁹ This position of power urged Himmler on to the contemplation of even more ambitious schemes, as the Reichsführer announced in March 1943:

'At the Peace Conference, the world will be appraised of the resurrection of the old province of Burgundy, formerly the land of the arts and sciences, which France has reduced to the role of an appendix preserved in spirits of wine. The sovereign State of Burgundy with its own army, its own laws and currency and postal system, will be the model SS State. It will comprise French Switzerland, Picardy, Champagne, the Franche-Comte, the Hainaut and Luxembourg. The official language, naturally, will be German. The National-Socialist Party will have no jurisdiction over it. It will be governed by the SS alone, and the world will be astonished by and full of admiration for this State in which the ideals of the SS will be embodied.'¹⁰

Fortunately, this ambition was left unfulfilled, and the SS instead played a part in the Third Reich that was similar to the roles of the Inquisition and the Jesuits combined in the great days of the Roman Catholic Church. Part of this resemblance was intentional, as Walter Schellenberg recalls in his *Memoirs*:

'The SS organisation had been built up by Himmler on the principles of the Order of the Jesuits. The service statutes and spiritual exercises presented by Ignatius Loyola formed a pattern which Himmler assiduously tried to copy.'[11]

Heinz Hohne has also noted the resemblance:

'The similarity between the two was in fact astounding; each was an Order conferring enormous privileges on its members, subject to no temporal jurisdiction, protected by the strictest conditions of entry and held together by an oath of absolute blind obedience to its lord and master – Pope or Führer.

'The history of the two organisations showed equally remarkable parallels: in the seventeenth century the Jesuits founded their own state among the Paraguay Indians – it recognised no temporal sovereignty; during the Second World War, the SS dreamed of an SS State outside the borders of the Greater German Reich . . .

'Even the crises which each faced were similar. There were always enemies of the Jesuits within the Catholic Church and enemies of the SS within the Party.'[12]

Another striking resemblance is the intensive training in the basis of magic, systematic visualisation, which both Orders employed. Not surprisingly, Hitler used to compare Himmler to Ignatius Loyola, while Karl Ernst, leader of the SA, referred to him as the 'Black Jesuit'. The other Order which helped to inspire the ideals of the SS was that of the medieval Teutonic Knights, whose legends Himmler incorporated in his concept of the SS Order Castle at Wewelsberg.

The stamp of the Grand Master's obsession with the esoteric was revealed even more plainly in one of the major departments of the SS, the Ahnenerbe, or Ancestral Heritage Department. This had its origins in an occult society founded in 1933 by one Friedrich Hielscher, an enigmatic character of whom we shall hear more. In 1935, Himmler made it into an official organisation, attached to the SS, under Hermann Wirth, the author of the *Uralinda Chronicle*, whom Himmler considered to be an expert on Aryan prehistory. A friend of Karl Haushofer, Wirth was an occultist whose cranky obsessions caused even Himmler to question the wisdom of the appointment, but under his leadership the Ahnenerbe recruited every expert on occultism whom it considered useful from the debris of the magical Orders which the Nazis had banned. In 1939, the Ahnenerbe was turned into a full department of the SS, and Wirth was eventually replaced by SS Colonel Wolfram Sievers, a black-bearded gentleman who cultivated a deliberately Mephistophelean appearance. Under Sievers's direction, the organisation grew swiftly until it numbered fifty branches. Extraordinarily enough, Germany spent more money on the researches of the Ahnenerbe than the USA did upon its first atomic bomb project.

What exactly did the Ahnenerbe do? Pauwels and Bergier have revealed the bizarre truth:

'These researches ranged from strictly scientific activities to the practice of occultism, and from vivisection practised on prisoners to espionage on behalf of the secret societies. Negotiations were entered into with Skorzeny with a view to stealing the Holy Grail, and Himmler created a special section for the collection of information 'in the sphere of the supernatural'.

'One is astounded at the list of reports drawn up at enormous cost by the Ahnenerbe on such subjects as: the strength of the Rosicrucian confraternity; the symbolism of the suppression of the Irish harp in Ulster; the occult significance of Gothic towers and of the Etonian top-hat, etc . . . When the German troops were evacuating Naples, Himmler gave repeated orders that they should not forget to take away with them the enormous tombstone of the last Hohenstaufen Emperor. In 1943 after the fall of Mussolini, the Reichsführer summoned to a villa in the outskirts of Berlin the six greatest experts in Germany on occultism to discover the place where the Duce was being held prisoner.

Meetings of the General Staff began with yoga concentration exercises. In Tibet, acting on orders from Sievers, Dr Scheffer was in contact with a number of lamas in various monasteries, and he brought back with him to Munich, for scientific examination, some "Aryan" horses and "Aryan" bees, whose honey had special qualities.'[13]

When German bombers failed to damage Oxford, the Ahnenerbe immediately investigated what they believed to be the magically protective powers of the city's cathedral bells.

Himmler displayed an intense and earnest interest in all of these activities. Of still greater importance to him were the activities of the Ahnenerbe's 'Institute of scientific research for national defence', which performed medical experiments on living human beings which were based upon the craziest occult speculations. Experiments included: high altitude simulation tests, the pressure of which caused victims to go mad before dying in acute agony; freezing experiments, in which men and women were frozen alive, after which various methods of reviving them were sometimes put to the test; vivisection without anaesthetics; the sterilisation of Jews by irradiating their testicles and ovaries with X-rays; and the amassing of a large collection of Jewish skulls and skeletons.

What type of man could even conceive of such revolting practices? The obvious, and unhelpful answer is, only a sadist. But there is not one scrap of evidence to lead us to believe that Heinrich Himmler was a sadist in the conventional sense of the word. In his private life he was a gentle man who loved animals and deplored hunting as a cruel and savage sport: when he witnessed the mass execution of several hundred Jews by shooting, he became violently sick. The truth is only distorted by the use of such commonplace concepts as sadism. The fact is that though many SS men, particularly in the lower ranks, were sadists of the most disgusting kind, the majority of SS officers had accepted a system of morality in which ordinary human feelings like conscience and compassion had no place. It was their duty to be hard: they boasted of their lack of feeling: they were beyond good and evil. They felt no more pity for their human victims than a modern British vivisectionist does for his monkeys, kittens or puppies, and few would accuse the latter of sadism.

But what of the original founder of the Ahnenerbe? He is of interest because it seems that he continued to affect both the organisation he had founded and the mind of Himmler. Friedrich Hielscher has rightly been described as 'one of the most mysterious figures of the twentieth century', for he may have influenced the SS on a scale far greater than is usually ascribed to him. Unfortunately much more research is required before we can ascertain the precise importance of Hielscher, though there is no doubt that he was indeed the spiritual mentor of SS Colonel Sievers, head of the Ahnenerbe. When Sievers was tried at Nuremberg, Hielscher gave evidence on his behalf, making intentionally absurd racial and political statements. He asked if he could accompany Sievers to the gallows, and this favour was granted, without anyone realising Hielscher's true motive. Within the confines of the condemned cell, the two magicians proceeded to intone the prayers of their secret cult. Sievers, who had shown no sign of remorse during the trial, then went peacefully to his death, while his teacher returned to a permanent obscurity.

Those who judged at Nuremberg failed to understand the significance of what they were judging. They were astounded by statements like that of the Commandant of Auschwitz, Rudolf Hoess: 'I am completely normal. Even while I was carrying out the task of extermination I led a normal family life and so on.' The judges were as baffled by the horrors of the camps as they were appalled. Though the executions they ordered are deserving of eternal applause, they might just as well have been sentencing men from Mars.

Yet to the SS men, their actions were perfectly comprehensible. They were the warrior élite of a new civilisation immeasurably superior to the old, the high priesthood of the New Age, the standard bearers of the coming Superman. Their leaders were magicians who had formed alliances with the mystic Tibetan cities of Agarthi and Schamballah, and had mastered the forces of the living universe. Crimes against humanity? Most men were little better than robots, and anyway they felt little. Compassion? A hateful and sickening virus. Conscience? An excrescence left over from the Christian era. Jews? Racial degenerates far removed from humankind, lower than the animal and twice as dangerous. Concentration camps? A model for the social order of the future. Extermination camps? A vital and necessary stage in the purification of Aryan Man. Gas ovens? Efficient sacrificial ceremonies dedicated to racial purity.

In their determined drive to bring about the New Order, the SS murdered 14,000,000 men, women and children: roughly 6,000,000 Jews, 5,000,000 Russians, 2,000,000 Poles, 500,000 Gypsies, and 500,000 others, including nearly 200,000 non-Jewish Germans and Austrians. This list does not include the millions who were subjected to slave labour, or who suffered through torture or unspeakable degradation. It is deeply disturbing to have to add that of the 53,000 SS men who managed the concentration and extermination camps, a paltry 600 have been brought to justice.

We have now plumbed the very depths of Nazism: on the one hand, for ninety-five per cent, 'a boot stamping on a human face – forever', to quote Orwell: on the other, for five per cent, the ecstatic intoxication of absolute power climaxed by the evolution of the Superman. Such was the main culmination of the eruption of the daemonic in twentieth-century Germany. If, as we have suggested, there was some mysterious force at work in the world, then the Nazi magicians knew of it and used it, but shaped it to their own ends within the severe limitations of their own personalities. For the sake of the magical vision of Adolf Hitler and his associates, the Second World War claimed the lives of almost 50,000,000 human beings.

It should be with a profound sense of relief that we contemplate the second half of 1942, for the events which then took place ensured the doom of the Nazi New Order and all that it stood for. At last there were men of stature to oppose Hitler, and they, whatever their innumerable personal failings, expressed the elemental strengths of their respective peoples: Churchill in Britain, Roosevelt in the USA, Stalin in the USSR. Whether rightly or wrongly from a purely strategic point of view, these three leaders were resolved upon the total extermination of National Socialism. American money and equipment poured into Russia. In North Africa, the British won a decisive victory over Rommel at El Alamein. Most important of all, there took place the great battle of Stalingrad.

It is arguable that Hitler could have won this battle had he displayed the calculating skills which had earlier brought him so much success. But the Führer had left the borders of the land of reason far behind him. Earlier in the Russian campaign, Hitler had had the opportunity of employing the Ukrainians and other nationalities who abhorred the rule of Stalin and had welcomed the Germans, and the adoption of a conciliatory policy towards them could well have won the war for Germany. Blinded by race-hatred, however, Hitler adopted the tactics of terror, and roused up against him a monumental surge of Russian patriotism which Stalin was quick to make use of.

This was a fatal error, as was the conduct of the entire Stalingrad campaign. The military details lie outside the scope of this work; suffice to say that the Führer's blunders were worthy of the First World War. The entire Sixth Army of 270,000 men was lost by Germany; a mere 91,000 survived as prisoners. The German offensive had been halted for ever, the German front smashed and reduced to chaos. Though the Army managed to recover somewhat after the final Stalingrad surrender (January 1943) it was henceforth reduced to fighting a long, bitter and bloody series of battles against the advancing Russians, battles which pushed it further and further back to the German soil from which it had originally set out.

The shock of the Stalingrad catastrophe could be felt throughout the whole of Germany. The myth of German military invincibility had been destroyed: national mourning was proclaimed in the newspapers. Hitler very nearly broke down, and was to make only four public speeches up until the war's end. The magnitude of the consequences of the Stalingrad defeat was at last comprehended by Dr Goebbels, who wrote:

'Do you realise what has happened? It is a whole school of thought, an entire conception of the universe that has been defeated. Spiritual forces will be crushed, the hour of judgement is at hand.'[15]

CHAPTER FIFTEEN

Goetterdaemmerung

'Pity not the fallen! I never knew them. I am
not for them. I console not: I hate the consoled
& the consoler.

'I am unique & conqueror. I am not of the
slaves that perish. Be they damned & dead!
Amen.'

The Book of the Law II 48–49

'When we depart, let the earth tremble!'
Joseph Goebbels

From 1943 until 1945, the Third Reich battled foes who
possessed between them seventy-five per cent of the world's
natural resources. It was a desperate and hopeless conflict,
yet the length of its duration is a grim tribute to the
stubborn and admittedly heroic resistance of the Germans.
No matter how disastrous the situation became, German
soldiers fought on and German citizens endured as though
they really were battling for an ideal. It was an extraordinary display of morale, and much of it was evoked by
the arts of that wizard of propaganda, Joseph Goebbels.
With one idea after another, ranging from the resistance of
the noble Germans against Asiatic barbarism, to the
existence of decisive secret weapons, Goebbels kept alive
the hope for ultimate victory, and the dampened flame of
idolatry for his beloved Führer. Now the cynical minister
was at last believing his own propaganda, a fate which had
also befallen Hitler. For Hitler continued to believe in his
eventual triumph with all the fervency of his wretched days
in Vienna. He continued to place his faith in the power of
his will. As he told his Generals in August 1944:

'Under all circumstances we will continue this battle

until, as Frederick the Great said, one of our damned enemies gets too tired to fight any more . . . I live only for the purpose of leading this fight because I know that if there is not an iron will behind it, this battle cannot be won.'[1]

Comments Alan Bullock:

'Hitler's faith was crystallised in the belief that if only he could survive the buffetings of the waves which were breaking over him, he would be saved by some miraculous intervention and still triumph over his enemies. Everything depended on the will to hold out.'[2]

During this period, Hitler employed the techniques of magic which he had so assiduously learned. An intense strain was put upon his personal magnetism. One could see that in his physical condition. Formerly youthful for his years, the Führer was now ageing prematurely. He suffered from bouts of giddiness, stomach cramps, and a trembling of his left arm and leg which was so violent, it obliged him to clutch his left hand with his right, and brace his left leg against a desk or wall. Tertiary syphilis or Parkinson's disease are incorrect explanations, for his doctors found no evidence at all for these, and thought Hitler's ailments to be psychological in origin. To combat these afflictions, Hitler took a variety of drugs, including strychnine, belladonna and morphine. Like so many drop-outs of our own age, he soon became a junkie. He was mastered by hysterical outbursts of rage and weeping, and an almost pathological desire to combat the plain facts around him. Yet despite this decomposition of his psyche, he retained his magnetic powers, shrinking though they were. When, for example, in the spring of 1943 he had a meeting with an exhausted and dispirited Mussolini, he was able to 'recharge' him:

'By putting every ounce of nervous energy into the effort I succeeded in pushing Mussolini back on to the rails. In those four days the Duce underwent a complete change. When he got out of the train on his arrival he looked like a broken old man. When he left again he was in high fettle, ready for anything.'[3]

With this for his weapon, he could still subdue the doubts and dominate the minds of the men around him. Said Admiral Doenitz:

'I purposefully went very seldom to his headquarters for I had the feeling that I would thus best preserve my power of initiative, and also because, after several days at headquarters, I always had the feeling that I had to disengage myself from his powers of suggestion. I am telling you this because in this connection I was doubtless more fortunate than his Staff, who were constantly exposed to his power and personality.'[4]

Albert Speer has also commented:

'They were all under his spell, blindly obedient and with no will of their own – whatever the medical term for this phenomenon may be. I noticed during my activities as architect, that to be in his presence for any length of time made me tired, exhausted and void.'[5]

Goebbels thought that this power could extend to the whole of Germany, writing after one speech of Hitler's in 1942:

'The address made a tremendous impression . . . We may now rest assured that the main psychological difficulties have been overcome . . . The Führer has charged the entire nation as though it were a storage battery.'[6]

After the losses of 1942 and 1943, however, Hitler's power over men's minds deteriorated, and so did his personal magnetism. It was as though the source of much of his power lay in his mediumistic oratorical contact with the masses, which now he denied himself. Various explanations have been offered for the lack of Hitler's public appearances: that he needed to report to the crowd a great German victory; that he felt tired; or that he lacked the time. The last two cannot be right, for Hitler needed the masses rather more than they needed him. As he once cried to them: 'Everything I am, I am through you alone.' In communion with the crowd he could intoxicate himself with words of hate, draw into himself the strength of the masses he had mastered, and emerge with renewed energy and will. His relationship with his audience was mediumistic: he would take 'from the living emotion of his hearers the apt word,' he once remarked, 'and in its turn this will go straight to the hearts of his hearers.' Francis King's explanation for Hitler's later avoidance of public oratory is therefore the most convincing:

'Knowing this, fully aware that when he spoke unrestrainedly, at his oratorical best, he was only reflecting the contents of the deepest levels of the minds of his audience, Hitler *dared* not face the crowds after January 1942. For he dreaded what, in his heart of hearts, he knew must be the truth – that in the secret depths of the German unconscious the resentments of the moment would no longer be directed against the Versailles Treaty or even "Judah", but against himself, the man who had taken Germany into war and had been individually responsible for the blood sacrifices of Stalingrad and the other great battles on the Russian Front. This was why Hitler could truthfully tell Goebbels that he could not make a public appearance until a major victory had been won. Once the unconscious minds of his listeners were again filled with a belief in his genius, his capacity to lead Germany to a glorious final victory, then Hitler could again be the great mediumistic orator, telling his people the things that were already present in their own hearts. Until then, however, Hitler could do no more than recite the occasional prepared speech, for should he exercise his mediumship the things he would say would be disastrous for the reputations of himself and the regime that he led.'7

Denied this source of energy, Hitler began to behave not as a man who is striding confidently forward, but as a man who is tenaciously hanging on. As Alan Bullock rightly avers:

'Until he could force events to conform to the pattern he sought to impose and reappear as the magician vindicated, he hid himself away in his headquarters . . . Hitler's ostensible reason for shutting himself up in this way was the demands made on him by the war. But there was a deeper psychological compulsion at work. Here he lived in a private world of his own, from which the ugly and awkward facts of Germany's situation were excluded. He refused to visit any of the bombed towns, just as he refused to read reports which contradicted the picture he wanted to form.'[8]

J. H. Brennan has demonstrated that in so doing, Hitler was simply acting as a magician would act:

'When he talks of the "picture Hitler wanted to form" Bullock hits the nail right on the head. Forming pictures was precisely what Hitler was doing. But it was not, as Bullock suggests, simply a psychological escape mechanism. The Führer was engaged on a typical magical operation, arranging his environment to help him visualise as clearly as possible the situation he wished to bring about. Western initiates, from the Golden Dawn to the present day, have done exactly the same thing in the secrecy of their temples. He became enraged when anyone interfered with his consistent visualisation with news about unpalatable facts. But even the raging pressure of his turbulent emotions, even the iron grip of his trained will, even the psychotic consistency of his victory visualisations were not enough to change the vast inertia of the opposing reality now ranged against him.'[9]

Hitler's approach was doomed to failure: a mere apprentice magician could have informed him that all successful operations make use of reality rather than engage in a futile endeavour to flout it. But the Führer persisted in denying the obvious and placed his faith first, in a will which he believed could overcome all obstacles, and second, in the protected relationship he was convinced he enjoyed with providence. Even so, his powers deteriorated relentlessly. His prophetic foresight was one of the first talents to desert him. It will be remembered that he had been right, against all odds, on numerous occasions; Francis King's analysis does much to explain the subsequent degeneration:

'The first, a purely materialistic explanation, is that he had never been anything more than a lucky guesser and that his luck had run out. The second is that he usually arrived at the trance stage at which his intuition came into play by overbreathing at the frenzied height of his public speeches. Once he gave up making these he never reached the trance state and from then onwards his intuition degenerated into mere guesswork. The third explanation is that he became too personally involved in the outcome of his prophecies of future political developments, threw his personal future too much into the calculations he made on the basis of his intuitions, and therefore failed to interpret them correctly. Similar failures are widespread in the history of psychic research.'[10]

Admittedly, there were still flashes of genuine predictive insight. One such was over the D-Day invasion. The Generals and strategic experts, including Rommel, were convinced that the Anglo-American landings would be in the region of Calais. Hitler, however, accepted instead the dictates of his intuition which told him that the invasion would be launched on the beaches of Normandy, ordered reinforcements to this area, and enjoyed a temporary satisfaction at being proved right. Another example is a prophecy made on 2 April 1945:

'With the defeat of the Reich . . . there will remain in the world only two great powers capable of confronting each other – the US and the Soviet Union. The laws of both history and geography will compel these two powers to a trial of strength . . . These same laws make it inevitable that both powers should become enemies of Europe.'[11]

But these were rare successes. More typical was his behaviour over the V-2 rocket bomb. This, the forerunner of today's intercontinental ballistic missiles, was one of the most destructive weapons of the war, and the mainstay of Dr Goebbels's 'secret weapon' propaganda. That the V-2s were not used to greater effect was as much due to the intuition of Hitler as it was to RAF bombing raids on launching sites. For Hitler experienced a prophetic dream which informed him that the V-2 would not work: this dream may have been caused by the advice of certain Horbigerians, who feared that the V-2 might disturb the global balance of ice and fire. Hitler's immediate reaction was to order total stoppage of all work on the rockets, a situation which lasted a full two months.

By January 1945, it was obvious that despite all the power of his will, Hitler had not succeeded in anything. 'Everything is as though under a spell,' he fumed. The Russian front had become a nightmare after the failure of the 1943 German offensive at Kursk, and the Red Army was pressing forward relentlessly towards its targets of Berlin and beyond. The Ardennes counter-offensive of the 1944 winter had failed to check the Anglo-American advance into Western Germany. On the Italian front, the German Army was engaged in a steady retreat. Germany was doomed, yet its leader still remained in his Bunker, poring feverishly over maps on which he obsessively directed imaginary divisions.

Within the crumbling Third Reich was hell finally made manifest in its purest form. Allied bombers turned German cities into flaming heaps of rubble. In the camps the cruelties and exterminations still continued. The Gestapo still maimed and tortured. The Nazi leaders still plotted to increase their power. Their intrigues had never been more feverish as when the territory of the Third Reich was daily shrinking. Only Hermann Goering, the discredited Reichsmarschall of the Luftwaffe, acted as though the war was irretrievably lost, dressing up in an endless series of splendid costumes in which he could indulge his morphine-induced fantasies. It was fitting that Hitler's official heir should in this way end his days of power, as it was that the post of de facto Number Two should now be occupied by Martin Bormann. In Bormann we find no baffling combination of the banal and the daemonic; he was merely banal. It is appropriate that in these last days, Hitler's chief subordinate should be a colourless and brutal thug.

Hitler did nothing to halt these intrigues, for they

sustained in his subordinates the faith that there was something worth intriguing for. Extraordinary though it is, he himself still had faith in ultimate victory. His hopes were now placed not so much in his weakened will as in the divine dispensation of providence. After all, he had miraculously survived many and repeated assassination attempts, the last of which had been the Generals' Plot of June 1944. As always, Hitler's escape had been as narrow as it was lucky, confirming him further in the conviction he voiced on the radio: 'I regard this as confirmation of the task imposed upon me by providence.' Appreciative though he was of this providential sign, his revenge upon the plotters had been quite savagely sadistic.

Just as it had done in the First World War, his repeated deliverances from almost certain death fanned the flame of his faith in a messianic destiny. It did not occur to him that perhaps Adolf Hitler had outlived his usefulness to providence. He thought he still had one more card to play, a magician's card. Like primitive peoples all over the world, and like many modern magicians, the Führer believed in the efficacy of human sacrifice. Sacrifice, he felt, would attract the attention of the powers, propitiate the powers, induce the powers to bring about a miraculous intervention on his behalf.

In the winter of 1942, Hitler had given the order for the Final Solution, which he thought was part of his mystic mission. Could he offer to the gods the charred corpses of the gas ovens? 'Faster!' he urged, 'it has to be done faster!' When this failed to produce any effect, he turned his attention to his own people, a worthier sacrifice, he suspected, to the powers which sustained him. 'Losses can never be too high!' he screamed at Field Marshal von Reichenau. When news of the deaths of so many young officers was brought to his attention, his reply was reminiscent of the Aztec priests: 'But that's what the young men are there for.'

He became caught up in this ecstasy of destruction. If providence would not answer, he would try to take the whole world with him. Was it the end of the Superman? Then let the end be a true Goetterdaemmerung!

'In his last days, in the days of Radio Werewolf and suicidal strategy, Hitler seems like some cannibal god, rejoicing in the ruin of his own temples. Almost his last orders were for execution: prisoners were to be slaughtered, his old surgeon was to be murdered, his own brother was to be executed; all traitors, without further specification, were to die. Like an ancient hero, Hitler wished to be sent with human sacrifices to the grave,'[12]

writes Trevor-Roper. 'If the war is to be lost,' Hitler informed a frightened Speer, 'the nation will also perish.' He issued order after order to the German people which commanded them to transform their nation into one vast flaming funeral pyre. When he learned that 300,000 people had taken refuge in the Berlin Underground, he had it flooded as a further act of murderous destruction. If he had had atom bombs, he would have rejoiced in triggering them all simultaneously.

Even in April 1945 there was still a final lingering hope that the smell of blood might cause providence to intervene. When Goebbels read to him an extract from Carlyle's biography of Frederick the Great, Hitler was moved to tears by the extent to which his own plight resembled that of one of his heroes. One passage in particular affected him:

'Brave king! Wait but a little while, and the days of your suffering will be over. Behind the clouds the sun of your good fortune is already shining and soon will show itself to you.'[13]

Hitler then heard how the Tsarina of Russia had died, and how peace proposals had followed from her heir, the famous 'Miracle of the House of Brandenberg'. Could these events repeat themselves for him? Was providence waiting to spring this surprise upon the world? Hitler called for astrological horoscopes of Germany, and excitedly compared the interpretations with Goebbels.

The two horoscopes they had before them were in accord. Both predicted war in 1939, German victories until 1941, and a subsequent series of defeats, the worst of which would be in the first half of April 1945. This would be followed by a temporary German success, a three month lull, peace in August 1945, and then, after three miserable years, a rise to greatness recommencing in 1948.

The two Nazi leaders had never been keen astrologers save when it suited them for propaganda purposes, but now they were desperate for any sign whatsoever. The sceptical Goebbels became a convert to the esoteric sciences, and proclaimed to the defenders of Berlin:

'The Führer has declared that even in this very year a change of fortune shall come . . . The Führer knows the exact hour of its arrival. Destiny has sent us this man so that we, in this time of great external and internal stress, shall testify to the miracle . . .'[14]

A miracle of a sort did occur. On 13 April, Goebbels received the news that President Roosevelt had died. Immediately he opened champagne and telephoned Hitler:

'My Führer, I congratulate you! Roosevelt is dead. It is written in the stars that the second half of April will be the turning point for us. This is Friday, April 13. It is the turning point!'[15]

But this astonishing coincidence turned out to be rather like a final providential joke. President Truman, Roosevelt's successor, was every bit as determined to extirpate Nazism from the face of the earth, and the American, British and Russian vice tightened speedily on the dying Third Reich.

There was still enough flickering magnetism in Hitler to convince those around him that the war might still be won by a final battle before the gates of Berlin. When, on 22 April, a largely imaginary counter-offensive under General Steiner failed to stop the Russians, Hitler finally admitted to himself and to almost all of his associates that it was indeed the end.

Even in defeat, he retained his hold on those around him, though his behaviour alternated between wild accusations that everyone had betrayed him, and a manic rejoicing in the destruction of Germany. In Speer's words he 'deliberately tried to make everything perish with him. He had reached a state in which, as far as he was concerned, the end of his own life meant the end of the world.' And as Trevor-Roper puts it: 'Hitler and Goebbels called upon the German people to destroy their towns and factories, blow up their bridges and dams and demolish the railways and all the rolling-stock, all for the sake of a legend – the Twilight of the Gods.'[16] The faithful Joseph Goebbels rejoiced with him:

'Under the ruins of our demolished cities the accomplishments of the stupid nineteenth century lie buried ... Our end will be the end of the whole universe.'[17]

Slowly the Führer made preparations for his own death, interspersing them with ravings of self-pity, which sought to pin the blame for his end in a cellar on everyone save himself. Outraged by Goering's offer to take over power, shattered by the news of Himmler's private attempts at negotiation with the Western Allies, he expelled them from all offices, and like a spoiled child, exploded into tantrums of screaming at the indignities which had been heaped upon him.

He drew up a wretched political testament which blamed the Jews for all the ills of the world, including the Second World War, and portrayed his own actions as noble and selfless. He jibed at his defeated Army. He even appointed a Government to succeed him: Admiral Doenitz as President, Goebbels as Chancellor, Bormann as Party Minister, a singular exercise in fatuity. On 29 April, with Russian shells falling on the Chancellery building above him, he married his mistress, Eva Braun as a reward for her loyalty. Then, at around 2.30 a.m. on 30 April, he said farewells to the inmates of his Bunker. His eyes were moist and far away, his body shrivelled as if it was decaying, his voice an inaudible mumble. As the broken man stumbled away to his wife, to enjoy a honeymoon consisting of two revolvers and a phial of poison, the wedding guests gave him a suitable send-off. As Hitler's door closed, the tension abruptly evaporated, and music and dancing suddenly erupted, soon developing into a jolly little party. It was a signal that the Führer's once omnipotent will no longer extended beyond the four walls of his austere room.

On the afternoon of 30 April, at around half-past three, Mr and Mrs Adolf Hitler committed suicide: he shot himself, she took poison. The bodies were then carried outside, soaked in petrol, and set on fire. Appropriately, it was the afternoon of Walpurgis Night, the greatest festival of satanism.

On the evening of 1 May, Dr and Frau Goebbels took their leave of the planet. They poisoned their six children, and were shot, at their request, by an SS orderly; their corpses were also set on fire. Martin Bormann, unwilling to die for the sake of a myth, fled from the Bunker shortly after: it is not known for certain whether or not he survived. The Bunker itself was consigned to the flames. On 7 May, the Third Reich, which had hoped to endure one thousand years, surrendered unconditionally after twelve.

The leading actors in this daemonic drama feverishly sought some means of escape from the reckoning that was upon them. Heinrich Himmler tried, but was apprehended by a British unit. He knew what he now had to do. Previously, he had issued instructions to the SS on the proper method of committing suicide, and so the Reichsführer proceeded to set the example. On 23 May, he bit on a concealed cyanide capsule and died in the utmost agony.

Most SS men decided that escape was preferable to honour, and an alarmingly large number of them succeeded. Those whom the Allies did apprehend were tried at Nuremberg: death sentences were passed on, among others, Kaltenbrunner, Rosenberg, Frank, Streicher and Goering; the latter cheated the hangman by swallowing poison two hours before his scheduled execution. Others received stiff prison sentences, though in the final analysis, when one notes the number of subsequent amnesties, the Nazi war criminals could congratulate each other on having escaped so lightly. Nevertheless, the Allies did keep one promise: they did exterminate the philosophy of National Socialism.

As for the National Socialist Prophet and Messiah, what had he achieved? He had achieved unprecedented power. What else? What had he done with his power? He had destroyed. All that remained to testify to his existence was the destruction around him. Ruins and corpses, millions and millions of corpses, maimed lives and spirits, tortured bodies, and pile upon pile of rubble. This was all that was left of the Hitler era: not the creation of a Superman but the destruction of a civilisation. Writes Fest:

'. . . Hitler did not destroy Germany alone, but put an end to the old Europe with its sterile rivalries, its narrow-mindedness, its selfish patriotism and its deceitful imperatives. He put an end too to its splendour, its grandeur and the magic of its *douceur de vivre*. The hour of that Europe is past and we shall never see it again. By the hand of the man whom it brought to power, the lights were really and finally put out over Europe.'[18]

Adolf Hitler had failed utterly in the fulfilment of his dreams, but succeeded perhaps in the fulfilment of some destiny. The more fanciful might see in him 'the unconscious tool of higher powers', the instrument of a God of War and of Vengeance, the perfect weapon for the destruction of the Old Aeon. The yet more imaginative might feel that Hitler was never meant to win, that his only use was to lash out and destroy buildings, people, ideas and ideals. Certainly there has never been a better human engine of annihilation. Certainly too, it was at last the end of Hitler and of Nazism, but it was by no means the end of the Age of Horus. For the men and women who fought the Third Reich with such superhuman faith, splendid courage and noble ideals once again had no inkling of the horrors that were yet in store for them. The acutest realisation of the Second World War's ultimate consequence is to be found in Thomas Merton's poem, *Adolf Eichmann*, performed by the late American 'sick comedian', Lenny Bruce:

'I, Adolf Eichmann
vatched through the portholes.
I saw every Jew burned
und turned into soap.
Do you people think yourselves better
because you burned your enemies
at long distance
with missiles?
Without ever seeing what you'd done to them?
Hiroshima . . . *Auf Wiedersehen*!'[19]

THE LAST CHAPTER?

'I am the warrior Lord of the Forties: the Eighties cower before me, and are abased.'
The Book of the Law III 46

'*The Book of the Law* takes us back to primitive savagery," you say. Well, where are we?

"We're at Guernica, Lidice, Oradour-sur-Glane, Rotterdam and hundreds of other crimes, to say nothing of concentration camps, Stalags, and a million lesser horrors, inconceivable by the most diseased and inflamed Sadistic imagination forty years ago.

'You disagree with Aiwass – so do all of us. The trouble is that He can say: "But I'm not arguing; I'm telling you."'
Aleister Crowley

It would be a grave mistake to think that the Age of Horus is dead.
So far we have only witnessed its beginning.
This is the Age of Horus.
This is the Age of War.

From 1945 to 1969, there were ninety-seven wars around the globe. The total duration of these conflicts exceeded 250 years. There was not a single day in which one or several wars were not fought somewhere in the world. The death toll amounted to tens of millions. At the present moment it is difficult to remember the exact number of wars in progress, or the exact number of places where war seems likely. Nor does the frequency of these wars show the slightest sign of diminishing. As soon as one war ends, another begins.

World War Three has hitherto been avoided, though not

for want of trying. The race for newer, more deadly and more destructive weapons continues to accelerate between the USA and the USSR, despite all talk of détente. A 1974 estimate put the combined raw megatonnage of these two nations at equal to 1,200,000 atom bombs of the type that annihilated Hiroshima. No longer does that grim prophecy of *The Book of the Law* strike one as being so foolish: 'Hail! ye twin warriors about the pillars of the world! for your time is nigh at hand.'

The world of 1889 has been wiped from the face of the planet and been replaced by a mask of anxiety and terror. Comments the conservative Henry Kissinger: 'The Western world seems to be floating without power or rudder on a sea filled with destructive events.' Even the rational and hopeful French President, Giscard d'Estaing admits: 'The world is unhappy. Unhappy because it does not know where it is going and because it guesses that, if it knew, it would be that it is going towards a catastrophe.' There is no point in ennumerating either the nature of the weapons of extinction which lie, begging for employment, in the military arsenals of our Great Powers, or the growing membership list of smaller Powers who have proudly joined the Nuclear Club. We know about that. We know too about the plight of the Third World and its increasing hostility to the West, of the scarcity of natural resources and the rapacity of our demands upon them, of a shrinking food supply and an accelerating growth in population, and of a pollution that will kill us in the long run even if the H-bomb does not destroy us in the short.

The West, which so recently ruled the world, has lost its values. All ideals sound unintentionally comic to the ears of its inhabitants. No new world outlook has replaced the debris of the old. There have been minor revolutions of consciousness in the young, but nothing enduring has emerged. We may instance the creation of a specifically teenage culture, based upon hedonism, that followed the emergence of rock n' roll in 1950: or the mass movement of the young towards an alternative culture during the so-called 'psychedelic revolution' of 1967–70; or the eruption of another occult renaissance which followed it, and which

210

has, among other things, resulted in Anton LaVey's occult Lodge, the Church of Satan, becoming the fastest growing religious body in the United States. Yet these phenomena, influential though they have been, have evoked only indifference or repression from those who govern and have not significantly influenced the course of history Instead the majority have endured an age of conformity, the 1950s, based upon the fulfilment of sterile materialist standards; a prosperous age of frivolous and in retrospect rather silly optimism, the 1960s; and are now through the dismal 1970s, which we may rightly term an age of anxiety.

In 1917, G. K. Chesterton felt able to write: 'The whole culture of our time has been full of the notion of "A Good Time Coming". Now the culture of the Dark Ages was full of the notion of "A Good Time Going".' A mere fifty-nine years later, the culture of our own Dark Ages is obsessed by the notion of A Good Time Going, and the entertainment industry makes millions from our collective wallowing in the comforting mud of nostalgia.

When we search for ideals which our culture holds strong, we find none, not even the concept of culture itself – that is unfashionable. Our much-vaunted 'Sexual Revolution' has merely destroyed the old taboos in order to replace them with a loveless promiscuity, which is definitely an improvement, but has nothing about it that is positive. Our controversial, so-called Permissive Society is just an impressive name which we give to our collective apathy. Our attempt to exclude ethics from education has resulted in a new generation which lacks faith in anything except an amoral and half-hearted pursuit of a narrow but ill-defined self-interest. Our endeavour to secure equality has been parodied by its consequences, drabness and bureaucratically ordained mediocrity. Our vision has been rendered obsolete by television.

We are still, it is true, better off than the people of the Third World: we eat, they starve – and then we forget our dependence upon their raw materials. We are still, it is true, better off than the citizens of Communist regimes: we boast of our freedom, pity their slavery – and then we forget the war economy of the USSR. We still think we are better off, which in material terms we are, but aside from this, no one ever stands up to acclaim our values for no one knows what they are. We are exhorted to defend ourselves from Communism, but no one ever tells us what it is that we are supposed to be defending, apart from the right to overeat. Others even have the temerity to assure us that Communism is a preferable system to our own despite the obvious fact that we can all enjoy the benefits of a Communist regime by going to Dartmoor. Only vote-catching Conservatives speak up against this last assurance, and invariably reveal thereby their utter ideological bankruptcy. Like citizens of the dying Roman Empire, we turn a blind eye to the future, for we do not wish to see what it has in store, and strain feverishly to forget our fears in the frenzied pursuit of what remaining luxury and pleasure is left to us. We have given up hope in the dismal nonentities who call themselves politicans and are no longer even surprised by their incompetence, dishonesty and corruption.

It is fitting that at this time much of the history taught in schools is not of the great deeds of great men, but of the little deeds of little men. It is as though we want to see ourselves as helpless pawns.

The Christian religion is no longer of the slightest importance; perhaps it is in poor taste to speak ill of the dead. Those desperate for religious values have turned to curious cults and allegedly divine gurus. Appropriately, the marketing of Messiahs has become big business, and techniques used for selling soap powder are employed now for selling a large range of products, variously packaged as 'God'. All this is a bleak and appalling picture, but there is no point in disguising its reality: surely we have suffered enough from this century of destroyed illusions?

To leave the reader flooded by this outburst of pessimism is less than helpful. It is therefore an opportune moment to summarise the main points of this work, and to glean from these statements any available scraps of optimism. The most important of the theses in this book are:

1   That nearly two thousand years of Christian civilis-ation, which ultimately led to the domination of the world by the values of the West, have come to an end.

2   That the end of the Old Aeon and the character of the New was foreseen by artists, poets and occultists in the dying years of the nineteenth century.

3   That a remarkable insight into ensuing events was written in the form of a prose-poem called *The Book of the Law*, which announced the New Aeon.

4   That the twentieth century has seen a swift and unprecedented transformation in the conditions of life on our planet, including two World Wars, the collapse of all European Empires, and the destruction or inversion of previous values.

4   That some kind of force, hitherto unsuspected by science, whether physical or psychological and moving in the depths of our collective unconscious, has impelled this destruction: in poetic fashion, we have personified it as Horus, the Egyptian God of War; or else referred to it as an eruption of the daemonic.

5   That certain individuals who practised the neglected and despised arts of magic and mysticism, which involved the comprehension of forces like the one referred to, invoked this current to further their own ends, whether the attainment of enlightenment and truth, or the achievement of political power.

6   That one of these individuals was Adolf Hitler, whom we may call the greatest black magician of the century, whose beliefs were a warped amalgam of the occult irrationalities which Western civilisation had for so long suppressed.

7   That both Hitler's success and Hitler's failure were due to the application of the magical world outlook he had acquired.

8   That the manner of his application was confined within the limitations of a completely contemptible personality,

and that in consequence, the Third Reich was the negation of the human spirit and a blasphemous parody of everything affirmed in the true principles of magic.

9 That Hitler's personality complemented both the frustrated hatred of his people, whom the First World War prepared for this adventure, and the nature of the daemonic force which he believed himself to control, and which instead came to control him, its demon of nightmare, vengeance and destruction, which it flung aside when its purpose had been served.

10 That this process of destruction, accompanied by repeated eruptions of the daemonic in the minds of groups and individuals, is continuing and will continue until the Old Order has been irrevocably obliterated, and that we can do nothing whatever that will halt this process.

Is it the end of the world? It is the end, unquestionably, of the old world, and there is no point in wasting time by pretending that it is not, or by sobbing lingering farewells. Our hours would be better spent in becoming aware of the fearful reality around us, adjusting to the new conditions, and making use of them for our own benefit. Man has survived disasters before, and it is impossible to accept that he has lost the evolutionary struggle and is doomed to self-extinction.

This is a terrifying time, but it is also a time of an exhilarating adventure. The next thirty years will test the ability of our species to cope with the new conditions prevalent upon this planet. If we are to avoid extinction, we had better employ every atom of our intelligence and imagination, our faculties, conscious and unconscious, that have enabled mankind to survive through all previous geographical and historical crises. And if indeed Do What Thou Wilt Shall Be The Whole Of The Law, then we had better start doing our Will.

BIBLIOGRAPHY

The Bibliography consists of those works which are cited frequently, and a few works which are of basic importance for thematic reasons. Other bibliographical information is given in the chapter notes.

BLAVATSKY, H. P., *The Secret Doctrine* (Adyar: Theosophical Publishing House)

BRENNAN, J. H., *Occult Reich* (Futura, London 1974)

BULLOCK, Alan, *Hitler, a Study in Tyranny* (Pelican Books Ltd, London 1960)

COLQUHOUN, Ithell, *Sword of Wisdom: MacGregor Mathers and the Golden Dawn* (Spearman (Neville) Ltd, London 1975)

CROWLEY, Aleister. *The Equinox of The Gods* (London 1936)
The Confessions of Aleister Crowley (Cape, London 1969)
Magick (Routledge, Kegan Paul, Ltd, London 1972)

FEST, Joachim C., *The Face of the Third Reich* (Pelican Books Ltd, London 1972)

FISHMAN, Jack, *The Seven Men of Spandau* (London 1954)

FULLER, J. F. C., *The Star in the West* (New York 1907)
The Decisive Battles of the Western World (Granada Publishing Ltd; Paladin, London 1970)

HITLER, Adolf, *Mein Kampf* (Hutchinson, Trans: Ralph Mangeim, London 1973)
Hitler's Table-Talk (Ed. Picker) (Bonn 1951)
Hitler's Secret Conversations 1941–4 (New York 1953)

JULIAN, Phillippe, *Dreamers of Decadence* (Phaidon Press Ltd, London 1974)

KERSTEN, Felix, *The Kersten Memoirs 1940–5* (London 1956)

KUBIZEK, August, *Young Hitler, The Story of Our Friendship* (London 1954)

KING, Francis, *Ritual Magic in England* (New English Library Ltd, London 1972)
Sexuality, Magic and Perversion (New English Library Ltd, London 1972)
Satan and Swastika (Mayflower Books Ltd, London 1976)

LAVEY, A. S., *The Satanic Bible* (Avon Books, New York 1970)
The Satanic Rituals (Avon Books, New York 1972)

LYTTON, Edward Bulwer, *The Coming Race* (California 1967)

MANVELL, R. & FRAENKEL, H., *Himmler* (New English Library Ltd, London 1973)
Dr Goebbels (New English Library Ltd, London 1974)
Goering (New English Library Ltd, London 1974)
MOORE, George, *Confessions of a Young Man* (Penguin Books Ltd, London 1939)

NIETZSCHE, F., *Thus Spake Zarathustra* (New York 1937)
PAUWELS, L., *Gurdjieff* (Douglas 1964)
PAUWELS, L. & BERGIER, J., *The Dawn of Magic* (Granada Publishing Ltd; Panther, London 1964)
PRAZ, Mario, *The Romantic Agony* (Oxford University Press 1970)

RAUSCHNING, Hermann, *Germany's Revolution of Destruction* (London 1939)
Hitler Speaks (London 1939)

RAVENSCROFT, Trevor., *The Spear of Destiny* (Transworld Publishers Ltd; Corgi, London 1972)

REGARDIE, Israel., *The Tree of Life: A Study in Magic* (Weiser and Weiser Inc., New York 1971)

SHIRER, William., *The Rise and Fall of the Third Reich* (Secker and Warburg Ltd, London 1964)

SPENCE, Lewis., *The Occult Causes of the Present War* (London 1940)

TAYLOR, A. J. P., *The First World War* (Hamish Hamilton Ltd, London 1965)
Europe: Grandeur and Decline (Penguin Books Ltd; Pelican, London 1967)
TERRAINE, John, *The Great War* (London 1965)
TREVOR-ROPER, H. R., *The Last Days of Hitler* (Pan Books Ltd, London 1970)

WAITE, Robert G. L., *The Psychopathic God Adolf Hitler* (Basic Books Inc., New York 1977)
WILSON, Colin, *Rasputin (* Granada Publishing Ltd, Panther 1964)
WYKES, Alan, *Nuremberg Rallies* (Purnell Books, London 1970)

YEATS, W. B., *Collected Poems* (Macmillan Publishers Ltd, London 1967)

NOTES

CHAPTER ONE

1 Nietzsche, *Thus Spake Zarathustra*.

CHAPTER TWO

1 Pauwels & Bergier, *The Dawn of Magic*.
2 George Moore, *Confessions of a Young Man*.
3 Letter by S. L. Mathers quoted in Francis King's *Ritual Magic in England* and in Pauwels & Bergier.
4 Quoted in Francis King's *Satan and Swastika*.
5 Letter to Machen from Wynn Westcott quoted in Pauwels & Bergier, *The Dawn of Magic*.
6 W. B. Yeats, *The Second Coming*.

CHAPTER THREE

1 J. F. C. Fuller, *The Decisive Battles of the Western World*.
2 M. Pavlovich, *The Problems of National and Colonial Policy and the Third International*.
3 J. F. C. Fuller, *The Decisive Battles of the Western World*.
4 William Shirer, *The Rise and Fall of the Third Reich*.
5 Letter from Lanz von Liebenfels quoted in both J. H. Brennan, *Occult Reich*, and Francis King, *Satan and Swastika*.

CHAPTER FOUR

1 Hitler's *Secret Conversations 1941–4*.
2 Quoted in Shirer, *The Rise and Fall of the Third Reich*.
3 ibid.
4 Hitler, *Mein Kampf*.
5 ibid.
6 ibid.
7 Konrad Heiden, *Hitler, a Biography*.
8 Hitler, *Mein Kampf*.
9 Alan Bullock, *Hitler: a Study in Tyranny*.
10 Hitler, *Mein Kampf*.
11 Bullock, *Hitler: a Study in Tyranny*.
12 Hitler, *Mein Kampf*.

CHAPTER FIVE
1 Goethe, *Dichtung und Wahrheit*.
2 ibid.
3 Aleister Crowley, *Book Four*.
4 ibid.
5 ibid.
6 ibid.
7 Crowley, *The Confessions of Aleister Crowley*.
8 A. J. P. Taylor, *Europe: Grandeur and Decline*.
9 Colin Wilson, *Rasputin*.

CHAPTER SIX
1 J. F. C. Fuller, *The Decisive Battles of the Western World*.
2 ibid.

CHAPTER SEVEN
1 Pauwels & Bergier, *The Dawn of Magic*.
2 Louis Pauwels, *Gurdjieff*.
3 Hitler, *Mein Kampf*.
4 Quoted in Shirer, *The Rise and Fall of the Third Reich*.
5 ibid.
6 Hitler, *Mein Kampf*.
7 ibid.
8 ibid.
9 ibid.

CHAPTER EIGHT
1 Hitler, *Mein Kampf*.
2 ibid.
3 Quoted in Heiden, *Hitler, A Biography*.
4 Francis King, *Ritual Magic in England*.
5 Pauwels & Bergier, *The Dawn of Magic*.
6 Joachim C. Fest, *The Face of the Third Reich*.
7 Quoted in Fest.
8 Bullock, *Hitler, a Study in Tyranny*.
9 Quoted in Brennan, *Occult Reich* and in Pauwels & Bergier.

CHAPTER NINE
1 Quoted in Fest, *The Face of the Third Reich*.
2 Quoted in Shirer, *The Rise and Fall of the Third Reich*.
3 Fest, *The Face of the Third Reich*.
4 Rosenberg, *The Myth of the Twentieth Century*.

5   A cameo of extracts from *Hitler Speaks* and *Hitler's Secre.*
    Conversations 1941–4.
6   Quoted in Brennan, *Occult Reich.*
7   Quoted by Francois Bayle, *Psychologie et ethique du*
    Nationalsocialismo, which is quoted in Fest, *The Face of the*
    Third Reich.
8   Quoted in Fest, *The Face of the Third Reich.*
9   ibid.
10 Quoted in King, *Satan and Swastika.*
11 Quoted in Shirer, *The Rise and Fall of the Third Reich.*
12 ibid.

CHAPTER TEN
1   Fest, *The Face of the Third Reich.*
2   A. J. P. Taylor, *Thus Spake Hitler* in *Europe: Grandeur ana*
    Decline.
3   Rauschning. *Hitler Speaks.*
4   Quoted in Pauwels & Bergier, *The Dawn of Magic.*
5   ibid.
6   Pauwels, *Gurdjieff.*
7   Quoted in Fest, *The Face of the Third Reich.*
8   Rauschning, *Hitler Speaks.*
9   Quoted in Pauwels, *Gurdjieff.*

CHAPTER ELEVEN
1   Quoted in Fest, *The Face of the Third Reich.*
2   Rauschning.
3   Quoted in Pauwels & Bergier.
4   Quoted in King, *Satan and Swastika.*
5   Quoted in Pauwels & Bergier.
6   William Shirer, *Berlin Diary.*
7   Bullock, *Hitler: a Study in Tyranny.*
8   Hugh Trevor-Roper, *The Last Days of Hitler.*
9   Quoted in Pauwels & Bergier.
10 ibid.
11 Rauschning.
12 King, *Satan and Swastika.*
13 Rauschning.

CHAPTER TWELVE
1   From a broadsheet issued by Crowley in 1936 when he
    published *The Equinox of the Gods.*
2   Gerald B. Gardner, *Witchcraft Today.*

CHAPTER THIRTEEN

1 Fest, *The Face of the Third Reich*.
2 ibid.
3 Quoted in Brennan, *Occult Reich*.
4 This tale is related in John Pearson's *Ian Fleming*.
5 Quoted in Pauwels & Bergier.
6 ibid.
7 *Hitler's Table Talk* (ed. Picker) quoted by Francis King in *Satan and Swastika*.
8 Rauschning, quoted in King, *Satan and Swastika*.
9 I owe this line of argument entirely to Francis King.
10 Quoted in Pauwels & Bergier.
11 ibid.
12 Rauschning.
13 Robert Ley, *The Way to the Order Castle*, quoted in Fest, *The Face of the Third Reich*.

CHAPTER FOURTEEN

1 Rauschning.
2 Quoted in King, *Satan and Swastika*.
3 Himmler's Posen speech (1943) quoted in Fest.
4 Pauwels & Bergier.
5 Quoted in Fest.
6 Quoted in Manvell & Fraenkel, *Himmler*.
7 Schellenberg, *The Schellenberg Memoirs*.
8 King, *Satan and Swastika*.
9 Quoted in Brennan, *Occult Reich*.
10 Quoted in Pauwels & Bergier.
11 *The Schellenberg Memoirs*.
12 Quoted in Brennan, *Occult Reich*.
13 Pauwels & Bergier.
14 ibid.
15 ibid.

CHAPTER FIFTEEN

1 Quoted in Bullock.
2 ibid.
3 Quoted in King, *Satan and Swastika*.
4 ibid.
5 Speer's evidence at Nuremberg.
6 *The Goebbels Diaries*, entry for 31 January 1942.
7 King, *Satan and Swastika*.
8 Bullock, *Hitler, a Study in Tyranny*

9   J. H. Brennan, *Occult Reich*.
10 King, *Satan and Swastika*.
11 2 April 1945, quoted in King.
12 Hugh Trevor-Roper, *The Last Days of Hitler*.
13 Thomas Carlyle, *Frederick the Great*.
14 Goebbels' appeal of 6 April 1945
15 Quoted in Trevor-Roper.
16 ibid.
17 Quoted in Pauwels & Bergier.
18 Joachim C. Fest, *The Face of the Third Reich*.
19 Quoted in *Ladies and Gentlemen, Lenny Bruce!!* by Albert
    Goldman, from the journalism of Laurence Schiller.

INDEX

227

Piercing the
REICH

BY JOSEPH E. PERSICO

*The remarkable true story of Allied undercover operations in
World War II*

PIERCING THE REICH tells for the first time the full
story of the infiltration of Germany by the Office of
Strategic Studies, a closely guarded secret for over
thirty years.

In 1944, the OSS parachuted highly skilled agents into
the heart of the Third Reich. Kitted out with forged
documents and false identities, which were based on
months of detailed research, the agents worked in
isolation to obtain information vital to the Allied war
effort. Their missions were many and varied, from the
organisation of resistance groups in strategic areas to the
masterminding of attempts to assassinate Hitler. Never
before had such a wide-scale operation succeeded in doing
the impossible – undermining the very foundations of
the Nazi State.

Written with full access to Central Intelligence Agency
files and with the cooperation of surviving OSS agents,
PIERCING THE REICH is both a gripping and
sensational read and a profoundly important piece of
secret history.

ILLUSTRATED

WAR/NON-FICTION   0 7221 6809 8   £1.75

THE
CULTURE OF
NARCISSISM

BY CHRISTOPHER LASCH

'Never has the case against narcissism been made with
such an all-embracing sweep'
NEWSWEEK

Freedom from religious superstition has left a gap in our
lives which has been replaced by the creed of self-love,
maintains Christopher Lasch. Emotional shallowness,
fear of intimacy, hypochondria, pseudo-self-insight,
promiscuous pansexuality and dread of old age and death
are the symptoms of the narcissist whose culture has lost
interest in the future. The frantic search for fulfilment –
in the new consciousness movements and therapeutic
culture; in pseudo-confessional autobiographies; in the
replacement of Horatio Alger by the 'Happy Hooker' as
the new symbol of success – is the world of the resigned.
THE CULTURE OF NARCISSISM points the way to a
world where new politics, new discipline and new love are
the only hope for a society moving helter-skelter towards
total self-absorption.

SOCIOLOGY/PSYCHOLOGY   0 349 12165 6   £1.75

keeper of the children

BY WILLIAM H. HALLAHAN

NOTHING CAN PREPARE YOU FOR
THE NERVE-WRENCHING FRENZY OF . . .
KEEPER OF THE CHILDREN

Alone in a child's bedroom in a suburban Philadelphia home,
Eddie Benson listens for footsteps on the stairs.

The footfall Eddie is waiting for will not be human.
It could be someone's pet cat, or a stuffed teddy bear,
or even a smiling marionette doll.

But whatever it is that comes creeping up the stairs it will
have two horrifying qualities: it will be propelled by a
diabolic force and it will have only one intention – murder.

If Eddie Benson wants his daughter back, he will have to
fight a battle no human has ever fought before. And he
must win. For only the victor can return with his life –
and soul – from the realms of such dark, unnatural evil.

**'Eerie, scary . . . utterly fascinating . . .
this is not going to be what you think'**
Publishers Weekly

HORROR   0 7221 4246 3   £1.00

Give them
the pleasure of choosing

Book Tokens can be bought
and exchanged at most
bookshops.

MENACE

THE LIFE AND DEATH OF THE TIRPITZ

BY LUDOVIC KENNEDY
(ILLUSTRATED)

THE GREAT WHITE ELEPHANT OF WORLD WAR II

Ludovic Kennedy tells the story, in graphic detail, of the
largest, fastest, most powerful European battleship ever built.
In the new light of the rich store of 'Ultra' signals – German
top secret coded naval signals – now available, he examines
her career from her completion in 1941 to her destruction in
November 1944. Stationed in a strategic position in the
Norwegian fjords, the **Tirpitz** acted as a fleet-in-being.
She presented a continuing menace to North Atlantic shipping
and the Arctic convoys where her greatest success was the
disaster to convoy PQ 17. Mr Kennedy captures all the drama
of the attempts to destroy the great white elephant until she
finally succumbed to the biggest bomb of all – a 'Tallboy'.

'Mr Kennedy extracts the full drama, technological data,
and the gallantry of all concerned'
OBSERVER

NON-FICTION/WAR   0 7221 5165 9   £1.25

A selection of bestsellers from SPHERE

FICTION

INNOCENT BLOOD	P. D. James	£1.50 ☐
HOLLYWOOD GOTHIC	Thomas Gifford	£1.50 ☐
STEPPING	Nancy Thayer	£1.25 ☐
UNHOLY CHILD	Catherine Breslin	£1.75 ☐
TO LOVE AGAIN	Danielle Steel	£1.25 ☐
THE ELDORADO NETWORK	Derek Robinson	£1.50 ☐

FILM & TV TIE-INS

RAISE THE TITANIC	Clive Cussler	£1.50 ☐
CLOSE ENCOUNTERS OF THE THIRD KIND	Steven Spielberg	85p ☐
LLOYD GEORGE	David Benedictus	£1.25 ☐
SOMEWHERE IN TIME	Richard Matheson	£1.25 ☐
THE GENTLE TOUCH	Terence Feely	£1.10 ☐

NON FICTION

WAR IN 2080	David Langford	£1.50 ☐
A MATTER OF LIFE	R. Edwards & P. Steptoe	£1.50 ☐
WORLD OF SALADS	Rosalie Swedlin	£2.75 ☐
SUPERLEARNING	S. Ostrander & L. Schroeder with N. Ostrander	£1.75 ☐

All Sphere books are available at your local bookshop or newsagent, or can be ordered direct from the publisher. Just tick the titles you want and fill in the form below.

Name ....

Address ....

....

Write to Sphere Books, Cash Sales Department, P.O. Box 11, Falmouth, Cornwall TR10 9EN.

Please enclose cheque or postal order to the value of the cover price plus:

UK: 40p for the first book, 18p for the second and 13p per copy for each additional book ordered to a maximum charge of £1.49.

OVERSEAS: 60p for the first book and 18p for each additional book.

BFPO & EIRE: 40p for the first book, 18p for the second book plus 13p per copy for the next 7 books, thereafter 7p per book.

Sphere Books reserve the right to show new retail prices on covers which may differ from those previously advertised in the text or elsewhere, and to increase postal rates in accordance with the P.O.